# HEARTTHROBS

CAROL DYHOUSE

# HEARTTHROBS

## A HISTORY OF WOMEN AND DESIRE

OXFORD
UNIVERSITY PRESS

# OXFORD
UNIVERSITY PRESS

Great Clarendon Street, Oxford, OX2 6DP,
United Kingdom

Oxford University Press is a department of the University of Oxford.
It furthers the University's objective of excellence in research, scholarship,
and education by publishing worldwide. Oxford is a registered trade mark of
Oxford University Press in the UK and in certain other countries

First Edition published in 2017

Impression: 1

Published in the United States of America by Oxford University Press
198 Madison Avenue, New York, NY 10016, United States of America

British Library Cataloguing in Publication Data
Data available

Library of Congress Control Number: 2016946643

ISBN 978-0-19-876583-7

Printed in Great Britain by
Clays Ltd, St Ives plc

*For Nick*

# CONTENTS

# LIST OF ILLUSTRATIONS

# ACKNOWLEDGEMENTS

I am grateful to the staff at the several institutions which enabled me to carry out research for this book. Every time I visit the British Library I find myself aware of just how privileged its readers are, and delighting anew in its riches. I rather miss the newspaper division in Colindale, where the staff trudged uncomplainingly back and forth delivering me bundles of *Boyfriend*, *Roxy*, and *Mirabelle*, but I don't miss the tube journey out there, and the periodicals arrive in the reading rooms at St Pancras, just as magically as before. Thank you so much, all the brilliant staff at the British Library, for your reliably friendly help over the telephone, for your efficiency in the reading rooms, and for uncomplainingly helping me (yet again!) with the photocopying machines and scanners.

My warm thanks, too, to the staff of Reading University's Museums and Special Collections Service, (which houses the Mills and Boon Archive), for guiding me through their holdings. Thanks also to Dr Phil Wickham and the staff at the Bill Douglas Cinema Museum at the University of Exeter. I am grateful, as ever, to the staff at the University of Sussex Library, and to those at The Keep, which now houses the University's Special Collections holdings, including the Mass Observation Archive.

Friends and colleagues at the University of Sussex have been extraordinarily generous and supportive while I've been working on this book. I am grateful to the History Department, to colleagues in the School of History, Art History and Philosophy and to Deborah Jackson-Smith and Ahmed Koyes, for continuing to provide me with facilities for research and writing. Ahmed has shown extraordinary patience in the face of my panics and often breath-taking technical incompetence with reprographics and software. It has been a real privilege to continue to work alongside older and newer members of the department: my special thanks to Ann-Marie Angelo, Hester Barron, Vinita Damodaran, Sian Edwards, Jim Endersby, Ian Gazeley, Tim Hitchcock, Rose Holmes, Hilary Kalmbach, Jill Kirby, Claire Langhamer, Ian McDaniel, Katharina Rietzler, Lucy Robinson, Claudia Siebrecht, James Thomson, Chris Warne, and Clive Webb. I have benefited from conversations about history and popular culture (among other things) with Claire Langhamer, Lucy Robinson, Owen Emmerson, Alexa Neale, Zoe Strimpel, and Angela Ferreira Campos. Claire, Hester, and Lucy have, all three of them, been inspirational, as well as mainstays of support.

My thanks, too, to the many people (some, but not all connected with the academic world) who have provided ideas and support while this book was coming together. I owe a particular debt of gratitude to Imogen Robertson, for introducing me to the riches of Charles Garvice. It says something about how much historians have still to learn about popular culture that even after some decades of teaching social history in universities, I had never before even heard of Garvice. Thanks to Stephanie Spencer and Penny Tinkler. Camilla Leach offered words of support which she's probably forgotten, but I haven't. I am grateful to Stephen Brooke, Lesley Hall, Selina Todd, and Amanda Vickery for their personal and intellectual generosity as well as for inspiring me with their own historical work and writing. Ulrike Meinhof has shared friendship, warmth and ideas over many years. Alison Woodeson, Monica Collingham, Jeanne Openshaw, and John Bristow have been wise and kind and buoyed me up through low times. I am hugely grateful to Jenny Shaw and to Marcia Pointon for their understanding, their ideas, and for their friendship. My thanks to Madge Dresser and Helen Taylor, too, for many years of friendship, intellectual stimulus, and emotional support. Alan Sinfield and Vincent Quinn have offered countless suggestions for more reading and thinking: it has been a real privilege to share conversations with them both.

I have benefited from the skills, professional expertise, and competence of a number of people in bringing this book to press. My warm thanks to Maggie Hanbury and her colleagues at the Hanbury Agency. Connie Robertson and Deborah Protheroe helped with textual and picture permissions respectively and both were impressively efficient. I am grateful to Pat Baxter for her copyediting expertise. Thanks also to Cheryl Brant who was painstaking and patient in seeing the manuscript of the book through to production. The team at Oxford University Press, Luciana O'Flaherty, Matthew Cotton, and Kizzy Taylor-Richelieu were always an absolute pleasure to work with.

My family, as always, has been a fount of encouragement and support. Conversations with Alex and Eugénie have never failed to stimulate, galvanise – or to puncture – my thinking about history and popular culture. I am boundlessly grateful for their sharp-wittedness, warmth, and common sense. Talking to, and learning from, Andrew Whitehurst and Mike Witcombe has also been both a privilege and a pleasure. The writer Georgette Heyer once observed through the heroine of one of her novels that 'a well-informed mind and a great deal of kindness' count as major assets in a partner. This book is dedicated to Nick von Tunzelmann, on whose intelligence, loyalty, and generosity I have so long been able to rely.

I need a hero
I'm holding out for a hero 'til the morning light
He's gotta be sure and it's gotta be soon
And he's gotta be larger than life

(Bonnie Tyler, Holding Out for a Hero, Dean<br>Pitchford/Jim Steinman, 1984)

I dreamed that you bewitched me into bed
And sung me moon-struck, kissed me quite insane.
(I think I made you up inside my head.)

(Sylvia Plath, Mad Girl's Love Song, 1951)

If thy desire have over thee the power
Subject then art thou and no governor.

(Sir Thomas Wyatt, sixteenth-century poet)

*through fantasy, we learn how to desire*

(Slavoj Žižek, Looking Awry: An Introduction to Jacques<br>Lacan through Popular Culture, 1992)

When I read for Entertainment, I had much rather view the Characters of Life as I would wish they were than as they are: therefore I hate Novels and love Romances.

(R.B. Sheridan, Letters, 1772)

# Introduction

W*hat did women want?* asked Sigmund Freud, founding father of psychoanalysis and excavator of the human mind.[1] Despite some thirty years probing the dark mysteries of the feminine soul, he confessed himself stumped for an answer. The question still intrigues: are women's desires completely different from men's? How far have their needs and wants been shaped or blocked by history?

This book narrows the question down to look at what women have found irresistibly attractive in men. Its scope is historical, with an emphasis on modern times. I am curious about the men—real and imagined—who inspired dreams, passions, and obsessions in women on a grand scale. Have there been patterns in all this sighing and longing? What do these patterns tell us about women and desire? The icons of romantic literature—Mr Darcy, Mr Rochester, Heathcliff, or Rhett Butler—were mostly, in the first instance, products of the female imagination. Movie stars and rock musicians acquire and cultivate images that in many cases have little to do with their 'real' selves. Many of the most successful 'romantic leads' in the past—Montgomery Clift, Rock Hudson, Dirk Bogarde, Richard Chamberlain, for instance—have been gay. Their performances nevertheless conjured visions of maleness which had women weak at the knees: how do we make sense of this?

What we now refer to as the 'alpha male' hero, rugged, square-built with a strong jawline, has never held indomitable sway over feminine emotions. Sensitive types, moody aesthetes, and men exuding androgynous charm have featured equally prominently in the cultural

1

landscape of desire. Lord Byron and Rudolph Valentino are obvious examples. Through history, any whiff of effeminacy in men who proved particularly attractive to women was likely to evoke censure from other males. A 'ladies' man' could be suspected of letting the side down. Male dancers of Valentino's ilk were castigated as gigolos, 'lounge lizards', or 'tango pirates' in North America a century ago. Army men in Britain used the pejorative term 'poodle-fakers' to mean ladies' men, implying some shortage of masculine grit, and almost certainly a disinclination for military service.[2] The weight of expectations around masculinity increased during wartime, when men were expected to fight. During the First World War, those who questioned this imperative were all too likely to be shamed with white feathers, often presented by women.[3]

Understanding the icons of masculinity who have served to invoke female desire is a step towards understanding the history of women's wants and needs, but it is more than that. It is also an inquiry into cultural history, an exploration of changing forms of communication, representation, and reinterpretation. There are similarities—but also crucial differences—between 'Byromania' in the nineteenth century and 'Beatlemania' in the twentieth. The young women who swooned over Byron got lovesick on poetry and the printed word via rumours and reputation. Beatles fans in the 1960s could listen to and watch their idols on record players and television screens in their bedrooms. They could, but didn't have to, storm concerts or converge upon airports for a glimpse of the real thing. Technology has reshaped patterns of desire and consumption. When air travel became possible, pilots and airmen started to feature large as romantic heroes both in novels and on the cinema screen. Voice recordings made it possible for women to fantasize about intimacy with 'crooners' such as Rudy Vallée, Bing Crosby, or Frank Sinatra. With the advent of cinema, mass publishing, and television, the possibilities multiplied. Icons of the past could be continually reinterpreted: John Barrymore as Beau Brummel; Richard Chamberlain as Byron; British actor Colin Firth as a particularly sexy incarnation in a long line of Mr Darcys. Since the

1990s, the impact of the internet has massively expanded opportunities for people to express, to play with, and to communicate their passions. The heartthrobs of the past gain a new lease of life as their appeal is reinterpreted and argued over through the media of YouTube, fan sites, blogs, or the discussion forum. Websites such as 'My Daguerreotype Boyfriend', described as a forum 'where early photography meets extreme hotness', even explore the sex appeal of long-dead men in history.[4]

Economics, as well as technology, impacted on desire. As the twentieth century progressed, younger women became more independent. As wage earners and consumers they began to express preferences. Sales of magazines like *Peg's Paper* and cheaply produced romances by Charles Garvice, E. M. Hull and Ethel M. Dell rocketed. Critics sneered at 'shop-girl romances' and worried about a decline in cultural standards.[5] Social aspirations—unlike literary standards—appeared to be rising apace. Were girls wanting too much and getting above themselves? Stories in early editions of *Peg's Paper* had heroines of modest birth entrapping mill owners and minor gentry, if not aristocrats. There was uneasiness about girls' new spending power and what was seen as their disinclination for self-improvement; their new and seemingly insatiable appetite for pleasure.

Such anxieties deepened as the habit of cinema going entrenched itself among the female population, with many women going to 'the pictures' regularly, two or three times a week in the 1920s and 1930s.[6] Film offered up new and potent images of masculinity for female delectation, especially following Rudolph Valentino's performance as Sheik Ahmed Ben Hassan in the screen version (1921) of E. M. Hull's (1919) best-selling novel, *The Sheik*. Contemporaries complained that courtship and common sense were being warped by romance reading and picture going. And meanwhile, the torrent of printed romance literature poured from the presses. New magazines—*Oracle, Miracle, Red Star, Glamour, Secrets and Flame*—thrilled female readers with a long procession of male romantic prototypes: sheiks, sultans, and foreign princes, captains of industry, film stars, aristocrats, and airmen. Even

**Figure 1.** *Peg's Paper*, cover image: Little servant girl, 22 Nov. 1921. There was a rich vein of fantasy around the possibilities of cross-class relationships.

those most in sympathy with the habits of young women expressed concern at the rate at which girls gobbled up cheap 'novels' and magazines of this kind, immersing themselves in a world heavy with escapist fantasy, even (or especially) in wartime.[7]

Young women's wages, and their levels of employment, continued to increase after the Second World War.[8] Teenagers began buying records and listening to new kinds of music.[9] Television began to compete with the cinema screen. Male pop stars—youthful, and casually dressed—began to replace sheiks, sultans, and airmen, particularly in the magazines aimed at the young female market. Another crop of new magazines—*Boyfriend, Roxy, Mirabelle, Romeo, Valentine*—mushroomed

**Figure 2.** Toffee tin, Keiller's Kinema Krunchies. A girl dreams about the men she would see on the cinema screen.

in the late 1950s, part and parcel of the teenage revolution. Singers and pop stars such as Elvis Presley, Lonnie Donegan, Tommy Steele, and Cliff Richard were heavily marketed through the pages of these magazines, which offered souvenir photos of pop heroes, transfers which could be ironed onto skirts and embroidered, and other 'personal keepsakes'. Teen magazines encouraged fan clubs and gossip. The Sixties accentuated these trends. Young girls retired to their bedrooms and swooned over Beatles recordings, played on treasured Dansette record players.

While teenage girls swore undying allegiance to pop singers, their mothers' hearts might have stayed with performers with a more mature style such as Mario Lanza, Frankie Vaughan, or Perry Como. Or older women may have sighed—along with their daughters—over one of the handsome doctors so popular with film and television audiences in the 1950s and 1960s: Dirk Bogarde as *Doctor in the House*, 'Bud' Tingwell in *Emergency Ward Ten*, Bill Simpson as Dr Finlay, or Richard Chamberlain as the handsome young intern, Dr Kildare. Married women confined to domesticity often had a hard time of it in the 1950s: the decade of Betty Friedan's *The Feminine Mystique*, housewives' psychosis, and pill popping. The consumption of tranquillizing drugs such as valium (diazepam) rose.[10] Medical romances were popular in these years. Marrying a doctor—with prospects of a steady income, and status in the community—could appear a safe bet for a comfortable, middle-class lifestyle. And some women invested a great deal of faith in family doctors, hoping for understanding of what had begun to look like a rising tide of female desperation, trusting that the medical profession would have some of the answers.[11]

For women's liberationists of the 1970s, on the other hand, medics—however paternalistic or avuncular their bedside manner—were too often identified with the social status quo. As representatives of patriarchy, they were something of a lost hope. They certainly couldn't be relied upon to diagnose women's social frustration and predicaments.[12] Indeed, as the feminist critique of patriarchy gathered steam, some of the more radically inclined theorists suggested that women's romantic preoccupations with men were altogether a big mistake. 'You start by sinking into his arms and it ends with your arms in his sink' was a warning often printed on tea towels. The catchphrase frequently (though probably wrongly) attributed to Gloria Steinem, 'a woman needs a man like a fish needs a bicycle', circulated widely at this time.[13] If women got sick, it was probably men's fault.

Feminists fell over themselves in their eagerness to deplore romantic dreams involving the finding of 'Mr Right' as deluded, and romantic fiction as a kind of hallucinatory drug which rotted women's minds. Germaine Greer, for instance, roundly condemned the 'titillating mush' of Barbara Cartland and 'her ilk'.[14] And yet notwithstanding the rising strength of second-wave feminism, sales of romance fiction, published by Mills & Boon and Harlequin, obstinately continued to rise. What was this trend about? Why were so many women seemingly addicted to the reading of romances?

Feminist academics argued about whether such readers were drugging themselves into compliance with a male-dominated social order, or compensating themselves for its miseries through escapist fantasy. There was no agreement about how these fantasies actually operated. Was romance fiction a place where uncompromising, manly heroes knocked women into shape? Or was it a place where female fantasy knocked men into shape, through narratives where heroes fell passionately in love, eventually prostrating themselves at the heroine's feet, their voices husky with lust, beseeching marriage? Was the romance plot, in essence, one of transformation, domesticating men for family life and love ever after? With advances in women's independence in the 1970s and after, the heroines of romance fiction became more varied and interesting, less prissy and more interested in sex. But the shape of the imaginary heroes who crushed these heroines to their manly chests, the templates of desirable masculinity, changed much more slowly.

The 1970s was a decade in which adolescent girls in Britain rushed to devour the trendsetting magazine, *Jackie*. The popularity of the magazine, with sales reaching some 606,000 in 1976, gave rise to much consternation among feminists. It was feared that young girls and even pre-teens were being seduced by strip cartoon romances which suggested that selfless, feminine behaviour would eventually earn them the prize of a boy's true love.[15] Any boy with flowing locks, a flowery shirt and bell-bottomed trousers could act the part of Prince Charming if a girl played her cards right. True love, it was assumed, would bring fulfilment and was what made a girl's life worth living. *Jackie*'s covers, and centre pages, sedulously promoted a new breed of boy-singer heartthrob: David Essex and David Cassidy were outstandingly popular in the early 1970s. David Essex featured in a centrefold for Valentine's Day in 1975 coyly grappling with a man-sized heart; a confection of satin ribbon and red roses. *Jackie* magazine's hegemony eventually gave way in the 1980s to more sexually sophisticated, celebrity-oriented magazines.

Boy bands increased their following among young girls in the 1980s, while the media through which they could be marketed and enjoyed changed rapidly. Performances could now be viewed and replayed at will through the click of a button. Pop videos, the rise of MTV, smart phones, and the mushrooming of social media through the internet have brought a new meaning to the mass adulation of boy performers by young teenage girls: witness the popularity of Justin Bieber, or boy band One Direction's massive and volatile fan base. With the rise of social media, the popularity of blogging, and the growth of fan and slash fiction, young women's expressions of desire—however ephemeral—have become louder and more difficult to ignore than they were even twenty years ago.

Have the objects of girls' passions changed much over the last half century or so? Is the frenzy of adulation surrounding One Direction in the twenty-first century essentially the same as Beatlemania in the 1960s? There are certainly continuities, but the styles and images of masculinity are very different, as are the media through which the fan base operates. The behaviour of fans is now notoriously hard to predict: witness the Twitter attacks on the editors of the British version of the magazine GQ when it decided to feature the members of One

Direction on its cover in the autumn of 2013.[16] The boys were represented in a way that many fans felt to be salacious and objectionable and a storm of 'death threats' and pungent abuse followed.[17]

Boy performers who can be described as 'pretty' or 'cute', many of whom have exhibited a tendency to clown around like puppies for public consumption, have evoked strong passions among young (and not so young) women fairly continuously since the 1980s. More recent is the widespread obsession with pretty-boy vampires evident over the last thirty years. The image of the vampire as an intensely desirable young man (physically youthful, if ages old) gained purchase with the popularity of Anne Rice's *Vampire Chronicles* in the 1970s and 1980s, together with their film adaptations, particularly *Interview with the Vampire* in 1994. Tom Cruise played vampire Lestat de Lioncourt, a heady mix of French aristocrat and rock superstar, Brad Pitt his moody, sensitive side-kick, Louis de Pointe du Lac. Edward Cullen, hero of Stephenie Meyer's vampire romance series, *Twilight*, famously described by his author as 'sparkling' and disturbingly beautiful, was played on screen by Robert Pattinson in the film version of 2008, immediately acquiring a cult following among girls and women worldwide. Internet communities of 'Twilight Moms' attested to his appeal across age groups. The massive increase in popularity of vampire romance over the last few decades has intrigued many observers. With it has come a new breed of heartthrobs: witness the many internet sites announcing readers' votes for 'the top ten sexiest vampire heroes' and suchlike.[18]

Vampires have become domesticated. The writer Stephen King recently commented that *Twilight* and its spin-off stories 'are not really about vampires and werewolves. They're about how the love of a girl can turn a bad boy good'.[19] This is of course the standard narrative of romance fiction, a narrative which underlies and partly explains the success of E. L. James's phenomenally successful volumes in the *Fifty Shades of Grey* series.[20] Such fantasies of transformation—embodied in the belief that a loving woman can elicit passion and devotion from a damaged and difficult man—retain a powerful hold in contemporary culture.

In 1972, art critic John Berger published an influential book (based on an earlier television series for the BBC) entitled *Ways of Seeing*.[21] In one of the most quoted passages from the book, Berger wrote that 'men act and women appear. Men look at women. Women watch themselves being looked at'.[22] This, he suggested, determines 'not only most relationships between men and women, but also the relation of women to themselves. The surveyor of woman in herself is male: the surveyed female.' Influenced by Berger's observation, a great deal of feminist literature has represented women as 'objects of the male gaze'. One of my primary aims in writing this book is to turn things round a little, and to look at the emergence of women as desiring subjects, linking this with their growing independence in a wage-earning, consumer society. I set out to explore ways in which patterns of romance and fantasy have changed over the last century, reshaping women's ideas about what they find desirable in men. It is a cultural history of desire from a particular perspective: the book will mainly look at men through the eyes of women.

# 1

# Her Heart's Desire

## *What Did Women Want?*

*T*he *Tiredness of Rosabel*, a short story written by Katherine Mansfield in 1908, offered a glimpse into the daydreams of a young girl working in a hat shop.[1] The young girl, Rosabel, is exhausted and frustrated: the gap between her desires and longings and the poverty of her everyday life is immense. Splashing out on a bunch of violets, she has to go without a proper dinner. She dreams of roast duck with chestnut stuffing but must resort to a Lyons Corner House to make do with a boiled egg. Travelling home to a shabby bedsit on a crowded bus, Rosabel is repelled by the stuffy, steamy atmosphere and her smelly fellow passengers. She sits next to a girl of her own age who is absorbed in reading a cheap paperback romance, noticing with distaste that the girl licks her fingers to turn the pages and mouths the words to herself as she goes along. Back home, Rosabel wearily trudges up several flights of stairs to her dismal rented room, then slumps down in the dusk with her head resting on the window ledge and begins to recollect the events of her day.

A glamorous young couple had burst into the hat shop, indulging in playful banter. Rosabel had found the girl a perfect hat, adorned with 'a great curled feather, and a black velvet rose ... They had been charmed,' she recalled. Asked to model this creation for her customers, Rosabel had experienced pangs of envy and resentment, made worse by a suggestive remark by the young man about her own 'damned pretty little figure'. Unsettled by these recollections, she found herself brooding on the attributes of the young man and his sexual appeal. What if she and the girl who had accompanied him were to change places? Rosabel imagined herself rich, privileged, loved, and desired. Conjuring up images of lush bouquets of roses, gorgeous clothes, and rich food in candlelit settings, her thoughts drifted into erotic reverie.

It is not just the man, Harry, who is at the heart of Rosabel's desire in this story. Rosabel dreams about and yearns for the voluptuousness of physical comforts, wealth, and position. In her fantasy, Harry provides a passport to a richer life, to a life of physical well-being where, protected by marriage to a powerful man, she counts for something in the eyes of others.

In the 1900s, femininity spelled frustration. Women's opportunities—for education, for well-paid employment, for political participation, for sexual expression—were limited. There was still a widespread assumption that female duties meant servicing others, and that true womanliness demanded purity and self-sacrifice.[2] Victorian images of 'the angel in the house' continued to haunt the imagination of young girls brought up on books stuffed with illustrations of maidens in white muslin, and garlanded with rosebuds. The writings of Ruskin and Coventry Patmore, pontificating about femininity, circulated widely as Sunday School prizes and featured routinely in the kind of 'improving literature' distributed by the Girls' Friendly Society.[3] Needy, desiring, or ambitious girls were frowned upon, especially if they set their sights on personal achievement at the expense of family and domestic obligations.[4]

It was easier to conform to social expectations about dutiful daughterliness, wifely submission, and motherly self-sacrifice if a woman had the protection of rich, liberal-minded males and wasn't too much plagued by her own ambitions and need for autonomy. In a society where women's crowning achievement was so regularly defined in terms of motherhood and domestic harmony, it is scarcely surprising that many women wanted to marry and raise children, hoping to find genuine and lasting happiness in family life.[5] But not everyone wanted or could achieve this ideal of the perfect marriage, the perfect family life. The odds were against it. For one thing, there weren't enough well-heeled, marriageable men to go around. And women in the early twentieth century were becoming ever more critical of a society which hemmed them in, depriving them of opportunities for self-development and independence. What were they to do if they chose not to marry, or if they couldn't find the man of their dreams?

Controversy over the 'woman question' or the 'sex question' had raged since the 1890s, intensifying in the early years of the twentieth century and peaking in the bitter conflicts and struggles around suffrage, on the eve of the First World War.[6] Openings for women in the workforce were widening during this period: although many girls still laboured in domestic service, increasing numbers of younger women turned to work in light industry, offices, and shops. Rosabel was a fictional creation, but her prototype could be met with any-where, in increasing numbers, in most towns and cities in Britain and America.[7] Living and working conditions for this growing army of young, white-collar female workers could be hard. And given the 'surplus women problem', their chances of marriage were slim. The devastating loss of young men in the First World War made this situation even worse.[8]

Ruth Slate and Eva Slawson were two young clerical workers in London in the 1900s. They left diaries and a collection of correspond-ence which allow us to reconstruct their friendship, and to learn something about what they wanted in their lives.[9] As a girl, Ruth found family life difficult; she was developing a mind of her own, which often brought her into conflict with her parents. Earning a living meant a great deal of drudgery for both girls. Eva was often bored by her job as a legal secretary. Ruth, employed by a grocery firm whose owners she described as 'slave drivers', chafed against exploit-ative conditions. Ruth and Eva's dreams of escape were less material-istic than those of the fictional Rosabel. Both of these young women wanted desperately to better themselves. Sharing a strong attachment to non-conformist religious principles, they hungered after education and self-improvement. They saw themselves very clearly as living through a time of change and upheaval in young women's lives.

Their letters and diaries are full of references to reading and discussion on social issues, to talk about the woman question, and to suffrage meetings and demonstrations. Both Ruth and Eva were inspired by 'rebellion against our old ways of living and thinking'.[10] Both were avid readers, trying to make sense of the heady new ideas of the day. South African writer Olive Schreiner's feminism and Edward Carpenter's radical visions of socialism and the new life made a particular impact. Both Schreiner's *Story of an African Farm* (1883) and Carpenter's *Love's Coming of Age* (1896) questioned traditional assumptions about what it meant to be male or female, and how the sexes should relate to each other, arguing for much more equality and comradeship.[11]

Ruth and Eva agonized over relationships. Ruth was uncertain about her feelings for the men in her life; they never quite seemed to measure up to her ideals. Her boyfriend Walter was less than sound on the woman question and she was hopping mad to find anti-suffrage leaflets in his lodgings.[12] 'Men have so little straightforwardness, unselfishness or backbone these days,' she grumbled in her diary in 1908.[13] Another suitor, Hugh, seemed incapable of emotional intimacy and Ruth wondered whether his heart had been frozen in his youth—although she did eventually marry him. 'My friendships with men seem disappointing things,' she confessed, wondering whether she was in part to blame for this.[14] And yet she found it hard to let go of 'the romantic idea of the one man for the one woman', which would give shape and meaning to her life.[15] Eva made no secret of her longing for a loving relationship with a man with whom she could have children; 'one heart, somewhere, to love and love'.[16] Several times she described herself as 'heartsick' and 'longing for the touch of baby fingers'.[17] But no Mr Right presented himself, and Eva's most intimate relationships were those she enjoyed with her women friends.

Ruth and Eva were adventurous, at both an intellectual and a personal level. Eva explored physical intimacy with her married woman friend, Minna, recording in her diary 'delicious' hours 'discussing the difference between passion, sensuousness and sensuality' and admitting that she had told Minna that 'if she were a man, I should feel absolutely completed'.[18] The two women came even closer after the sudden death of Minna's husband, when Eva moved in to help with the birth of Minna's baby. But both continued to think of sexual love as something that could only exist between men and women, in a different category from intimacy and physical tenderness between women. Discussing the women's movement in 1913, Eva's diary tells us that 'Minna said she thought if we could get an ideal man our difficulties would be solved' although Eva herself feared that no ideal man could exist until women themselves became 'spiritually and economically free'.[19]

Helping to care for Minna's new baby intensified Eva's longing for a man who would love her passionately and for children of her own. The friends discussed all kinds of radical ideas. Might sharing men be one answer to the man shortage of the time? Would it be possible to have a baby with a friend, rather than a fully committed lover? But the idea of one perfect love died hard. For a while, in 1914, Ruth toyed with the idea of marrying her good friend and benefactor, Mr Thompson, but confessed that though she respected him, the idea of marrying him was repugnant to her: 'I could not enter into sexual union with a man who was not *My Lover*', she explained, 'either to satisfy desire or curiosity, or for the sake of having a child'.[20] We know from Eva's diary that she had been reading H. G. Wells and that she found Wells's ideas about sexual freedom troubling. Eva, too, revolted against any suggestion that sexual gratification could be taken lightly, without real love and commitment. In June 1913 she commented on *The New Machiavelli*, which she found 'a brilliant but shallow book':

> Wells reminds me of sherbet which when shot into water causes it to effervesce—he is stimulating, but I think transitory. I dislike the manner in which early sexual episodes are related—I am perhaps fastidious, but to seize opportunities for sexual intercourse merely for self-gratification appears to me to be the attitude of the drunkard and glutton.

This certainly wasn't because she didn't understand the strength of physical desire, but:

> Even in my most rampant moods, when nature *thunders* in me and almost *demands* expression I feel in the depth of me that unless as an expression of love and completion the act would have but little satisfaction for me.[21]

Eva worried about Wells's effect on the minds of young men, who she thought would be encouraged to adopt too low an ideal of manhood and virility. Like many feminists of her time, she was sceptical about the idea of passion being too strong for restraint in young men, insisting that women, too, experienced powerful bodily desires. In her view, a single standard of good behaviour should govern the actions of both men and women.[22]

In the summer of 1914 Eva felt restless, but was reasonably optimistic about the future. Her diary records happy hours spent with Minna and her children. She delighted in playing with the baby in the garden, burying her face in her plump little body and hearing the child laugh and gurgle. Even so, she was haunted by the sense of something missing in her life, of a gap between desire and fulfilment, writing:

> How full of desire life is—*my* life is. Often I have felt as though on the very verge of infinite beauty—whether in friendship, nature or art—yet it has never quite revealed itself to me, neither have I ever *quite* succeeded in unfolding into its essence—ever it eludes me, hovering just at the extremity of one's grasp, luring one on and on.[23]

At the point at which she wrote this (4 July 1914) war had not yet been declared. Over the year which followed, Ruth and Eva continued their correspondence, Ruth writing from Woodbrooke, a Quaker study centre in Birmingham, where, thanks to Mr Thompson's generosity, she was at last able to devote herself to full-time education. The friends planned that Eva should follow Ruth to Woodbrooke, which she did, in 1915. Their correspondence came to an abrupt end, however, in the spring of the New Year, when sadly and unexpectedly, Eva died.

Ruth and Eva had read widely: alongside serious literature on religious subjects, and on social and political reform, they both managed to get through a large amount of romance fiction. After tea with Minna in the summer of 1913 Eva recorded that they had 'retailed romance after romance' and that Minna had impressed her by having read so many romances.[24] Minna's marriage was not altogether happy, and she may have read partly as a form of escape. But far from being carried away by sentimental fantasies, she suggested to Eva that too much romance was built up around the idea of marriage and that often 'the less romantic' marriages, based on kindness and trust, were the happiest.[25] It becomes clear from the discussions among these women friends that reading romance fiction was one way of thinking about the relationships between men and women, and trying to work out what it was that they actually wanted.

By the 1900s women were consuming novels in large quantities.[26] Whereas in Victorian times, reading had served to fill long hours of leisure, girls in the 1900s would often pop a book into a bag to read on the way to work, by train or omnibus. The market for cheap literature burgeoned. Books could be borrowed or bought. Circulating libraries supplied some of the demand: W. H. Smith had set up bookstalls on railway stations in the late nineteenth century, and Boots Booklovers' Libraries operated out of the chain of drugstores from 1898.[27] The publishing firm of Mills and Boon was established in 1908, although their specialization in romantic novels for women came later, after the First World War. Heavy, three-volume novels went out of fashion in the 1900s and readers went increasingly for single volumes in light bindings, often with colourful, seductive covers. These were easier to prop up in bed, as well as to carry on journeys.

Women wanted novels about adventures in love, and both male and female writers set out to supply these. The popular genre was much denigrated by literary critics who sneered at the tastes of typists, cooks, and domestic servants, and dismissed what was increasingly referred to as 'the shopgirl romance' as unworthy of serious attention. The sneers were based on snobbishness, misogyny, and social unease, as well as the conviction that such writing lacked any literary merit. No doubt jealousy also played a part: best-selling authors could make a great deal of money.

One writer, almost completely forgotten today and whose books sold in phenomenal quantities in the 1900s, was Charles Garvice. In 1910, Arnold Bennett described Garvice as 'the most successful novelist in England': he was said to have 'the largest sales of anyone in the world' by 1914.[28] In one of his broadcasted letters from America in the 1980s, Alistair Cooke remembered Garvice's immense popularity, 'a great many slim novels palpitating with romance—what my headmaster called with a snort, "housemaids' literature"'.[29] Garvice wrote prolifically; there are some two hundred book titles, in addition to serials in periodicals.[30] In North America, he published under the pseudonym 'Miss Caroline Hart' as well as in his own name. With titles such as *In Cupid's Chains* (New York, 1893, London, 1902), *A Woman's Soul* (1900), *Just a Girl* (1898), and *She Loved Him* (1908), Garvice was a writer who deliberately set out to cultivate the female reader.[31]

Garvice was confident that he knew what women wanted in a hero. He industriously delineated a range of desirable masculine types, all of them decently British, however, sporting guts and good taste. There were often references to service in the empire, which had allowed such men to hone their masculinity in combat with recalcitrant natives or wild beasts. Some but not all of his heroes were rich aristocrats. Blood and breeding definitely mattered in Garvice's books, and true gentlemanliness was deemed to be rooted in both. Rich parvenus were inevitably shown up as vulgar and the wrong sort.[32] They usually had terrible taste.

In *Her Heart's Desire* (1908), for instance, the hero is a world-weary aristocrat whom the author deemed just 'the sort of man to catch a young girl's fancy': rich, brave, good-looking, and debonair.[33] Lord Gaunt, we are told, had in abundance that quality of cool courage 'which has made the Englishman master of half the world'.[34] He had a slightly grim appearance and the reputation of a wicked past. This was a coded reference. 'A Past', as the contemporary reader would understand, added appeal to a man, whereas it would destroy a woman absolutely. It emerges that Gaunt's past was ruined by a calculating seductress. In contrast to this evil sophisticate, the heroine of the story, Decima Deane, is childlike and unsullied. She wears modest, dove grey silk and coos over small animals in cages. Decima is described as Gaunt's 'girl-love'. There isn't that much character development in a Garvice novel: there are goodies and baddies. The good types win and the baddies lose, but only after pages and pages of suspense and intricate plotting. As a master of fast-paced plot and narrative, Garvice's skills as a writer were unequalled. It isn't hard to understand his appeal in the 1900s: reading his books is like watching a speed driver negotiate a series of hairpin bends at full throttle. You hold your breath at every turn.

Garvice was careful about his heroines; he wanted his readers to root for them. They had to be girlish and modest but not like 'the impossible heroines in goody goody novels'.[35] Nor should they be 'brilliant or witty' types; this, too, might stand in the way of reader approval or identification.[36] But he took pains not to condescend to women in his writing. The heroines weren't all limply feminine: some were resourceful and adventurous in their own right. Many of them had to deal with inadequate fathers and brothers: eccentric, unworldly men, older men losing their marbles, younger wastrels, gamblers, or financial incompetents. Heroines stressed out and feeling abandoned in this wasteland of dysfunctional patriarchy are shown as vulnerable to predators (grasping types, often *nouveau riches* and unscrupulous) from whose clutches the gentleman-hero must rescue them.[37] He always makes it in the end.

Charles Garvice's heroes may have given women much of what they wanted at a fantasy level but he was always very careful to avoid direct references to sex or to sexual problems. He prided himself on his reputation as clean-minded: an irreproachably moral writer, read by men as well as women, recommended by churchmen, with a healthy, decent tone that could brook no harm to impressionable daughters.[38] This was a difficult area: many critics were all too keen to damn any kind of romance with clear popular appeal—especially to young women—as 'sex-obsessed' rubbish. As in the remark made by Alistair Cooke's headmaster, the word 'palpitating' was often used as shorthand to suggest too much sensuality embedded in debased emotional claptrap.[39]

Women writers had long come in for this kind of put-down. Male critics in the late Victorian years loved to sneer at the writings of Marie Corelli, 'Ouida', or Rhoda Broughton.[40] The 'New Woman' literature of the 1890s had attracted particular derision from those who dismissed it as pathological, the outpouring of 'erotomaniacs' and 'neurasthenics'.[41] Generalizations about romance fiction as low-brow, sensational, and second-rate were all too often based on contempt for women writers and readers. It is worth trying to sidestep this critical disdain in order to ask why, at this point in history, women turned to romance reading on such a large scale.

Katherine Mansfield wrote of a girl on a bus, entirely absorbed in a romance. She was specific about the text. The girl on the bus in *The Tiredness of Rosabel* was intent on a cheap edition of *Anna Lombard*. This was a novel by Annie Sophie Cory, using the pseudonym 'Victoria Cross'.[42] Published in 1901, the year of Queen Victoria's death, this novel created a huge stir and became an immediate bestseller. It was to go through some thirty editions, and to sell six million copies, and is almost completely forgotten today.[43] Mansfield's contemporaries, Ruth Slate and Eva Slawson, were charmed by *Katharine Frensham*, a novel by Beatrice Harraden first published two years later in 1903.[44] Harraden was a feminist intellectual.[45] Again, her work is now mostly forgotten. What were these books like to so enthral their readers?

*Anna Lombard* was set in India under the Raj. It is about the unruliness of female desire. Anna, the central character, loves two men. Her relationship with a socially acceptable, upstanding English civil servant, Ethridge, is endangered by her physical passion for her Pathan servant, Gaida Khan. Gaida's proud demeanour is matched by an exquisitely beautiful body, and he is described as graceful and majestic in his rich oriental dress. Anna finds Gaida erotically mesmerizing. She looks upon him as something of a 'beautiful toy'. It is hard for the selfless but slightly stiff Ethridge to compete. He has to wait, patient and miserable, for Anna's lust for his rival to work itself out. Conveniently enough Gaida Khan succumbs to cholera. But there is still a problem in that Anna finds herself pregnant with his child. This small mixed-race obstacle to narrative closure has to be disposed of before Anna can fully commit herself to Ethridge. The story—and the Indian landscape in which it is set—are as steamy as the atmosphere on the bus boarded by Katherine Mansfield's Rosabel. It is easy to see why *Anna Lombard* created shock waves.

*Katharine Frensham*, a more 'highbrow' example of romance, was also about female desire. The eponymous heroine is an intelligent and resourceful woman. Although she has several suitors, she has resigned herself to spinsterhood. She doesn't want to marry unless she can love passionately, and is all too aware that this may never happen. And then it does. She falls for a widowed academic, Clifford, whose first wife had failed to understand him. Clifford and his son had become emotionally withdrawn: they are described as 'icebergs'. Katharine's warmth, her exceptional intelligence, and her sensitivity allow them to thaw. We begin to understand why Ruth Slate, prone to describe the men in her life as 'emotionally frozen', might have responded to this text.[46]

These novels, with their desiring women and their sensitive, introspective, or wounded heroes, rarely appealed to male critics. There were some exceptions. The journalist and critic W. T. Stead defended *Anna Lombard* for the way in which it boldly reversed gender roles, showing not only that women could be sensual beings, but that men as well as women could love unselfishly and learn to govern their passions.[47] But most dismissed Ethridge as unmanly and reprehensible, if not altogether unbelievable. Nor did Beatrice Harraden's Clifford appeal. A reviewer in *The Spectator* thought him 'particularly unsatisfactory', grumbling that:

> He is intended to be an interesting and romantic figure, but he is so fond of taking out his emotions to see how they are getting on, as children dig up the seeds in their gardens, that the reader loses all patience with him.[48]

The long list of 'sensational' novels of the 1900s derided by male critics included Elinor Glyn's erotic romance, *Three Weeks* (1907) and Ethel M. Dell's *The Way of an Eagle* (1912).[49] Again, both of these focused on female sexual desire and the kind of hero who might offer a woman fulfilment. The central female character in *Three Weeks* is a lady of mysterious Balkan origin who seduces a young Englishman, Paul Verdayne. Paul's class background is impeccable (Eton and Oxford), and he is described as a 'splendid young animal', if somewhat wet behind the ears and socially immature. The lady both mothers him and inducts him into cultural and erotic sophistication. This involves a great deal of petting and squirming about on tiger skins. The well-worn doggerel 'Would you like to sin with Elinor Glyn on a tiger skin/ Or would you prefer to err with her on some other fur?' was prompted by *Three Weeks* and helped to establish it as a landmark in popular culture. The text is heavy with the clichés of Edwardian sensuality: fur, perfumes, orchid-coloured silks, and banks of tuber-oses. More 'modern'—and shocking to contemporaries—was the idea of a woman taking the sexual initiative and teaching a young man something about what turned women on. Under the lady's tutelage, we are told, Paul learned 'that he could always affect her when he pretended to dominate her by sheer brute force', and that 'a woman will stand almost anything from a passionate lover', although it's never in doubt that these are power games which leave the lady firmly in control.[50]

We know comparatively little about Ethel M. Dell, although among largely male critics, her name became a kind of shorthand for roman-tic rubbish. *The Way of an Eagle* was Dell's first novel; she had found it difficult to interest a publisher. Eventually taken on by T. Fisher Unwin in 1911, the book was an immediate success with women readers and had been reprinted thirty times by 1915.[51] The book tells the story of a young woman, Muriel, and her growth towards sexual awareness, emotional maturity, and understanding of the meaning of love. Muriel is the daughter of a brigadier who has raised her in British India. Her father, about to perish in a savage native revolt, entrusts his daughter to Nick Radcliffe, a maverick and physically unattractive young soldier who has impressed the brigadier with his qualities of daring and resourcefulness. Muriel mistrusts Nick, even after he has performed the astonishing feat of lugging her on his back across the Himalayas, strangling a hostile-looking tribesman with his bare hands, and cherishing her with gentle and devoted care. It is a distinctly odd story. Nick is a queer fellow, though women are shown as drawn to him. He's eligible as a husband, with property in the South of England. Ethel Dell portrays him as somewhat physically repulsive, with sun-wizened, 'wrinkled yellow skin', and a face 'like an Egyptian Mummy', while emphasizing his tender, 'motherly' solicitude and absolute devotion to Muriel. For a time, Muriel is attracted to a more conventionally handsome soldier, Blake. Nick despairs and goes off to fight again, losing an arm in the process. Eventually Muriel realizes her deep, primitive desire for Nick, who has by this time turned to stalking her, dressed as an old woman. This time, *she* proposes marriage. Yellow wrinkles notwithstanding, she can't resist him. But Nick still makes her take the initiative, even after all the stalking. She marries him, and the book ends with Muriel happy and fulfilled—and pregnant.

This is scarcely first-rate fiction. But it is worth thinking about what made *The Way of an Eagle* so popular among women readers of the day. The book's popularity coincided with women's struggles for the vote, years in which the problems and difficulties of power relationships between men and women were everyday matters for discussion.[52] The book shows women as self-determining, and struggling to make sense of their own desires and futures. It problematizes masculinity, and asks fairly searching questions about what women might find physically attractive in men. It recognizes the importance of physical courage and the intrepid masculinity of the imperial adventurer, while suggesting that women want and need more sensitivity and gentleness in their heroes. The book is peopled with men who both respect and protect women. Its characters may be unconvincing, but it offers a benevolent, comforting vision of patriarchy, where there can be harmony between men's and women's desires.

Much less comforting to Edwardian patriarchs were Dr Marie Stopes's writings on the subject of what women wanted from men. *Married Love* crashed like a juggernaut into the walls of English reticence in 1918. Stopes dedicated *Married Love* to 'young husbands and all those who are betrothed in love'.[53] It was certainly not addressed to young unmarried women, although this didn't stop them reading it if they could get hold of a copy. The first chapter of the book was entitled 'The Heart's Desire'. 'Every heart desires a mate', insisted the author: men and women needed each other for completion. Stopes slid straight into purple, pulsating prose. Bodily union between a man and a woman:

> is the solid nucleus of an immense fabric of interwoven strands reaching to the uttermost ends of the earth; some lighter than the filmiest cobweb, or than the softest wave of music, iridescent with the colours, not only of the visible rainbow, but of all the invisible glories of the wave-lengths of the soul.[54]

We can't know how many readers skipped this kind of passage to get to the nitty-gritty, but this was easier said than done, because so much of Stopes's more helpful information about physiology was embedded in language about the essences of the soul. We find her getting more graphic in Chapter 3, which is entitled 'Woman's "Contrariness"'. Here, Marie set out to explain to her imagined young, male audience why they so often found their womenfolk capricious and cold. Why was this? It was partly because society had effectively schooled young women into neglecting their own sexuality and desires. This process of repression was so effective 'that most women would rather die' than admit their randiness, even though they might feel 'a physical yearning indescribable, but as profound as hunger for food'.[55] Female desire came and went in waves, Marie explained, abandoning her poetic strain for the moment to hold forth about 'what I call the law of

Periodicity of Recurrence of desire in women'.[56] She helpfully drew graphs to illustrate this. Men needed to respect these wave crests and sexual tides, and to woo with tenderness before every act of coitus.[57] They should also remember that a woman's love was stirred primarily through her heart and mind and couldn't be wholly physical.

There followed a series of pronouncements and recommendations akin to an instruction manual for the male. Not all of it was reassuring. Between 70 and 80 per cent of married, middle-class women, Stopes alleged, were deprived of orgasms through their husbands' incompetence.[58] Either their lovers didn't know about the clitoris or they came too fast—arrived too quickly at 'the explosive completion of the act'.[59] Many men didn't realize that it could take a woman ten to twenty minutes of intercourse before she was able to climax, as opposed to a man's two or three minutes.[60] It was nerve-racking if a man fell asleep straight after his own climax, leaving his wife wakeful and on edge. This could cause terrible injury to the woman's health as well as destroying marital harmony. Men should pull themselves together and stop complaining about their wives as contrary beings, or whingeing about their coldness; it was their own inadequacies as lovers they needed to look to, to solve the problem.

The tone of this horrified many. Were women to be the judges of male sexual competence?[61] This was radical indeed, and to some, quite unacceptable. Stopes had trouble finding a publisher for *Married Love*. Walter Blackie told her that he found the subject displeasing and thought that there was too much talking and writing about 'these things' already. After the war, he objected, 'There will be few enough men for the girls to marry, and a book like this would frighten off the few'.[62] *Married Love* was banned as obscene in America until 1931. By then it had gone through nineteen editions in Britain and sold some three-quarters of a million copies. In a later book, *Enduring Passion*, a sequel to *Married Love* which was first published in 1928,[63] Stopes contended that she had been bitterly attacked by an unnamed aristocratic male for having told women about the joys of sex. 'Lord X' is alleged to have accused her of breaking up the home by giving women a taste for things that only prostitutes should know about, insisting that:

> Once you give women a taste for these things, they become vampires, and you have let loose vampires into decent men's homes . . . We do not want that sort of thing in our own homes. The wife should be the housekeeper and make the home a place of calm comfort for the man. Instead of that you have made my home a hell: I cannot meet the demands of my wife now that she knows.[64]

'If you create these vampire women', Lord X is alleged to have threatened her, 'you will rear a race of effeminate men'.[65] According to Stopes this man was elderly.[66] If so, he probably avoided the cinema. But it wouldn't be difficult to predict what he would have thought about the slave-braceleted contemporary cinema-screen heartthrob, Rudolph Valentino.

Edith Maud Hull started writing novels while her husband was away in the First World War. *The Sheik* was first published in 1919.[67] *The Sheik* told the story of a plucky young aristocrat, Diana Mayo, bent on adventure in the desert. She gets more than she bargained for when she is carried off by Sheik Ahmed Ben Hassan, a testosterone-fuelled Arab warlord with that clichéd feature of so many romantic heroes, a 'cruel mouth', who treats women like horses. He clobbers Diana into submission in his richly adorned, luxuriously appointed tent, strewn with silk cushions and Oriental knick-knacks. We learn that Ahmed chain-smokes, but is fastidious about his personal hygiene. Diana resists his advances at first, and is bitter and miserable. Ahmed doesn't give a toss. She tries to escape and he hunts her down. However, all of a sudden Diana realizes that she's enjoying this and that she has actually fallen in love. After all, Ahmed is a lot sexier than some of the wimpy English toffs she's accustomed to. Even so, and rebel though she is, she feels that she must hide her change of heart from Ahmed, who she's pretty sure gets off on the idea of her resistance and will be bored by any soppy confession of love. But his feelings are beginning to change, too. When Diana is captured by a rival sheik—a

fat, smelly one, this time, with disagreeable habits and dirty finger-nails—
Ahmed rides to the rescue. He's just in time, but gets badly wounded.
This gives Diana the opportunity to display some self-sacrificing,
feminine devotion. While Ahmed is delirious, his friend tells Diana
that her sheik isn't really an Arab, he's of mixed English–Spanish
blood and actually has a title (Lord Glencaryll). Ahmed begins to
understand the social predicament in which he has mired Diana and
makes plans to pack her off home. But by this time she's so desirous of
staying with him that she threatens to shoot herself if he sends her
away. So Ahmed presses her shuddering, quivering little body to his
big manly chest with promises that he'll never let her go.

**Figure 3.** Rudolph Valentino as *The Sheik*.

Generations of critics have loved to satirize *The Sheik*. Q. D. Leavis snootily dismissed it as the ultimate 'typist's daydream'.[68] But the text is pacey and engaging, and even today it attracts enthusiastic recommendations on internet sites like Goodreads.com. Others find Hull's novel offensive in its suggestion that Diana needed to be forced into sexual compliance to discover the meaning of passion, or even womanliness. At a fantasy level, though, the story worked and was a runaway success, spawning countless imitations over the next century.[69]

The impact of Hull's story was sealed by the Paramount silent film which it inspired, starring Rudolph Valentino in the title role, and first screened in 1921. The film greatly sanitized the novel. There is no suggestion of rape on screen. Valentino's sheik is a lot less craggy and cruel than his fictional equivalent. He's introduced early on as a romantic idealist, prone to encouraging marriages for love among his tribespeople. Like Diana, he's a bit of a prankster. The two of them lark around like a couple of Bright Young Things, making eyes at each other. In a scene inserted early in the film, Diana disguises herself as a native dancing girl to get into the Arab, male dominated casino. Amused by this, Ahmed unmasks her. After he carries Diana off to his tent the only thing forced on her is an outfit of sparkly harem pyjamas. When she resists his embraces he looks miserable and crestfallen. Next morning he hopefully tosses a white rose on her breakfast tray, but she stroppily hurls it to the floor. Much of the sexual charge loaded into the original text is displaced, in the film, onto the weather: winds batter and rage, and sandstorms swirl. Rudy projects an endearing tenderness throughout.

Valentino's performance as the sheik may have been boyish and rather camp, with a great deal of eye-rolling suggestiveness, but he was already establishing himself as what writer H. L. Mencken described as 'catnip to women'.[70] The extremely successful anti-war film *Four Horsemen of the Apocalypse* had also launched in 1921. In it Rudy played Julio, a dashing young Argentinian whose emotional development to manhood, and eventual destruction, takes place in a Europe falling apart through war. Rudy undergoes a powerful process of transformation, from gigolo into war hero, but also from strutty male into sensitive soulmate. The film featured a scene in which Julio danced an outrageously sensual tango in a Buenos Aires nightclub. It brought Valentino instant celebrity. Jesse Lasky, Vice-President of Famous Players-Lasky, was awed by the performance. Looking back in 1957, he judged that Rudy showed 'more sheer animal magnetism than any actor before or since'.[71]

These two films together cemented Valentino's reputation. Both were particularly attuned to the needs and concerns of women at the time. *Four Horsemen of the Apocalypse* dwelt on the cost of war for men, but also for women. Julio stood for all the dashing young men, full of promise, who had been lost by mothers, sisters, wives, and lovers. What *The Sheik* offered was very different. The book described a handsome, powerful tribesman with the culture of a discerning European and aristocracy in his blood, who learned to love an English girl. The film offered a tamer version, with a still potent but more good-natured story of seduction. Rudy is a smooth-skinned lover boy, perfectly at ease with flappers in Biskra, the 'Monte Carlo of the Orient', but possessed of sufficient English graces to allow the modern girl to imagine taking him home to meet her mother.

The 1920s were years of social dislocation following wartime. It was a decade of uncertainty, uneven aspirations, loss, disappointment, and frustration for women of all ages, all over Britain. It is hardly surprising that many sought escape through romance in novels or on the cinema screen. *The Sheik* was the perfect escape fantasy; book and film between them offered a multifaceted vision of desirable masculinity, both masterful and tender: just about all that the heart could desire.

# 2

# Unbridled Passions

There are many stories in history and legend where rampant females are seen as posing a particular threat to the social order. In classical mythology it was the maenads, or 'raving ones', the followers of Dionysus or Bacchus, who frenziedly tore Orpheus apart. Dolled up in fawn-skins, wine-fuelled, and brandishing their *thyrses* (long sticks wreathed in ivy and tipped with a pinecone), on a night out the maenads were uncontrollable. In the seventeenth century, women were often seen as more lascivious than men, their passions ruled by nature rather than reason.[1] Nineteenth-century physiologists clung to this notion that women were governed more by nature than by civilized thought. But they fiddled around with the concept of female nature, adjusting it to preconceptions about social class. They argued that women—at least the decent, middle-class sort—were pure at heart and not driven by physical passion in the way that men were.[2] Lower-class women might be seen as more physical (read, more in touch with their animal nature) than their middle-class equivalents. In a certain male mindset this helped to explain why some middle- or upper-class men turned to prostitutes. It could even be suggested that a class of 'prostitute' women was a necessary evil, so that men could relieve their lusts on one group without compromising the virtue of 'respectable' females.[3]

Where this Victorian illusion that respectable women were passion-free beings prevailed was often in the face of plenty of evidence to the contrary and at great cost to women themselves.[4] All women—whatever their class backgrounds—were effectively lumped into one of two categories: 'respectable' or 'fallen'. That men were allowed a degree of licence while women were caged in by expectations of chastity and virtue was all part of a distinct double standard of sexual morality which has persisted up to the present day. For a woman, giving vent to passion has always carried serious risks, quite aside from the physical risk of unwanted pregnancy.[5] The social cost of being labelled unfeminine—or of being seen as a loose or fallen woman—has been high. Loss of reputation could expose a woman to the worst features of masculine exploitation: there was the danger that she would be seen as worthless and therefore 'fair game'.

Passionate feelings of all kinds could look unfeminine. Even writing about them was risky. Charlotte Brontë felt obliged to apologize for her sister Emily's rendering of the 'harshly manifested passions, the unbridled aversions, and headlong partialities' of northern folk in *Wuthering Heights*.[6] That a quiet, well-behaved girl could even imagine a Heathcliff was somewhat unseemly. Emily had been unworldly, a home-bred country girl, Charlotte explained, much accustomed to the rough folk of the rugged moorlands, and it showed in the 'perverted passion and passionate perversity' of her characters. Not that Charlotte herself was able to fully disguise her passions: her love for the (married) French teacher, Professor Constantin Héger, with whom she lodged and worked in Brussels in the 1840s, was a disruptive influence in her life and erupts through the surface of her novels.[7]

Women sometimes colluded with the idea of themselves as modest and passionless because that way they could look pure and innocent, avoid censure, and appear stronger candidates for masculine protection.[8] In a world in which the balance of power between the sexes was so unequal, having a protector counted. It was extremely risky to look knowing, experienced, or in any way sexually needy as a woman. But it has also been hard for women to give expression to what they want, or even to recognize their own desire in the first place.

As Marie Stopes had explained to her 'young husbands', social conditioning could be very effective in blocking off desire.[9] Understanding this goes some way towards explaining the vexed question of the appeal of 'rape' scenes in imaginative literature, such as the episodes in E. M. Hull's The Sheik, as discussed in Chapter 1. Hull tells us that Diana's body 'throbbed with the consciousness of a knowledge that appalled her'.[10] Even once sexually awakened, she feels that she has to keep her desires hidden, to protect herself.[11] The fact that the heroine is overwhelmed by a strong, desirable hero at an imaginative level frees her from responsibility, excuses what otherwise might be interpreted as her own risky, culpable, or even unrecognizable sexual longings. That this 'rape' only takes place within the realms of fantasy, where the woman/fantasist is in control of both the characters and the narrative, is crucial.

Dance was one medium through which women could express and explore desire and passion. The 1900s saw the eruption of what was widely described as 'dance mania' or a 'dance craze' in America and Britain, regularly linked—in the minds of both contemporaries and later historians—with new forms of liberation for women.[12] The dance craze had various manifestations. There was the impact of Russian ballerina Anna Pavlova, choreographed by Mikhail Fokine in The Dying Swan in 1905. There was Diaghilev's Ballets Russes, reinforcing an already fashionable orientalism.[13] There was ragtime; a passion for the tango in London, Berlin, and New York; the Charleston and Josephine Baker in Paris between the wars.[14]

Dance allowed transgressive fantasies about both gender and power. Scheherazade, performed for the first time in Paris in 1910, was based on the first chapter of One Thousand and One Nights (Arabian Nights). In this story a despotic Persian king goes off hunting, and while he's away his favourite wife, Zobeide, persuades the eunuchs guarding the women to free the king's slaves. The black, male slaves are seduced by the concubines. Zobeide chooses the king's exquisite 'golden slave' (Njinsky) as her lover. Scenes of breathtaking, orgiastic sensuality follow, before the king returns and massacres everyone except Zobeide, who takes her own life.

As cultural historian Mica Nava has emphasized, this was shocking and exciting on many levels.[15] Lustful, libidinous women were shown dancing a defiance of patriarchy and initiating erotic adventures with black subordinates. Vaslav Njinsky, gorgeous and bisexual, became a cult figure. Whether androgynous as a bejewelled sex slave in gold harem pants, or stitched into silk elastic and rose petals, he fired the imagination of both men and women. After his performances in Fokine's *Le Pavillon d'Armide*, *Le Spectre de la Rose*, and *Scheherazade*, Njinsky found himself the object of what classical scholar and critic James Davidson has described as 'a great geyser of sexual and romantic fantasies'[16] across the world.

Highly significant for women were the performances of individual female dancers such as Isadora Duncan and Maud Allan.[17] Isadora Duncan moved from California to London in 1898. She described her innovative, expressive form of dance as inspired by a mixture of classical sculpture (she studied Greek vases and bas-reliefs in the British Museum) and American ideals of freedom. She drew heavily on fantasy and imagination, performing barefoot in flimsy draperies or a Greek tunic. Ruth Slate, introduced in Chapter 1, recorded in her diary that she had been particularly keen to see Isadora Duncan perform at the Duke of York's Theatre in London in 1908.[18] Ruth's then boyfriend Wal, less keen, had stood her up, so Ruth decided to go alone. She found the performance a revelation, recording children dressed as sprites and fairies frolicking around with ferns and lilies; but it was Isadora's expressiveness and freedom that made such an impact: 'I do not think I have ever seen anything more exquisite than Miss Duncan's dancing and my heart went out to the woman herself and loved her,' Ruth enthused.[19] Isadora Duncan's dance style was controversial: her lifestyle even more so. She was bisexual, and in 1906 had given birth to her first child without marrying the father.

Canada-born Maud Allan created even more ructions with her interpretation of Salome, first staged in 1908. Allan performed what dance historian Judith Mackrell has summed up as 'an audacious choreography of desire'.[20] She wore very little apart from ropes of pearls and a wispy skirt. There were many who dismissed this expression of a young girl's physicality as the height of decadence, but it fascinated nonetheless. Like the ballet *Scheherazade*, it opened up a register of expression for female lust which was both shocking and appealing to many women. In 1918 the right-wing Noel Pemberton Billing, editor of a magazine called *Vigilante*, denounced and derided such eroticism as 'the cult of the clitoris', by which he meant deviant and depraved.[21] He further declared it unpatriotic, contriving to suggest that Maud Allan's close friendship with Margot Asquith, wife of the former prime minister, was implicated in a web of German conspiracy to bring down Britain. Allan sued, but in the context of wartime uneasiness Pemberton Billing got away with it.

Women's freedoms were both amplified and attacked as a consequence of the First World War.[22] Young women moved into munitions work and previously male occupations, and many had their horizons widened by travel, work, and cinema. These new opportunities generated moral panics, such as that over 'Khaki Fever': the belief that young women were turning into nymphomaniacs, throwing themselves at soldiers. Popular travel writer Mrs Alec Tweedie alleged that as soon as war was declared, 'girls went out like cats on the tiles', looking for mates and shrieking madly.[23] During the war, there were fears that young women's passions were being inflamed by cinema-going. As cinema historian Chris Brader has pointed out, films with titles such as *The Shop-Soiled Girl* or *A World of Sin* weren't calculated to reassure the censors, however mild the content.[24] There was concern about improper goings-on in the dark of the picture palace, in dance halls, or indeed anywhere where young people hung about together.[25]

Girls gathered together in groups were held to egg each other on to unruly behaviour. Anxiety about this is clearly reflected in a story written by D. H. Lawrence, which was published in 1922.[26] The story, entitled *Tickets Please!*, features a group of girls working as conductors on trams during the war years. Described as 'fearless young hussies', we are told that 'they fear nobody—and everybody fears them'. One of the girls, Annie, develops a passion for a young male inspector, John Thomas Raynor, who is something of a Don Juan. When she shows a desire for a fuller, more intimate relationship with him, the inspector, wary of her possessiveness, cries off. Annie and her mates lure John Thomas into the Ladies' Waiting Room and taunt him about his behaviour, seeking some kind of retribution. They press him to make a choice, to commit himself to one or other of them. He gets uneasy, feeling himself cornered, and then the girls set on him like Bacchantes, ripping his clothes and drawing blood. When they let him go, crestfallen, Annie is left miserable, and the girls completely nonplussed.

The idea that women should know their place and behave with modesty was deftly satirized by Anita Loos in her 1925 comic novel, *Gentlemen Prefer Blondes*, and its sequel, *But Gentlemen Marry Brunettes* (1928).[27] Originally subtitled *The Intimate Diary of a Professional Lady*, *Gentlemen Prefer Blondes* focused on the adventures of a pair of resourceful, libidinous American flappers, Lorelei and Dorothy, who travel around Europe creating mayhem. High-spirited and irrepressible, they zestfully pursue pleasure and personal gain. They are magnets for men wherever they go, and though good-natured, they exploit their suitors shamelessly. The men are shown as gullible, shallow creatures, somewhat infantile and often at the mercy of their wives and mothers. Lorelei, as narrator, is something of a philosopher. Twisting men round her little finger is to her a skill, a sensible strategy for the ambitious girl. And ambition in a girl, she reflects, is a form of prudence. Through the voice of Lorelei, Loos makes hay with the strictures of a society structured by class and patriarchy, up-ending double standards of morality. Courted by the rich Henry Spoffard, a moralist and prohibitionist, Lorelei suggests that a girl might be considered to be 'more reformed if she knew what it was to be unreformed'.[28] Experience, to her, is invaluable: for how else can a girl learn what she wants? In Vienna, concerned about Lorelei's state of mind, Spoffard sends her to Sigmund Freud ('Dr Froyd'), who confesses that he can find nothing wrong with Lorelei apart from her lack of repression. He advises her to cultivate some inhibitions.[29]

The fashionable young woman, characteristically casting off her stays and inhibitions, caught the imagination of the 1920s. This image of the pleasure-seeking flapper could be tongue-in-cheek, but still basically positive. The term 'It', denoting sexual attractiveness, was widely discussed at this time. Elinor Glyn, invited to Hollywood to turn her hand to screenwriting in 1920, claimed ownership of the term, based on her short story, 'It', which she developed for the cinema screen in 1927.[30] Glyn kept insisting that 'It' was not merely sexual, but rather a quality of 'potent romantic magnetism', but the public wasn't in the mood for such fine distinctions. Clara Bow's legendary performance as the 'It' girl in this silent movie broke box office records in America. She played the part of a shop girl, Betty Lou, who set her sights on seducing and marrying the handsome owner of the department store in which she was a lowly employee. After a number of misunderstandings, and a lot of scheming, she pulls this off. The film—carried by Clara Bow's bubbly, appealing performance—celebrates Betty Lou as full of *joie de vivre*, irresistibly attractive and winningly feminine as well as having a shrewd eye for self-advancement.

Two other films of the period featuring girls on the make pushed the boundaries further. Warner Brothers' *Baby Face* (1930) starred Barbara Stanwyck as Lily Powers, a girl who survives sexual abuse and a deprived background by being inspired by Nietzsche and learning to exploit men before they exploit her. In an uncut version of the film she's advised to 'crush all sentiment' and to face life 'defiantly and unafraid', not to waste any energy 'yearning for the moon'.[31] A publicity poster for the film showed Stanwyck in a sexually challenging pose, declaring that 'She had "It" and she made "It" pay!' Lily sleeps her way up through the management structure of the company she works for before eventually falling in love. The screenplay of MGM's *Red Headed Woman* (1932) was written by Anita Loos. In this film, Jean Harlow plays Lil, an out-and-out exponent of sexual opportunism who stops at very little to get what she wants, destroying marriages in the process. Lil is lustful and sexually self-possessed, juggling between her own sexual needs and determination to marry wealth as it suits her. The film proved highly controversial, and was banned in Britain. Both of these films starred uninhibited female characters who had no difficulty with owning or expressing desire, or in deploying various forms of sexual opportunism. Both characters, Lily and Lil, profited from such sophistication, and went unpunished. They stood as examples of precisely the kind of licence and moral laxity that the Motion Picture Production (Hays) Code, which took effect in America from 1934, was designed to censor and clamp down on.[32]

In films like *Baby Face* and *Red Headed Woman* the men's roles are undeveloped. They are like cardboard cut-outs, characterized by, and differentiated from each other simply by age, wealth, and handsomeness, serving as ciphers for, or objects of, feminine desire. This is in contrast with the male icons of celebrity culture of the 1920s and 1930s. Here, the Hollywood 'star' system, together with the production of movie magazines and other forms of journalism, encouraged mass adulation among female fans, usually involving a near-forensic interest in stars' personalities and private lives.[33]

While it was risky for individual women to lose control or to surrender to passion, there could be safety in numbers. The maenads, after all, went around in a gang. In North America, by the late nineteenth century, groups of adoring girls had haunted matinée performances at the theatres in pursuit of actors whom they elevated to the status of 'matinée idols' on account of their desirability.[34] Displays of collective passion became commonplace around matinée and movie stars, as fans fought to see and to touch their heroes, and to secure autographs and mementoes. There were historical precedents for this kind of thing. Back in the early nineteenth century, the composer and pianist Franz Liszt had inspired women to heights of devotion which contemporaries dubbed 'Lisztomania'.[35] Women were said to have collected Liszt's cigar stubs, which they would encase in jewellery or hoard as relics.[36] Such behaviour has long been deplored and labelled hysterical. Late nineteenth-century observers spoke of a new disease affecting young women, which they dubbed 'idolitis'.[37] In his historical study of matinée idols (published in 1972), writer David Carroll commented on 'the hundreds of palpitating, breast-beating females' who cornered such performers in the 1890s and 1900s 'like wolves surrounding a stag, some reaching out to stroke his coat, his shoes, anything; some standing planted to the earth on which he walked, in mute adulation'.[38]

Rudolph Valentino, variously described as 'Love-God', prototype 'Latin Lover', or the 'greatest screen lover of all time' was a phenomenon on quite a different scale.[39] An estimated 125,000 people rushed to see *The Sheik* within weeks of its opening in New York. Valentino is said to have received thousands of letters a week from adoring women in his heyday, although as in many of the stories which surround his popularity, it isn't easy to separate fact from fiction. Women were said to swoon or shriek at the very mention of his name. When he appeared in public, they snatched at his clothing, jewellery, or cuff-links for mementoes. After Valentino's shockingly sudden, untimely death from peritonitis in 1926, huge unruly crowds jostled to file past his body; there were faintings, hysterics, and even reports of women driven to suicide with grief.[40] Valentino was, and remains a superstar, whose cult status has endured: his sex appeal is anatomized and hotly debated on the internet even today.[41]

A significant part of Valentino's appeal on screen was transgressive. In *The Sheik*, a brown-skinned man, ostensibly an Arab, carries off a pale-skinned girl, likened in the text to a pretty boy or a white gazelle.[42] The frisson of difference is there although ultimately we're reassured that Ahmed is the son of an English lord and not really an Arab at all. But fears about miscegenation were on the rise in the late 1920s, and soon the Hays Code set out explicitly to clamp down on suggestions of interracial romance.[43] More generally, the movie production code asserted that scenes of passion, 'impure love', and lustful kissing might threaten moral standards everywhere.[44] Adultery should never be made to look attractive, in order to protect the sanctity of marriage and the home. All this had an impact. Film historian Molly Haskell noted that before the mid-1930s, American cinema could show women as sexually desiring in their own right 'without being freaks, villains, or even necessarily Europeans'.[45] Stars such as Jean Harlow, Norma Shearer, Marlene Dietrich, and Barbara

Stanwyck all played convincing roles as women of uninhibited sexuality, pursuing men, enjoying sex, and challenging sexual double standards head on. In the later 1930s this changed, and sex had to take cover under metaphor. 'It is the difference between Ginger Rogers having sex without children—*Gold Diggers of 1933, Upper World* (1934)—and Ginger Rogers having children without sex—*Bachelor Mother* (1939)', Haskell explained.[46]

If it became harder to show women as explicitly sexually desiring, several films made just before and after the Second World War focused on heroines driven by unruly passions and worldly appetites. The most famous of these was of course *Gone with the Wind*, the historical romance epic based on Margaret Mitchell's 1936 novel of the same name, set in the American South during the Civil War. The novel was a huge hit when it was first published, and has continued a best-seller, with estimates of between 26,000 and 30,000 copies having been printed worldwide.[47] In the text, the young Southern belle Scarlett O'Hara is introduced as trouble from the start. Her education at Fayetteville Female Academy has schooled her in feminine demeanour and taught her how 'to conceal from men a sharp intelligence beneath a face as sweet and bland as a baby's'; but her green eyes are a give-away, 'turbulent, wilful, lusty with life'.[48] She is passionately in love with Ashley Wilkes, who is bent on marrying the much more conventionally feminine Melanie. Scarlett is 'fast'. She throws herself at Ashley but gets nowhere. Ashley—represented in the book as a gentle, gallant, and cultivated young man—will never leave Melanie, however much Scarlett tries to push him into doing so. A man of honour, he is aghast at her lack of loyalty to a friend. In the meantime, Scarlett goes from man to man, marrying variously out of pique, out of self-interest, and for survival. Sex is *not* one of her goals: indeed it is really to be avoided; Scarlett wasn't keen on having babies. She feels nothing much for Rhett Butler, the handsome, debonair 'hero' who watches her behaviour with amused detachment and even admiration. Although Mitchell suggests that Scarlett experiences the odd sexual frisson in Rhett's company, when he is in gaol and teases her for her manipulative behaviour, she owns that she wouldn't care very much were he to be hanged.[49]

The reader/viewer roots for Rhett, but Scarlett continues to be driven by her 'wild dreams, her mad desires' for the unattainable Ashley.[50] In the film version of *Gone with the Wind* Leslie Howard, not altogether keen on the role, played the part of Ashley Wilkes. His performance failed to appeal to women viewers. Helen Taylor, who has made an extensive study of women's reactions to the film, was surprised by the vehemence with which most of her respondents dismissed Ashley as a 'wimp' and couldn't understand why Scarlett would waste her time on him.[51] Clark Gable's Rhett Butler, on the other hand, was every woman's dream.[52] Nevertheless, when Scarlett and Rhett do eventually marry, the marriage degenerates into a mutually destructive power struggle, with neither character able to respond positively to tenderness in the other. We have to get to page 1,016 in this (very long) book before Scarlett starts to realize that her obsession with Ashley has had a negative impact on her life. But then she has a sudden revelation: 'I loved something I made up' she confesses to herself:

> I made a pretty suit of clothes and fell in love with it. And when Ashley came riding along, so handsome, so different, I put that suit on him and made him wear it whether it fitted or not. And I couldn't see what he really was. I kept on loving the pretty clothes—and not him at all.[53]

In the book, and at this point, Scarlett begins to respond to Rhett sexually. She realizes that Rhett's earlier accusation had substance: that she had been behaving all along like 'a child, crying for the moon'.[54] But it's too late. The tragic death of their daughter, Bonnie, and a row with Rhett, in the course of which she falls and miscarries another potential child, sharpens their mutual resentments and misunderstandings. The ending is well known. After a night of heady passion, when Rhett, in his cups, carries her upstairs and forces her into sex, Scarlett starts to feel something like love and compassion for him.

The film shows her smiling coyly to herself in the morning light. But Rhett's had enough. And so off he goes, frankly not giving a damn.

Kathleen Winsor's blockbusting bodice ripper, *Forever Amber*, was published in 1944, and a film version followed three years later.[55] Like *Gone with the Wind*, the story was set in historically turbulent times: in the case of Winsor's novel, Restoration England, against a background of political intrigue, plague, and the Great Fire of London. Amber St Claire is introduced, like Scarlett, as brimful of independence and appetite for life. Impatient with a lack of opportunities in the village in which she has grown up, she falls for a handsome young cavalier, Bruce Carlton, who just happens to be riding by. Amber has bags of initiative, of a both social and sexual kind. She falls hard for Bruce, who appreciates her physical charms but can't regard her as his social equal, so there's no way he'll marry her. She has to figure out how to fend for herself (and for her illegitimate offspring), which she does very effectively; scheming and planning and working hard. Sexual opportunism, with a judicious deployment of her beauty, wit, and talents, allows her to work through a series of rich men. Undaunted by setbacks (a spell in a debtor's prison, a husband killed in a duel, a bout of the plague, and so forth), she becomes wealthy in her own right, a mistress of the king, and a duchess. But Amber never lets go of her obsession with Bruce Carlton, whom she dreams about and pursues relentlessly through the novel. Bruce eventually marries a rich and pretty heiress, the epitome of gentle femininity, quite unlike the greedy and lustful Amber. But nothing can stop Amber's scheming about how to get him back. She's become a consummate stalker.

*Forever Amber* caused a sensation, selling 100,000 copies in its first week of publication.[56] It was banned in fourteen US states and denounced by the Catholic Church. The screen rights were snapped up by Twentieth Century Fox and the Hays office went on red alert.[57] The Attorney-General of Massachusetts, explaining objections to the book, famously referred to a count of 70 references to sexual intercourse, 39 to illegitimate pregnancies, 7 abortions, 10 descriptions of women undressing in front of men and another 49 'miscellaneous objectionable passages'.[58] There was also concern about the way that the publishers were marketing the book. One example of advertising blurb, for instance, promised that readers of *Forever Amber* would encounter a heroine 'who will remind them of Scarlett O'Hara and Catherine the Great rolled into one dainty package of dynamite and surrounded by a score of inflammable young Casanovas from the corrupt court of Charles II'.[59] Winsor herself attracted a great deal of attention in the media. She was still in her early twenties when the book was published, and her press photographs show her looking poised and lustrous, like a film star. This added fuel to the scandal—how could someone so young and fresh-complexioned dream up such racy goings-on? Winsor herself was unrepentant, retorting that she'd only written two explicitly sexual passages, both of which had been excised by her publisher, Macmillan.[60] She made a fortune, but had to endure a great deal of notoriety. Ava Gardner recorded that her then husband, bandleader Artie Shaw, had sneered when he caught her reading what he condemned as a low-brow, trashy novel.[61] Their relationship didn't last: interestingly, Artie Shaw married Kathleen Winsor two years later.

Scarlett and Amber were women full of appetite and resourcefulness. 'Fast' was the only word for Scarlett, wrote Margaret Mitchell.[62] Both of these fictional creations could be described as loose women. Both were named to suggest colour and vibrancy (Margaret Mitchell abandoned her original idea of calling her heroine 'Pansy', which it was thought would convey the wrong kind of message).[63] Both Scarlett and Amber were driven by romantic obsession and plagued by their own unruly passions. The passion in Amber's case was explicitly sexual; in Scarlett's less so: her sexual interest in Rhett is slow to develop, and an idealized Ashley Wilkes and the landed estate, Tara, are what really drives her on. Neither of these fictional heroines has ever made an easy role model and neither gets what they ultimately come to realize that they want, but it is their vital, driving, desiring, and imperfect selves that have always appealed to women readers. Countless women named their daughters after

Scarlett or Amber: film actress Joan Collins called one of her daughters Tara.[64] Winsor's novel had another dimension of appeal in the context of Britain in 1945. It took a while for the country to emerge from wartime austerity, which included the rationing of clothes and luxury goods. *Forever Amber* was a feast of imagined gorgeousness. Amber's outfits have been described by feminist critic Elaine Showalter as 'marvels of fashion pornography'.[65] She wafts round London in emerald velvet, rich furs, and cloth-of-gold, a spray of emeralds pinned to her sable muff.

The spectacle of such richness was exciting to women in post-war Britain, who were sick and tired of cheeseparing and 'make-do-and mend'. Reaction against the long years of penny pinching underlay the enormous appeal of Christian Dior's 'New Look', with its profligate use of expensive materials, and huge silky roses nestling in luxuriant, swirly skirts.[66] British historian Carolyn Steedman has written eloquently of her mother's frustrations during these years, her yearning for glamour, style, and a New Look skirt.[67] Austerity had cramped desire on more than one level: there had been a pinching of the emotions, too, as people gritted their teeth and learned to deal with deprivation. A mood of this kind suffuses *Brief Encounter*, David Lean's classic film version of Noel Coward's play, released in 1945. Celia Johnson plays Laura, a middle-class housewife who falls for a young doctor (also married) after a chance meeting at a railway station. It's touch and go whether their mutual attraction will spill into an affair, but in the end moral fibre wins out, and passion is—with great difficulty—restrained. Laura briefly considers finishing herself off under a train, but then, as if in a trance, goes back to her comfortable, understanding husband. 'Whatever your dream was, it wasn't a very happy one, was it?' he asks, sympathetically, looking deep into her eyes. Clipped tones prevail over sexual desire and self-expression; family values triumph.[68]

But the audience of course, weeps. Laura's dream may not have been an altogether happy one, but neither was coming back to earth with a bump. Some of the films of the post-war era presented women with a choice between sexual excitement and family values, often contrasting the allure of devastatingly attractive but unreliable Lothario-types with the less glamorous appeal of the boy down the road who was clearly better husband material. Ealing Studios' *Dance Hall* (1950, directed by Charles Crichton) focuses on four young working-class girls whose lives revolve around the factory floor and the Palais, a local dance hall.[69] At the Palais they meet up with boys and check out potential marriage partners. In this sense the film is a fair reflection of contemporary reality. Social worker Pearl Jephcott described how in the 1940s dancing was:

> one of the recognized ways in which to meet and look over men, with an eye to selecting a husband. The dance-hall, and relatively few other institutions, now that churchgoing has so declined, provide[s] that range of young masculinity which the girls very properly desire to explore. To say that you will go dancing implies that you are going man-hunting, in a perfectly reputable sort of way.[70]

In *Dance Hall*, Eve is tempted away from steady, Welsh-born Phil (Donald Houston) by foxy American Alec (Bonar Colleano) who drives a flash sports car. Cue lots of angst and misunderstanding, before Eve comes to realize that Alec is something of a spiv and Phil, inevitably, a good sort. Back to respectability and family values triumph again. But in spite of starring Petula Clark and Diana Dors, *Dance Hall* wasn't a great success with British audiences.[71] In terms of popular appeal, the big hits of the 1940s were the screen melodramas produced by Gainsborough Pictures, a British studio twinned with Gaumont-British and under the direction of Michael Balcon. These films, which in the 1940s included *The Man in Grey* (1943), *Madonna of the Seven Moons* (1944), *Fanny by Gaslight* (1944), and *The Wicked Lady* (1945), were particularly enjoyed by women.[72]

The Gainsborough melodramas were all about unruly passions, about women stifling themselves or letting rip, about female rebellion, sex, and desire. They turned the message of *Brief Encounter* upside down. These deeply subversive costume dramas, predictably panned by the critics, were some of the most financially successful films of their time.

Narratives which drew on ideas about psychoanalysis to explore the idea of repressed desire in women had strong appeal in the first half of the last century. Ideas about psychoanalysis were often mixed up with popular ideas about hypnosis. Warner Brothers' 1931 Gothic horror film, Svengali, starring John Barrymore, had thrilled the public with the story of a woman whose desires are wholly appropriated by an evil male control freak. In 1945, The Seventh Veil, produced by British film company Ortus Films and written by Muriel and Sidney Box, proved a smash hit. Seen by an estimated 17.9 million people, The Seventh Veil featured James Mason as the masterful controller who 'creates' a successful female concert performer.[73] Though without the anti-Semitism that infused Svengali, the story is in some respects similar. Mason's performance as Nicholas, the guardian of the young Francesca, is chilling. There is a horrifying scene where he brings his cane down, thrashing the hands of his piano-playing ward when she is set to defy him and go off with a lover. Like Marian Marsh, who played the part of Trilby in the 1931 film, Ann Todd, as the pianist Francesca in The Seventh Veil, is a limpid blonde. But Todd's Francesca, less vivacious, more vulnerable, has even less autonomy: she can't act on her own desires because she is stuck in a web of male control. There is her guardian, the sadistic Nicholas, her would-be (and not very confidence-inspiring) lovers, and her shrink, Dr Larsen (played by Herbert Lom). Frustrated in her attempt to commit suicide, Francesca is subjected to hypnosis by Larsen, who tries to cure her by helping her to find out what—that is, who—she really wants. The film ends with her walking towards the shadowy figure of her guardian. She might have been better off drowning.

The heroines of some of the Gainsborough melodramas were rather less amenable to male control. In The Man in Grey, the ambitious, dark-haired Hester Shaw (Margaret Lockwood) turns up at a school for young ladies and is surrounded by trilling, girly-girls with their hair in ringlets. Sourly, Hester refuses the offer of a sugared violet: she doesn't go for sugary things. Hester schemes her way to what she wants, riding roughshod over friendship and sisterhood. Lying and murdering her way to her heart's desire (James Mason as Lord Rohan), she is eventually exposed as the adventuress she is. Retribution follows. With Hester, it's not just her hands that suffer from James Mason's crop-wielding sadism; Rohan furiously thrashes the wicked woman to her death.

Like Francesca in *The Seventh Veil*, we are given to understand that Maddalena, the heroine of Gainsborough's *Madonna of the Seven Moons*, suffered trauma as a young girl. In Maddalena's case, this involved some kind of sexual harassment by a stranger. This is supposed to explain why Maddalena develops a split personality as an adult. Following her father's wishes, she marries a rich, cultivated bourgeois, Giuseppe Labradi. But every now and then she runs off to enjoy a secret, passionate life with the gypsies. Wearing long earrings and a flouncy skirt, she tucks a knife in her knickers and hauls up in a thieves' kitchen as Rosanna, mistress of the hot-blooded Nino Barucci (Stewart Granger). Meanwhile, back at home her husband and a doctor scratch and shake their heads over what's going on. 'One Woman . . . Living Two Kinds of Love, Loving Two Kinds of Man!' shrilled the lobby cards, which provided a clue.[74] But clearly, this *couldn't* go on. Defending her daughter from sexual harassment by Nino's brother, Rosanna/Maddalena suffers a knife wound. She dies, mourned by both of her men. Her husband Giuseppe arranges a cross on her bosom; Nino tosses a white rose.

If *Madonna of the Seven Moons* showed femininity as something of a conundrum, not altogether fathomable or controllable by the men in the picture, *The Wicked Lady* went further. Here was a woman entirely driven by her unruly passions. Lady Barbara Skelton (Margaret Lockwood) is all desire and no conscience. She seduces and steals her best friend's fiancé because he's rich. Bored silly by her role of lady of the manor, she turns to gambling. When she loses, she turns to robbery, masquerading as a highwayman. Challenged by a real highwayman— the inevitably dashing Jerry Jackson (James Mason)—she joins him for a hearty feast of stewed carp and lusty revels in the bedroom of a local hostelry, 'The Leaping Stag'. Barbara's husband's loyal retainer, Hogarth, gets wind of what's going on so she poisons him, finishing the job off by suffocating the poor old buffer with a feather pillow. All the men in *The Wicked Lady* are decent types, chivalrous, honourable, or loyal—even Jackson is a gentleman. Barbara is bad, through and through. She gets her comeuppance at the end though, sure enough: dying, distraught, surrounded by those who have come to see her for what she really is. But it's been a thrilling romp. Barbara's boldness, her impatience with the restraints of femininity, her gorgeous clothes and lush looks left an indelible impression on the memory of many a female filmgoer. The film was a huge box-office success.

Women both longed for, and were frustrated by domesticity after the Second World War. It could be difficult to adjust to peacetime conditions, to abandon the freedoms of wage earning for economic dependence, housekeeping, and the raising of children. Leisure and pleasure were often in short supply for working-class wives. Even the dance hall could be out-of-bounds for married women, who were supposed to stay at home once they had 'settled down'.[75] Many wives tried to conform, even if they felt fettered and hemmed in by family responsibilities, but their daughters were frequently more rebellious. Often better-educated than their mothers, and raised in a setting of comparative affluence and security, young women's aspirations, and their expectations of marriage and men were beginning to change. There was a trend towards marrying at younger ages than in the recent past, and older traditions of courtship, where parents exercised a considerable degree of control, were increasingly contested.[76]

Younger women were beginning to sense the changes associated with the teenage revolution. There is a hint of this generational change in *Madonna of the Seven Moons*. When she's at home, and not running off with the gypsies, Maddalena wears her hair in coiled braids. She's very elegant—somewhat like a Medici princess in Dior's New Look clothes. Daughter Angela, by contrast, is all slacks and modernity: she whizzes round in a sports car driven by a young man in shorts. Angela thinks nothing of spending a night with her beau in a luxury hotel and (of course) concealing this from her parents. At home, she manages to shock Maddalena by cavorting around her bedroom dressed only in her underwear: reproved for this, she retorts that if being ladylike means behaving like a tame mouse, it's not for her.

Ten years later, a British screwball comedy directed by J. Lee Thompson, *As Long as They're Happy* (1955) took a light-hearted look at a 'new' phenomenon: the influence of popular music on a household of women. The film features John Bentley, a stockbroker and paterfamilias living in Wimbledon. Bentley's ordered, suburban lifestyle falls apart when his daughters—and even his wife, and their female maidservant—all succumb to the charms of 'crooner' Bobby Denver, played by Jerry Wayne and modelled on American singer Johnnie Ray. Johnnie Ray had become famous for his emotional rendering of the song 'Cry', which had his audiences weeping. On the flipside of the single was 'The Little White Cloud that Cried', and Columbia later released an album, *I Cry for You*. All this lachrymosity earned Ray the soubriquet the 'Prince of Wails'. As a precursor of the rock and roll idol, Ray became something of a sensation in the 1950s.[77] Teenage girls went nuts over him.

The sight of young women screaming and fainting over favourite male performers—film stars, crooners, pop singers—became commonplace in the later 1950s. An early example of such a heartthrob in the United States was Frank Sinatra. The New York correspondent for the British newspaper, *The Guardian*, commented on his impact: 'Psychologists have written soberly about the hypnotic quality of his voice and the remarkable effect upon susceptible young women'.[78] Was this a form of hypnosis, or trance? Sinatra seemed to inspire adulation on a scale comparable with Valentino. Young women signalled their devotion by sitting through performance after performance, and by sporting polka-dotted bow ties and short white socks (hence 'bobby-soxers') of the kind worn by their hero. Historian Jon Savage heralds Sinatra as 'the first modern pop star'.[79] He singles out the scenes of mass hysteria which greeted Sinatra's performance at New York's Paramount Theatre in October 1944 as the first key event in the history of pop music, signalling the birth of the teenager and particularly, the collective power of young women.[80] This new power of the teenage fan as consumer underpinned the rise to fame of Elvis Presley in the late 1950s, and shortly afterwards, the British pop phenomenon of the Beatles.

Films such as *Bye Bye Birdie* (1963) parodied the behaviour of teenage fans, with fresh-faced girls in puff-sleeved prom dresses fainting in a controlled, ladylike fashion over the seductive aura of singer Birdie, a kind of Elvis-pastiche, gyrating his crotch invitingly, bulging in gold satin. For if Frank Sinatra and Johnnie Ray had pulled at the heart-strings, Elvis—and later the Rolling Stones—exuded a more blatantly sexual charge. The Beatles were more boy-next-door, not quite so challengingly sexy. But the frenzy they evoked challenged concert organizers and pushed many contemporary observers into panic. Music writer Dorian Lynskey has recorded how Scottish concert promoter Andi Lothian brought the Beatles to Glasgow in October 1963. The local police—and Lothian himself—became extremely nervous, fearing that

[t]he girls were beginning to overwhelm us . . . It was like the Relief of Mafeking! It was absolute pandemonium. Girls fainting, screaming, wet seats. The whole hall went into some kind of state, almost like collective hypnotism. I'd never seen anything like it.[81]

Contemporaries struggled to explain 'Beatlemania', and the behaviour of seemingly ever younger female fans whose passions were stirred to boiling point by pop idols and boy bands. Some just condemned the girls. In a startlingly misogynist article in the *New Statesman* in 1964, British journalist Paul Johnson hit out at what he called 'The Menace of Beatlism', describing fans as mindless and vacuous, 'bloated with cheap confectionery and smeared with chain store make-up', 'with open, sagging mouths and glazed eyes'.[82]

**Figure 4.** Beatles fans, Empire Pool, Wembley, 1964.

Singer Marianne Faithfull, girlfriend to Mick Jagger in the late 1960s, was more sympathetic. Recording some of the ways audiences responded to the Rolling Stones, she recalled one performance where

> [a]lmost from the first note of 'I'm a King Bee' an unearthly howl went up from thousands of possessed teenagers. Girls began pulling out their hair, standing on the backs of their seats, pupils dilating, shaking uncontrollably.[83]

The 'ululating teenage girls acted as if drugged,' she observed. Reflecting on the appeal which different members of the group had for their audience, Marianne suggested that where Keith Richards's style was Byronic, that of the injured, romantic hero, Jagger's swagger and androgyny were Dionysian: 'Mick was their Dionysus, he was the dancing god'.[84] Half a century later, biographer Fiona McCarthy, curating an exhibition on Byron for the National Portrait Gallery, suggested that it was Jagger himself, 'the focus of hysterical sexual fantasy', who should be seen as a twentieth-century Byron.[85] At the Rolling Stones rock concert in Hyde Park in 1969, Jagger, wearing a ruffled shirt, recited Shelley's poem *Adonaïs* in memory of band member Brian Jones, who had drowned just before the concert. Jagger was clearly aware of the associations.

Feminist social scientist Barbara Ehrenreich has argued that 'Beatle-mania' constituted 'a huge outpouring of teenage female libido' which we might see as having represented an opening salvo in the sexual revolution.[86] In this sense, fandom opened up a space in which teenage girls could express desire. This had revolutionary potential in the 1950s and 1960s, decades in which 'good' girls had it drummed into them that female sexuality was a precious commodity which should only be deployed in exchange for an engagement ring.[87] Fan behaviour offered more than just release: girls could begin to recognize and acknowledge their sexuality, knowing that their mates often felt the same way.

Teenage girls' outpourings of passion in more recent decades have usually been in response to younger, more boyish performers. Boy bands such as the Bay City Rollers, New Kids on the Block, the Backstreet Boys, and One Direction were and are carefully managed and marketed to appeal to young girls, although the managers don't always get it right. These boy performers function as a kind of starter-kit for girls, at an age when they are beginning to try out their own feelings and to experiment with desire. A sense of bonding with same-sex friends and peers over shared enthusiasms is also important: the sense of belonging to a youthful community.[88] The digital revolution, rising use of smartphones, and the popularity of social networking sites have expanded and amplified the opportunities for such bonding on a scale which can take the breath away.

# 3

# Packaging the Male

Many of the iconic romantic heroes in literature were dreamt up by women. Jane Austen's Fitzwilliam Darcy, in *Pride and Prejudice*, looms large as an archetype, one of the most powerfully attractive fantasy males in literature, who has inspired countless imitations. Austen may have drawn upon her reading of—and her critical reaction to—Byron in her novels. The two authors held very different values, but both were writing about what constituted gentlemanly behaviour, and they shared the same literary tradition.[1] Darcy incorporates many of the traits of the Byronic hero—pride, passion, elegance, and a sharp, satirical eye.[2] He is a man of substance, master of Pemberley, a large estate in Derbyshire. It is precisely when she drives through the park gates of this impressive inheritance that Elizabeth Bennet awakens to her changing feelings for the man.[3] Rich, aloof, but fundamentally generous and capable of emotional growth, Darcy's attraction has proved irresistible to generations of women, many of whom have grown up on televised or cinema versions of the text and may never have read the original. In the twenty-first century, scientists working on pheromones in mice discovered a protein in the urine of the male mouse which was irresistible to females. They named it after Jane Austen's character, 'Darcin'.[4] There are many ways in which Darcy has proved a money spinner.

But what made for irresistibility in a man? Men and women often had very different ideas about this. Another writer who influenced Jane Austen's thinking on the subject was Samuel Richardson.[5] In *Pamela; or Virtue Rewarded* (1740) and *Clarissa, or the History of a Young Lady*

(1748), Richardson gave us two examples of central male figures, highly eligible in terms of their persons, status, and worldly endowment, but not at all respectable in terms of ethics and conduct. Mr B. is Pamela's employer, and he seeks to have sex with her without commitment. Socially his inferior, she is strongly attracted to him but valiantly holds out against repeated forays on her virtue. Eventually Mr B. comes to respect Pamela and so her chastity reaps its reward: the couple marry and are happy together. Clarissa faces more severe trials in fending off the charismatic but disreputable Lovelace; her attraction to him fades as she comes to realize just how unprincipled he is. There is no happy ending. Clarissa is raped and then dies. Richardson was dismayed to find that many of his lady friends found Lovelace a beguiling figure, in spite of (or because of) his rakishness.[6] Further, he was peeved by the success of his rival, Henry Fielding's portrayal of an intemperate but loveable rogue in *Tom Jones*.[7] His lady friends urged him to respond by creating an image of a genuinely good man, a gentleman hero whom women could safely desire.

The result was the seven-volume *History of Sir Charles Grandison* (1753). Grandison is chivalrous and brave. He rescues ladies from seducers and bandits. He is handsome, generous, and honourable. He avoids bloodshed and is kind to animals—refusing, for instance, to dock his horses' tails. At one point he has as many as seven women sighing over him.

The trouble is that Grandison comes over as rather *too* perfect, an impression not helped by the fact that the author and his other characters laud Sir Charles's virtues to the point where the reader has really heard too much of them. No-one actually *fell* for Grandison. Art critic John Ruskin was an admirer.[8] The French critic and historian Hippolyte Taine, on the other hand, irreverently suggested that he was insufferable as a character, and should be canonized, and then stuffed.[9]

Women readers nevertheless studied Richardson's text assiduously. Over a century later, Benjamin Jowett, Master of Balliol, recorded that 'A young lady, a friend of mine, has read *Sir Charles Grandison* three times over and can pass an examination in it.'[10] He himself thought the novel 'one of the best'. Jane Austen similarly knew the text almost by heart: Richardson's writing was much discussed in her family. Austen parodied Sir Charles Grandison while being both inspired and influenced by the substance of the novel.[11] As she confessed to her niece later in her life, 'pictures of perfection' made her feel 'sick and wicked'.[12] But in the 1800s the choice of a husband shaped the whole of a young lady's life, and well she knew it. A girl needed a dependable gentleman provider, not a rake. Austen's male figures, Henry Tilney, Edmund Bertram, and George Knightley, all owed much to Richardson. Renowned Austen scholar Brian Southam pointed out that the scene in *Pride and Prejudice* where Lizzy Bennet is shown round Pemberley by a housekeeper who extols Darcy as a paragon of male virtue is strikingly reminiscent of Harriet Byron's first sight of Grandison Hall, as described in the earlier work by Richardson.[13] Fitzwilliam Darcy owes a great deal to Sir Charles Grandison.

The history of the novel reflects vigorous debate over what constituted desirability in the male. In the context of early nineteenth-century romanticism, 'Byromania' was both cult and potent stimulus. Byron's poetry, his concern with his self-image, and the details of his life made him a celebrity: his appeal to women was legendary.[14] Women wrote to him out of the blue, swearing devotion, suggesting assignations, regaling him with confidences and locks of their hair.[15] For over a century after his death, the Byron collection in publisher John Murray's archive in Albemarle Street, London, enshrined a large collection of such propositions and *billets-doux*.[16] There is also a tin box containing a mass of yellowing, small screws of paper, each containing a lock, braid, or ringlet of women's hair. These were catalogued, each packet marked with a name or initial in Byron's own handwriting.[17]

Byron's attitude to female adulation—like his sexuality—was complex and ambivalent. On the one hand he was impatient with his fans and followers, seeing himself as a victim of female voraciousness.[18] On the other hand, his reputation rested on women's passion for his person and their appetite for his verse. The letters and hair offerings were hoarded, as trophies. Byron was astute enough to realize that he

**Figure 5.** Lord Byron. Engraving after portrait by Thomas Phillips.

was a screen onto which women projected their fantasies: Canto XV
of his epic poem *Don Juan* expresses this idea succinctly. With women,
Juan was what:

> They pleased to make or take him for; and their
> Imagination's quite enough for that:
> So that the outline's tolerably fair,
> They fill the canvass up—and 'verbum sat.'
> If once their phantasies be brought to bear
> Upon an object, whether sad or playful
> They can transfigure brighter than a Raphael.[19]

The offices of John Murray in Albemarle Street house a bust of Byron
by the Danish sculptor Bertel Thorvaldsen.[20] Over the years it has

been subject to kissing by women who clearly regard it as an object of devotion. Where female devotees have worn lipstick this has necessitated expensive operations by conservators to remove reddened stains.[21] Byron might have objected to this fetishism, to being thus reduced to a passive sex object. On the other hand, the trophy hair collection shows that the fetishism operated both ways.

Byron's legacy thrums with sexual politics. Caroline Lamb, bruised and miserable after the break-up of her relationship with the poet, penned *Glenarvon*, in part a novel of revenge, but also a desperate attempt to fathom the riddle of Byron's sexual appeal and the nature of female desire.[22] One of Lamb's characters in *Glenarvon*, Lady Augusta, suggests that there are three kinds of men in demand among women of the day: ruffians or desperadoes, exquisites, and literary men, poets, or politicians being included in this third category.[23] Byron might be thought to have melded something of the lure of all three. Lord Ruthven (Glenarvon) is a version of Byron, represented as satanic or vampiric in the way he feeds on women's desire and lures them to their deaths. A heady mix of Gothic melodrama, incoherent plotting, and feminist insight, *Glenarvon* was a scandalous success when first published (1816) and influenced both Byron's approach to *Don Juan* and Polidori's story, *The Vampyre* (1819).[24]

Male and female writers continued to pen competing versions of masculine virtues and desirability throughout the Victorian period, with the differences often heightened at times of significant social change. The 'New Woman' fiction of the 1890s, for instance, was in part a reflection of advances in women's education and their struggles for independence in the labour market. Heroes in these novels tend to be companionable, treating women with respect and easy friendliness, as 'chums', or colleagues.[25] Nevertheless, arrogant and scornful Byronic types loomed large in attractiveness throughout the nineteenth century—in the fiction of the Brontës, for instance—but they required taming and domestication to be fully considered romantic heroes. Emily Brontë's Heathcliff remained untamed, a terrifying force of nature rather than a hero. He is unforgivably brutal and sadistic, and the author warns women, through Heathcliff's own words, to curb any fantasies about such a reprobate. Upbraided by the housekeeper, Nelly, for his cruel treatment of Isabella, Heathcliff retorts that the young woman is deluded, worthy only of his contempt for 'picturing in me a hero of romance' and expecting chivalry.[26]

In the early twentieth century, cinema began to rival the novel in portraying ideas about heroes, heroines, and romance. Since women made up so large a proportion of cinema-goers, there was profit in giving them what they wanted.[27] Ethel M. Dell's *The Way of an Eagle* was made into a film by G. B. Samuelson in 1918.[28] The Norma Talmadge Film Corporation, set up in North America by silent screen actress Norma Talmadge and her husband, Joseph M. Schenck, filmed in 1918 *The Safety Curtain*, another story by Ethel M. Dell.[29] In Britain, the Stoll Picture Company in Cricklewood had filmed by 1922 an impressive total of eighteen of Dell's stories.[30] Film historian Nathalie Morris pointed out that Stoll's publicist, Pearkes Withers, was quite clear about the attempt to appeal to women and girls in order to fill the cash box.[31] The storyline in these films, as in the original texts, was often one of women choosing between different types of men, or of wives escaping from brutal husbands to find love and safety in another (decent) man's arms. The settings were exotic or picturesque.

Some women made names for themselves in the early days of film-making by knowing exactly what would appeal to other women. It was screenwriter June Mathis, often described as one of the most powerful women in Hollywood in the 1920s, who saw the potential in the then relatively unknown Italian youth, Rudolph Valentino, and who insisted that he play the part of Julio in the 1921 silent film, *The Four Horsemen of the Apocalypse*.[32] Her fellow studio executives were uneasy about Valentino's Latin looks, but she stood firm, enlarging the role of Julio to showcase his dancing skills in the famous tango scene. June Mathis wrote the screenplay for *Blood and Sand* (1922), another huge hit for Valentino.[33] Dorothy Arzner edited the film, mixing footage of bullfights with close-ups of Valentino strutting and smouldering, nostrils a-flare.[34] The film casts Valentino as bullfighter Juan Gallardo, represented as the ultimate female fantasy: adored by (and adoring of) his mother, and his first sweetheart, Carmen, who becomes his wife. As Gallardo, Valentino moves with consummate sensuality: even his hair undulates seductively, in sinuous coils. But tragedy looms. Juan is powerless to resist the snake-like charms of sexual sophisticate Doña Sol, played by Nita Naldi. Carmen, pure in white lace, is even more helpless, snuffling miserably into her bouquet of lilies. But Gallardo is no simple seducer: fearless in confronting mad bulls, he is nevertheless putty in the hands of women.

June Mathis continued working with Valentino, on and off, in a close, though sometimes strained relationship up to his death in 1926. Many other women were instrumental in helping to craft his career. Elinor Glyn famously schooled Valentino in how to make love to Gloria Swanson in the 1922 film version of Glyn's 1906 novel, *Beyond the Rocks*. Glyn is credited with having suggested that kissing the open palm, rather than the back of a woman's hand, made the more sensuous statement.[35] Actress and film producer Alla Nazimova worked on Valentino's appearance, urging him to lose weight and tweezing his eyebrows into elegant arcs.[36] Valentino's second wife, Natacha Rambova, costume designer and photographer, exerted a powerful (if often controversial) influence on her husband's image.[37] These influences, alongside his immense appeal to the feminine public, explain why contemporary critics so frequently derided Valentino as 'a woman-made man'.[38]

An article by Lorine Pruette in *The Nation* in 1927 helped to focus the accusation. 'If it is true that man once shaped woman to be the creature of his desires and needs,' wrote Pruette, 'then it is true that woman is now remodelling man. If it is true that this was once a man-made world, then it is a certain fact that the world is now fast becoming woman-made.'[39] She added an important rider to the effect that what was *really* going on was a continuing dialogue between men and women, an exchange in which the voices of women, in the 1920s, were increasingly audible. And men were becoming less dominant and more defensive as women became more confident, assertive, and powerful. But she saw this as an eternal dynamic, and confidently expected the pendulum to swing back.[40]

Pruette's perception of men losing ground to women was one shared by many contemporaries and it was a perception which caused a great deal of anxiety among those who weren't so sure that the pendulum *would* eventually swing the other way. The impact of the 1914–18 war had knocked certainties and damaged the lives of many. Fears about employment, immigration, and an unstable economy between the wars all added to a high level of unease in North America and Europe. Much seemed to depend on a nation's manhood. Was this in decline? Conservative thinkers and dyed-in-the-wool patriarchs were horrified by Valentino's popularity among women, seeing him as a soft touch, pandering to the ladies, a male butterfly. There were doubts about his ethnicity—he wasn't 'white'—was he Italian or an Arab?[41] Slurs on Valentino's virility reached a height in the now infamous editorial which appeared in the *Chicago Tribune* in July 1926, associating him with a fashion for cosmetics and 'pink powder-puffs' among young men, and accusing him of perverting and undermining manhood. Valentino was furious at the allegations—and deeply hurt. In the short time he had left before he died he fought hard to defend himself against such slurs, offering to punch his detractors if they were man enough to come forward.[42]

Valentino's ambivalent public statements about his particular brand of manliness didn't always help matters. In conversation with interviewers and the press he was wont to attribute his own success with women to skills, understanding, and finesse which he claimed generally lacking in the American male. He would flaunt his elegant clothes and jewellery, but insist that he remained a humble farmer at heart. The contradictions were not easy to resolve, but made for piquancy: the slave bracelet gracefully encircling a muscular, manly arm.[43] However much some observers might express squeamishness about the new 'types of male beauty with water-waved hair adored by stenographers and work girls'[44] there can be little doubt that Valentino reconfigured ideas about masculinity. Among young men, fashions changed.[45] His style was widely emulated and used to sell products. Valentino was enduringly associated with the image of the Sheik: in North America the word 'Sheik' came to denote a lusty young man, and a brand of 'Sheik' condoms was introduced and became popular in the 1930s.[46]

There were attempts to reproduce the Valentino formula in Hollywood, where Ramon Novarro and Antonio Moreno were both cast as 'Latin lover' types.[47] In Britain, Welsh-born composer and singer Ivor Novello enjoyed considerable success as a matinée heartthrob whose style of soulful-eyed male beauty was often compared with Valentino's.[48] Novello's performance certainly owed something to Valentino: in the film version of *The Rat* (1925), he stars as amorous bad-boy of the Parisian underworld, Pierre Boucheron. In a scene set in the 'White Coffin' nightclub, Boucheron grabs his partner, rips her skirt, and thrusts her round the dance floor in an Apache dance. The scene was clearly influenced by Valentino's tango performance in *Four Horsemen of the Apocalypse*.

As technology moved on, silent films were replaced by 'talkies', and another criterion for sex appeal rose to prominence: the voice. Radio stars of the 1920s began crooning to women not only on the dance floor but also in their own bedsits and living rooms.[49] Whether Gene Austin singing caressingly of the joys of domesticity in 'My Blue Heaven', or the velvet baritone of 'Whispering' Jack Smith begging his girl 'for one more chance' this development suggested new intimacies. Rudy Vallée, Russ Columbo, and Bing Crosby were the new lover boys.[50] In the summer of 1929 young journalist Martha Gellhorn betook herself to the Brooklyn Paramount for a Rudy Vallée revue. As he sang 'I Kiss your Hand, Madame', she observed the female audience 'carried up to Parnassus on this insinuating, wooing voice'.[51] What was this all about, she wondered?[52] It wasn't just Rudy Vallée's good looks, or his tasteful simplicity in dress. Nor was it simply the voice. But it had a lot to do with the tender, coaxing lyrics, the pleading, intimate love songs that women heard as if whispered, personally, to themselves.[53] Russ Columbo was labelled 'the vocal Valentino'.[54] Male critics ventured crude comments: one dismissed Vallée as 'the guy with the cock in his voice'.[55] But they missed the point. This was about women imagining themselves as adorable and irresistible: imagining men as supplicants, begging for commitment.

Twenty years later crooners were being displaced by pop and rock. The style was changing, as were ideas about manliness. The end of the Second World War brought an end to universal conscription: in the UK, National Service was abolished from 1960.[56] In the USA, a selective service system remained: Elvis Presley famously received his draft notice in 1957. But long hair was replacing the short back and sides, and adolescent angst gained appeal against the stiff upper lip. Singer Johnny Ray's anguished laments made women weep along with him, as much in sympathy with his sensibilities as in thrall to his masculinity. Performers who set out to rock the system and singers with a slick, bad-boy image could stir up gratifying reserves of female passion when they begged for love. This kind of ambiguity—sharp style and a soft heart—underlay the success of many young male stars during the post-war years.

Young male performers with the capacity to drive girls wild were a potential gold mine. Wolf Mankowitz's West End musical, *Expresso Bongo* (1958), satirized this: Johnny, a cynical and opportunistic 'manager', sets out to exploit the young, working-class Bert Rudge, turning him into pop sensation 'Bongo Herbert'.[57] Herbert, 'the hope of Hoxton', is backed by a skiffle group called The Beasts, described as 'hungry for pizza and applause'.[58] A film version of *Expresso Bongo* starring a sleazy Laurence Harvey in the role of Johnny followed a year later. 'A plump lad named Cliff Richard' took 'the flabby and unpleasant role of the teenage bongo-basher . . . set on the road to fame', commented a reviewer in the *New York Times* shortly after-wards.[59] Mankowitz portrays the music industry as ruthless and dog-eats-dog: in the text version of *Expresso Bongo* Johnny watches Bert 'being salivated over, bone-like, by hordes of managerial canines';[60] but there were other, more benign models of musical promoters, some of whom emphasized avuncular feeling or even paternalism.

Larry Parnes, a Londoner, has often been claimed as the first major manager of pop musicians in Britain.[61] In the late 1950s, Parnes, originally working with freelance photographer John Kennedy, set out to turn Tommy Steele (born Tommy Hicks) into Britain's answer to Elvis Presley. Parnes helped to sanitize Tommy Steele's image away from Teddy boy and towards clean-cut family entertainer. As historian of pop management Johnny Rogan has pointed out, in 1950s Britain the newspaper press was eager to portray Teddy boys as yobs, and 'in many peoples' eyes, rock n'roll was synonymous with hooliganism and venereal disease'.[62] Parnes and Kennedy later split, but Parnes built on his experience with Tommy Steele, launching a whole bevy of less sanitized young male would-be stars with stage names which brought together the idea of the boy-next-door with that of the leather-jacketed rebel: Billy Fury (real name Ronald Wycherley), Marty Wilde (Reg Smith), Vince Eager (Roy Taylor), Johnny Gentle (John Askew), and several more. Parnes 'groomed' his protégées, seeing himself as taking a fatherly interest in their welfare. On one of the 'package tours' of rock shows around the country which he energetically promoted, he emphasized his responsibility for seeing that they took regular meals when on the road. But his shrewd business sense earned him the nickname of 'Mr Parnes, Shillings and Pence' and he was frequently lampooned as a Svengali-type figure, or puppeteer, skilfully manipulating his boys.[63]

The marketing of young Canadian singer Paul Anka as a teenage heartthrob was examined in a short documentary, *Lonely Boy*, made by Wolf Koenig and Roman Kroitor for the National Film Board of Canada in 1962.[64] This set out to show 'the astonishing transformation of an entertainer into an idol'. Anka confesses on screen that he had been 'a fat kid' who had had to work hard on his appearance. He'd lost weight, persisted with his hair, and had a nose job. Groomed by managers Irvin Feld and 'Uncle Julie' (operator of New York's

Copacabana nightclub, Jules Podell), he was filmed surrounded by sobbing young girls in gingham dresses trimmed with rickrack braid. The sobbing became hysterical as he chucked one or two of the most lachrymose girls sympathetically under the chin. 'I truthfully believe that Paul will be the biggest star this world has ever known,' announces Feld, solemnly, warning the 20-year old Anka that 'you no longer belong to yourself, you belong to the world'. Anka seems happy enough to go along with this, although he looks completely worn-out in the final scene, trying to rest in the car on his way to yet another engagement, against the soundtrack of his hit song, 'Lonely Boy'.

*Lonely Boy* influenced British film-maker Peter Watkins's 1967 film *Privilege*, which starred Paul Jones as a young pop idol, packaged and exploited to within an inch of his life by managers, profiteers, and in this case, sinister forces of the church and establishment.[65] Paul Jones plays Steven Shorter, a kind of suffering, Saint Sebastian figure pierced by the arrows of fame and everyone else's commercial interests. Girls weep as he sings on stage, helpless in handcuffs, begging for freedom. This rather odd film has its prescient moments and was certainly a powerful critique of both pop management and the cult of celebrity: Shorter, in the end, flips, screaming abuse at an audience who have gathered to see him presented with a silver trophy 'to our platinum boy' at a prestigious award ceremony. 'You worship me as if I was a sort of God', he screeches, 'I hate you', 'I'm a person, I'm a person, I'm a person'.

Music management, and the public relations industry, were changing rapidly. As young male singers rose on a tide of female adulation, the way that they were marketed—and used for marketing purposes—was becoming ever more complex. Peter Watkins satirized this trend in *Privilege* by making Steven Shorter a poster boy for the Apple Marketing Board, sponsored by the Ministry of Agriculture. As a knight in shining armour he is surrounded by hapless film extras bizarrely dressed as apple-men. When they've finished with him, Shorter is appropriated by the established church, which seeks to invigorate itself through 'Christian Crusade Week'. This is staged with Union Jacks, burning crosses, and mass singing of the hymn 'Jerusalem'. It sounds improbable, but three years after the film was made, the grassroots Christian revival movement, the Festival of Light, was staging rallies in Trafalgar Square and concerts in Hyde Park, supported by pop star and poster boy Cliff Richard.[66]

In the 1950s, entrepreneurs such as Larry Parnes and Elvis Presley's manager, Colonel Parker, had been making things up as they went along. Parker's inventiveness and his eye for a business opportunity were legendary.[67] Soon after becoming Elvis's manager he had accepted $40,000 from a Beverley Hills movie merchandiser, Hank Saperstein, to turn Elvis into a brand name. This licensed the production of countless Elvis-themed articles: charm bracelets, lipsticks in 'Hound Dog' orange, scarves, paper dolls, glow-in-the-dark busts, and plastic guitars. According to Colonel Parker's biographer, Alanna Nash, at venues Parker even came up with the idea of hawking 'I Hate Elvis' badges alongside 'I Love Elvis' badges.[68] Cash sent by fans to Elvis's first official fan club was said to have mounted so fast that no-one had time to deposit it. For some time Elvis was overwhelmingly grateful to Colonel Parker: it was only much later that the scandal of his exploitative practices (such as taking 50 per cent of profits) gained a hold.[69]

Milking the commercial potential of male performers became standard practice. There were tie-ins with teenage magazines, cut-out figures and posters, gossip columns, transfers for T-shirts, mugs, and key rings. The launch issue of *Roxy* in 1958 offered a tiny plastic brooch, modelled on Tommy Steele's guitar.[70] Teen magazine *Boyfriend* was heavy with marketing plugs for Cliff Richard. 'Cliff's Birthday Issue' in October 1959 offered a locket with his birthstone and photograph.[71] Undercutting the hard edge of rock, there were endless attempts to widen appeal by packaging pop stars as exponents of family values. Marty Wilde was presented as a boy who was mad about his mother.[72] Vince Eager was said to have practised kissing on

**Figure 6.** Elvis in concert, 1957.

his sister, and hoped he'd find a sweetheart as good as her.[73] Although on an altogether different scale, many of the marketing strategies we see today have their roots in the 1960s.

Even after death, male stars could live on as legends, like Byron. These days they live on through official websites. Commercially exploited, they become brands. Their estates continue to generate money, long after they themselves are gone. Elvis Presley's official website advertises an astonishing range of merchandise from its 'ShopElvis' worldwide internet store.[74] Elvis Presley Enterprises, originally founded and co-managed by Elvis's former wife, Priscilla Presley, controls Graceland, Elvis's mansion in Tennessee, which has been open to the public as an international tourist attraction since 1982. The estate of teenage rebel James Dean flourishes into the twenty-first century, profiting from endorsements of other brands of merchandise such as jeans and cameras.[75] Quite recently, it has advertised a choice of James Dean design VISA cards for those who want to flash his legacy every time they pull out their wallets.[76]

Some male heartthrobs may have basked in female adulation, enjoying their celebrity status along with its profits. But we certainly get glimpses of unease. Film stars and pop stars, like matinée idols before them, suffered the physical hazards of being mobbed by their fans. Cars and hotels were monitored and invaded. Clothing was snatched at and torn. Sir Dirk Bogarde's success as a romantic lead was such that he claimed it necessary to sew up his fly buttons at premieres.[77] Could celebrity itself erode more respectable forms of professionalism? Women stars sometimes saw glamour as undermining their status as 'serious' actors. Bette Davis, for instance, had insisted that she wanted to be known 'as a serious actress, nothing else . . . I don't want some glamour girl stuff'.[78] In her study, The Star Machine, film historian Jeanine Basinger argued that Tyrone Power's overpowering good looks worked against his reputation as a serious actor: he was too easily cast as an object of desire for the female gaze, too easily reduced to being sold as the perfect product.[79]

Was it a little demeaning to be regarded as a sex object by hordes of panting and wailing women? Male critics often thought so. The Times was scathing about British singer Frankie Vaughan, for instance, popular among women in the 1950s.[80] Sneering about the way Vaughan's publicity machine had introduced him as 'the latest model' of masculinity, 'like the latest in American cars', the writer continued: 'Mr Vaughan sings, but that is almost beside the point. His aim is to act as an erotic stimulant, and his swarthy good looks and big voice are single-mindedly addressed to that end'.[81]

In 1974, pop idol David Essex starred in the English film directed by Michael Apted, Stardust, billed with the tag line 'Show me a boy who never wanted to be a rock star and I'll show you a liar'.[82] Like its predecessor Privilege, this set out to demonstrate the hollowness of fame. Though supported by a sympathetic manager (played by Adam Faith), rock performer Jim MacLaine (David Essex) becomes sickened by the way he is turned into a commodity and loses control over his life; 'I'm an artist, not a bloody jukebox,' he complains. Alienated and bitter, he falls into drugs and depression and dies. Being known as a teenage idol could understandably get wearisome as performers aged. David Essex himself, who had a massive following of young girls in the 1970s, went on record many years later protesting about the way he was stuck with a reputation as a teenage heartthrob well into middle age. Almost every news item still introduced him as such. He vastly preferred being known as 'an actor and composer who was awarded an OBE in 1999 for his role as ambassador to the Voluntary Services Overseas'.[83]

Criticism of male performance styles could be particularly barbed at times of rapid social change, when any consensus in values between the generations was more likely to be challenged. In the 1960s, for instance, young men in Britain, freed from the requirement to do National Service, were wearing their hair longer and dressing in styles considered flamboyant and even girlish by an older generation. Social

Figure 7. Teenage girl in bedroom, 1970s, with huge poster of David Essex.

commentator Peter Laurie, writing in 1965 on *The Teenage Revolution*, was one of many to express uneasiness about this trend towards 'unisex'.[84] What exactly was going on, he wondered? Was virility in decline? Laurie thought girls were to blame. Unusually in history, he averred, young women now had 'a surplus of marriageable young men at their disposal' and they could pick and choose.[85] As consumers of men and goods, young women were in a powerful position and Laurie claimed that they were the force behind the teenage revolution:

> [T]hey impose a respect for fashion and neatness and quiet behaviour on the boys. They elect and cast down pop stars at their pleasure, they pull their hair and wail in mock dionysiac frenzies, and sometimes not so mock: a favourite who falls into the hands of a crowd of teenage girls will be fondled almost to death, his clothes will be ripped up for souvenirs and locks of his hair pulled out.[86]

Laurie's anxieties echo those of the 1920s, when contemporaries similarly worried about girls becoming boyish and having an emasculating effect on young men. And we hear the same unease about the destructive potential of female passion.[87]

Laurie argued that the pin-up magazines of the 1960s such as *Fabulous* (a publishing success in the UK in 1964) reversed assumptions about sexual superiority and now objectified boys rather than women.[88] But some attempts at marketing men as sex objects fell flat. In April 1972, the new British version of the magazine *Cosmopolitan* decided that the time had come to feature a naked man as centrefold, suggesting that the reason why women resented being seen as sex objects was because they 'weren't permitted to return the compliment'.[89] The magazine's choice was Paul du Feu, a literature graduate turned construction worker with a good body and an engagingly relaxed manner. His main distinction was to have been married to Germaine Greer since 1968, although by mutual consent they had separated, fast. The marriage seems to have been effectively over within a couple of weeks. Paul du Feu must have appealed to intelligent women—he later married Maya Angelou. He had all the right views, a strong respect for female independence, as well as 'the air of a man who knows about women'. But commenting on the breakdown of his relationship with Greer, du Feu reflected that their expectations of each other had been unrealistically conventional:

> I had the delusion that marriage meant tea in bed and she had the delusion she was marrying 'some enormous, broad-shouldered man who would crush (her) to his tweeds, look down into my eyes and leave the taste of heaven or the scorch of passion on my waiting lips'.[90]

Paul du Feu didn't last in the public eye. His image, at face value, failed to capture the female imagination. More successful as a female pin-up, in the 1980s and 1990s, was Fabio Lanzoni, an Italian male model who looked like a cross between a blond-haired, bare-chested Viking and a hunky comic-book superhero.[91] Fabio was hired by Avon Books to pose for the cover illustrations of romance novels with titles like *Defy Not the Heart*, *Scoundrel's Captive*, or *Savage Thunder*. He appeared on countless such covers, skin bronzed and gleaming, long blond locks blowing fetchingly in the wind.[92] His body towered over the forms of wilting and swooning females. Fabio's looks—and the books—sold well. Fabio gained riches, and he relished his fame. But just occasionally he worried that his image distracted women from his real self. 'I'm a person just like anybody else,' he insisted. 'But they treat me like a fantasy.'[93]

Standards of physical beauty change through time. In the 1900s, bodybuilder and showman Eugen Sandow had often been described as 'the perfect man', thought to epitomize 'the Grecian ideal'.[94] Women threw jewellery on to the stage after his performances and were said to have queued up after shows, avid to fondle his muscles.[95] By today's standards Sandow looks stocky, and perhaps too burly. A quarter of a century on from the heyday of Fabio Lanzoni's career, the fashionable aesthetic has changed again and former professional footballer David Beckham and male supermodel David Gandy are often singled out as embodying women's dreams of physical perfection in the male. Both Beckham and Gandy are associated with advertising and product placement on a huge scale. Effectively, they are modelling lifestyles. Gandy's style is urbane, suave, and sophisticated. Beckham

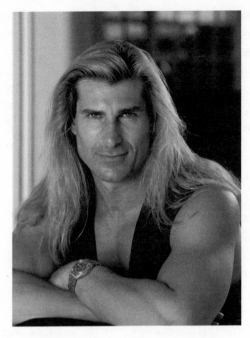

**Figure 8.** Fabio Lanzoni, 1980s model.

exudes physical fitness but at the same time an almost feminine sensibility: he has been confident enough in his maleness to sport jewellery, and to wear his hair in corn-braids or a ponytail. Beckham's appeal to women is also tied up with family values: his commitment to his wife and children is tattooed all over his body.

The products endorsed by Gandy and Beckham range from sports and fitness equipment to underwear and high fashion. Both men have made significant incursions into the fragrance market. Perfume, of course, is the very stuff of dreams. Boy bands such as One Direction have lent their imprimatur to a range of scents, with names such as 'Our Moment', 'Between Us', and 'You and I'. Resonant with notes of sweet flowers and candyfloss, these fragrances together with their names are designed to suggest young love and a special bond of intimacy between the adolescent girl who wears them and the object of her devotion. The perfumes endorsed by Gandy and Beckham are more grown-up, and tailored for the adult male: the suggestion is that they will enhance his power to attract women.[96]

Perfumes, bodies, clothes, and imagined lifestyles carry complex cultural meanings. Even so, for many women, these on their own haven't been enough to fuel fantasies, dreams, and desires: they have needed to imagine a *story*.

# 4

# Once upon a Dream

### Prince Charming, Cavaliers, Regency Beaux

The song, 'Some Day my Prince Will Come', which featured in Walt Disney's animated film version of *Snow White and the Seven Dwarfs* (1937) was ranked by the American Film Institute in 2004 as the nineteenth greatest film song of all time.[1] Being carried away by a perfect prince to his castle, and cocooned in a love which will last for ever, were enduring elements of a fairy tale consumed by generations of young girls. What did they have to do to be chosen? Very little. Just snooze on a daybed, or rest in a glass coffin, and wait for the kiss. Maybe do a bit of housework. Rather too much of the heavy stuff, if like Cinderella, you had a mean stepmother and bullying older sisters. A lot less, if like Snow White, you were surrounded by cute, domesticated woodland creatures, squirrels, and bluebirds with a taste for washing up and polishing furniture. Sooner or later Prince Charming would find you. Either he'd be smitten by your irresistible goodness and beauty at a ball, or he would hack his way through the brambly forest on a white horse, ready to rescue and carry you away. There were many versions of Snow White, Sleeping Beauty, and Cinderella, but the basic storylines are familiar, buried deep in our hearts and minds.

Who was Prince Charming? According to the Oxford English Dictionary he descends from French fairy tales of the seventeenth century: *le roi charmante* was a hero of the Baronne d'Aulnoy's *L'Oiseau Bleu*.[2] The term was in regular use by the late nineteenth century, sometimes to suggest idyllic dreams of a perfect lover. The *New York Times* published a haunting little story in 1891 about an elderly woman tramp in Madison Square, who was found scrabbling in the mud and between horses' hooves for fallen rose petals. She had explained 'in faultless Italian' to the paper's reporter that, 'of her triumphant youth she regretted nothing, nothing but the roses which a Prince Charming had sent to her every morning in Milan'.[3] The term was not infrequently used ironically, especially by male writers. A year earlier the *New York Times* had told 'a tale of roses and roguery' in which a young man, 'a veritable Prince Charming before whom all women go down', had duped four women staying in the same hotel into thinking that he wanted to marry them.[4] He had asked each girl to think about his proposal overnight, and to tuck a red rose in her belt at breakfast if she wished to signal acceptance. The 'gay cavalier' then hopped onto a midnight train to New York. In the morning, finding themselves all sporting roses, the women began to compare notes....

In a young girl's imagination a Prince Charming represented looks, class, and valour. Blood and noble birth counted for a great deal, but Cinderella's prince didn't need much individuality or character development, once he (or his valet) had played his part with the shoehorn. Clothes—and appearances—mattered, as an indication and reflection of rank, manners, and manly virtues. Victorian girls had grown up accepting Admiral Lord Nelson and the Duke of Wellington as national heroes. Their images were everywhere, as statues, in portraits, in china figurines and teapots, and even on the lids of biscuit tins. Young ladies swooned over Nelson: it was fashionable to wear cameo jewellery and to carry fans adorned with his likeness, or to dress in fabrics printed with gold anchors.[5] Hero worship was part of the culture, and thought to be improving, because it might inspire emulation.[6] Girls couldn't aspire to *be* great men, of course, but heroes could still be venerated as masculine ideals, and potential husbands measured against their stature. As historian Kate Williams has shown, Nelson, in spite of his unprepossessing physical appearance, and the sad loss of an eye and a leg, became, effectively, a sex-object.[7] So, too, did Wellington. The Brontë children had grown up venerating the Duke of Wellington.[8] Their early literary productions were in essence a kind of fan-fiction devoted to his deeds. For Charlotte, the Duke had been something of an obsession, a 'demi-god', the template for a knight errant, or a devoted lover.[9]

Lemuel Abbott's and Sir William Beechey's portraits of Nelson show a palely handsome face of 'proud resolve', a softness and fullness around his mouth and lips. In Abbott's portrait now in the National Maritime Museum, he glitters with gold and jewellery: the Star and Ribbon of the Bath, his Imperial Ottoman Order of the Crescent, and best of all, the feathery spray of diamonds in his hat.[10] This aigrette or turban ornament (*chelengk*) had been presented by Sultan Selim III in honour of Nelson's heroism at the Battle of the Nile.[11] One of the best-known images of the Duke of Wellington is the Thomas Lawrence

**Figure 9.** Lord Nelson. Engraving after portrait by Lemuel Francis Abbott.

portrait of c.1815 which hangs in Apsley House.[12] The Duke's arms are crossed, adding to the expression, again, of pride and determination. His features are manly, his chin shaded by gritty 'designer stubble'. Resplendent in his Field Marshal's uniform, with Garter star and sash, he wears the badge of the Golden Fleece. His hauteur implies disdain for such baubles.

Cavalier and military touches suggested valour. Trappings of gold braid, sashes, epaulettes, and frogging indicated rank and princely or noble status. Cossacks, Hussars, and cavalrymen wore extremely dashing uniforms, which became legendary for their appeal to women. Sir Arthur Conan Doyle's fictional Hussar, Brigadier Gerard, boasted that the arrival of his company could 'set a whole population running, the women towards us and the men away'.[13] Cossacks sported impressive tailored greatcoats, and Hussars were kitted out

**Figure 10.** The Duke of Wellington. After the portrait by Thomas Lawrence.

with tight-fitted jackets, gold braid, fur hats, and hessian boots. In *The Eagle*, a silent film of 1925 based on a story by Alexander Pushkin, Rudolph Valentino is fetchingly costumed as Dubrovsky, a Russian Cossack whose virility stirs lust in the loins of the formidable Catherine the Great. Dubrovsky's dashing uniform, with beribboned bullet cartridges (*gaziri*) decoratively lined up, slantingly, over the breast, was by costume designer Adrian (Adrian Greenberg), whose talents were early recognized by Natacha Rambova: he had previously designed stunning costumes for Valentino in the sadly now lost film *A Sainted Devil* (1924).[14]

The costumes of princes drew upon romantic and soldierly precedents. History can be a rich resource, a bran tub for the imagination. The romance associated with clothing styles of the past has persisted in the image of a prince. Princes and cavaliers can dress up without looking unmanly. In costume dramas their virility thrives on feathered hats, laced-up jerkins, and ruffled shirts with billowing sleeves. In the eighteenth century, men could enjoy powdered curls, satin embroidered waistcoats, silk tights, and twinkly shoe buckles. But as is well known, all this began to change in the 1800s.[15] Followers of the Regency fashion leader Beau Brummel began to tone things down.[16] Out went the wigs, powder, and embroidery. In came understated dark stuffs and tailoring. Ruffled shirts were acceptable for poetic types, but spotlessly white, carefully folded cravats indicated true gentility.

The French Revolution brought with it a reaction against too much extravagance in dress. In Britain, an industrial revolution altered work patterns and imposed a new discipline on the routines and rhythms of daily life. Partly in response to this, men's everyday clothing became more sombre, even dour, by the mid-nineteenth century. In turn, this fed dreams of a more romantic past. Queen Victoria liked consort Albert rigged up as her own fantasy prince. A Landseer portrait of them costumed for a ball in 1842 shows him richly arrayed in medieval garb: poppy-coloured tights, scarlet cloak, and gold brocade.[17] Another of the same period has Albert in tailored velvet, sporting startling, russet-coloured knee boots. He looks as if he's been costumed for a production of *Der Freischütz*, but relaxes in the drawing room at Windsor Castle surrounded by his family, dogs, and a heap of dead game.[18] Hunter-prince and family provider, his magic bullets have even done for a kingfisher: his infant daughter, Princess Vicky, toys with its small feathered corpse in a corner. The Queen looks on adoringly.

Historical flights of fantasy allowed a measure of freedom from contemporary expectations, where one could play with ideas about gender and the self. Costume designers working for stage and screen have always drawn rich inspiration from history. Natacha Rambova imagined Rudolph Valentino as a dandified prince of the blood in powdered wig and satin for *Monsieur Beaucaire* (1924); British designer Elizabeth Haffenden created dreamy, expressive costumes for the 1954 film production of *Beau Brummel*.[19]

Princes were supposed to be gallant, a word which originally meant gorgeous or showy in appearance.[20] They were expected to be courteous (in the sense of playing court to ladies), and exemplars of chivalry. But chivalry was associated with medieval times, and it wasn't clear how it should play out in later centuries. The debate about masculine behaviour that had been evident in the writings of Samuel Richardson and Jane Austen had widened in the early nineteenth century, with the popularity of a work by journalist and sportswriter Pierce Egan, *Life in London*.[21] Originally published as a series, this chronicled the adventures of two young men about town, Jerry Hawthorne and Corinthian Tom, in London during the Regency period. Masculinity was held to be a matter of fine distinctions. Pierce Egan was keen to emphasize that his hero, Tom, was no goody-goody. He declared that Tom was nothing like Richardson's Sir Charles Grandison, whom he dismissed as a bit of a ninny, 'almost afraid of a splash of dirt', and 'who moved through society by rule and measure and did nothing wrong'.[22] But nor was he a Lovelace, or anything like Fielding's Joseph Andrews.[23] Tom liked his drink, and he could gamble and whore and enjoy a dogfight with the best of men. But at the same time he was much concerned with his tailoring, and with

**Figure 11.** Rudolph Valentino as *Monsieur Beaucaire*.

looking fashionable and well turned out. The lines were carefully drawn: Tom was no fop or dandy: 'although one of the FANCY, he was not a fancy-man'.[24] He was a character designed to appeal to men, and not just to women.

How far could men go towards that princely elegance of manner and dress which seemed to please women, without looking effeminate? Unease about dandies and Mollies, together with British prejudice against the French as rather *too* preoccupied with fashion, had been evident during the Regency period; but the same issues were fought out all over again a century later, in the production of films and in the construction of the historical novel. This renewed unsettling of ideas about masculinity and manners in the early twentieth century is particularly evident in two silent films from 1924, Paramount's *Monsieur Beaucaire* and Warner Brothers' film of the life of Regency dandy *Beau Brummel*. The issues were also the central concern of an early novel by Georgette Heyer, *The Transformation of Philip Jettan*, first published by Mills and Boon in 1923.

*Monsieur Beaucaire* was based on a novel by American writer Booth Tarkington about a young French 'Prince of the Blood', the Duke of Chartres, played by Rudolph Valentino. For a young princess at court, Henriette (Bebe Daniels), Beaucaire is a handsome prospect, a 'King of Hearts', and 'a dream come true'. But the couple are uneasy about an arranged marriage and misunderstandings result in the duke taking flight to England. Disguised as a humble barber, he settles in the fashionable town of Bath. There he falls in with the wrong set of gamblers and social parasites and loses his heart to Lady Mary, 'the belle of Bath'. Not knowing his true identity, Lady Mary rejects him as of too lowly a status. Eventually, a disillusioned Chartres returns to France and to the arms of his first love.

The film, like the novel, questioned ideas about nobility and a man's honour, his relationship to women and true love. The set design and costumes are sumptuous: contemporary reviews commented on their Watteau-esque loveliness.[25] Valentino is gorgeous in powdered wig and eighteenth-century court dress. Episodes of chest-baring and muscular fencing were calculated to defend him against charges of too much prettiness. 'If the star's appeal is subordinated to silks and laces in making Valentino into something of a valentine', wrote a reviewer in *Photoplay*, 'there is nevertheless enough to set feminine hearts fluttering everywhere'.[26] But the film's reception fell short of expectations. Valentino's performance as Chartres was judged by many to be too feminine to be really charming. Valentino's biographer, Emily Leider, points out that Natacha Rambova bore much of the blame for this at the time. She was accused of encouraging her husband to take on 'perfumed parts' which audiences found arch and not manly enough.[27] *Monsieur Beaucaire* was swiftly parodied in a short American film entitled *Monsieur Don't Care* (1924), Stan Laurel playing the part of 'Rhubarb Vaselino'.[28]

The 1924 film *Beau Brummel*, starring John Barrymore and Mary Astor, was based on a play by American dramatist Clyde Fitch, and it engaged similarly with ideas about style, romance, and manhood.[29] Brummel, a prince of fashion, comports himself with taste and decorum, in marked contrast to the regally born but vulgarly mannered Prince Regent. Barrymore gets to wear splendid clothes. He's kitted out first as a dashing hussar, then as a Regency beau in the most revealing of high-waisted trousers. When he is forced to tear himself away from his true love, Margery (Mary Astor) following a touching farewell scene in a garden, he swirls a heavy cloak about himself, manfully. We then see his eyes fill with tears, which he dabs at, delicately, in order not to smudge his mascara.

Barrymore camps it up in this film, and we know that in spite of a genuine attraction for his co-star (he and Mary Astor were having an affair at the time), he was uneasy in the role. His brother Stephen recorded how John was continually afraid of being dubbed a 'pretty boy'.[30] He hadn't been happy with what he described as his 'pansy role' as the soulful Peter Ibbetson in the highly successful Broadway play based on George du Maurier's story of the same name in 1917. This experience fed Barrymore's determination to interpret one of his next roles, that of Shakespeare's Hamlet, in an unambiguously manly way. He famously declared that he wanted his Hamlet to be so male 'that when I come out on the stage they can hear my balls clank'.[31]

The young English writer Georgette Heyer used the pseudonym 'Stella Martin' when Mills and Boon published her novel, *The Transformation of Philip Jettan* in 1923. The novel was later republished, without its final chapter, by Heinemann as *Powder and Patch*. Set in the eighteenth century, the story was about what made for masculine desirability. Golden-haired Cleone Charteris is attracted to Philip Jettan, a local landowner who would be a highly suitable match, but he's rather too rough and ready for her increasingly refined tastes. Her fancy strays when she comes across Mr Bancroft, who impresses her with his urban sophistication. Bancroft's appearance has a startling effect on the population of the rural Sussex village in which Cleone has grown up. The locals all come out to stare at his elegantly cut pale apricot coat, his embroidered waistcoat, and his fashionable, red-heeled shoes. Philip bristles. He squares his shoulders at Bancroft's affectations and his mincing, affected manner. For him, foaming lace is more suited to the wrists of a woman than a man and he is repelled by Bancroft's 'sickly scent' and his 'fat soft hands'.[32] But Cleone is entranced, and increasingly inclined to see Philip as a graceless clod-hopper, a country bumpkin.

The story then centres on Philip's initially reluctant decision to polish up his manners and demeanour with a style makeover, fencing lessons, and a trip to Paris. Cleone is perplexed. Something irreducibly virile in Philip's character—Georgette Heyer describes this as his 'capacity for mastery'—draws her.[33] Now her childhood sweetheart has dress sense and cultural capital he seems more attractive than before. Moreover other women are attracted to him, too. Cleone is jealous, but a sense of pride holds her back from declaring her love. Philip is taken to one side by a woman of the world, Lady Malmer-stoke, who knows what women want. She counsels him to show manly determination and mastery. Duly propped up by this advice he takes action and Cleone falls into his arms.

Philip Jettan was an early version of a 'Heyer hero', in whom the author worked to bring together 'mastery' with gentleness and refined taste.[34] Today's readers sometimes baulk at the mastery, but the template proved itself to have enduring appeal, especially when envis-aged alongside a form of personality development which entailed the hero accommodating himself to feminine inclinations. This is more than just the classic romantic narrative where the hero mellows under the influence of true love. He has to abjure boorishness, to show a softer sensibility, a capacity to understand and to respect feminine desires. As one reader pointed out on Amazon's Goodreads review site in 2013, Jettan is effectively 'Cinderella-ized': here it is the prince, and not the scullery maid, who gets the total makeover.[35]

Heyer's heroes follow a formula. She herself referred to them as falling into one of two categories; they were either 'Mark I' or 'Mark II' heroes.[36] The first she defined as the 'brusque, savage sort with a foul temper'; the second tended to be suave, well-dressed, and rich. But there is considerable overlap. The charming eighteenth-century duke or marquis boasting exquisite taste, manners, and clothes sense, while having nerves of steel, is instantly recognizable in her work. He appears on the first page of *These Old Shades*, first published in 1926, in the form of His Grace the Duke of Avon. Avon strolls 'mincingly' through Paris at night in high, red-heeled shoes and a full-skirted coat of purple satin. He flaunts jewels, wears a powdered wig, and twirls a beribboned cane.[37] But this foppish exterior and languid manner conceal a rapier wit, alongside formidable resourcefulness, courage, and strength. Translated into the English Regency, Avon becomes the Earl of Worth, hero of one of Heyer's best-loved books, *Regency Buck* (1935). Worth is a touch grumpy and terse, but also 'the epitome of a man of fashion'. When he first appears in the text he wears a 'beaver hat set over black locks carefully brushed into a semblance of disorder', a faultlessly starched and folded cravat, and a driving coat with fifteen capes and a double row of silver buttons.[38] The heroine Judith Taverner finds him very handsome, if rather too full of 'self-consequence'.

The princely dukes and aristocrats in Heyer's novels all share one particular characteristic, and that is their horsemanship. As the etymology of the word suggests, chivalry had long been associated with horsemanship, as well as formal courtesy towards ladies. Heyer's heroes know their horseflesh, and indeed their own social credentials and breeding can usually be inferred from this knowledge: it really is 'in their blood'. Her heroes are often 'famous whips'. Heyer had read her Pierce Egan attentively. Egan's Tom was 'a perfect hero with a whip' and his skill in 'handling the *ribbons* and turning the corner of a street with his barouche and four' was described as unsurpassable.[39] The acme of a man's carriage-driving skills was to be able to remove a fly with a flick of his whip from the leading horse's ear.[40] Her immersion in Regency social history and style manuals gave Heyer a redoubtable knowledge of horsemanship, tackle, and carriage-driving. She understood the intricacies of pacing and reining, and the exclusivity of the Four Horse Club.[41] She revelled in detail of the advantages and disadvantages, as well as the social significance, of driving barouches, curricles, and high-perch phaetons. Horsemanship didn't just test breeding, it served also as a test of competence and virility. Skill in riding and driving served to mitigate any unease about masculinity which might be suggested by too much interest in fashion. A man who could command horses stayed in control. Men who couldn't ride or drive well were not real men; they were either immature or socially inferior. It wasn't so bad if *women* lacked confidence with horses. When Charlotte in *The Nonesuch* (1962) confesses her dislike for horses because she finds their behaviour unpredictable and 'if you pat them, they twitch', her male companions find this an endearing indication of feminine frailty.[42]

Heyer's more independent heroines, such as Judith Taverner in *Regency Buck*, are nonetheless competent horsewomen and enjoy driving themselves about. This can elicit admiration in the male but it may also provoke a test of strength. When Judith flouts convention and her guardian's authority to participate in an ill-judged carriage race, she has to climb down from her high horse and admit that she has behaved ill-advisedly.[43] Horses and horsemanship as metaphors for gendered power relations are rarely far from the surface in the literature of romance. In Georgette Heyer's writing this can lead to some unforgettable *double entendres*. When Ancilla in *The Nonesuch* rides out on an excursion on the back of an inferior hack her admirer, Sir Waldo, protests: 'I wish I had the mounting of you', he exclaims.[44]

Horses and sexual interest have long been linked in a tradition stretching back at least to the days of courtly chivalry and forward to Jilly Cooper's 'Rutshire Chronicles' (*Riders*, *Rivals*, and *Polo*), in the 1980s and 1990s.[45] We may recall how in *Jane Eyre*, Rochester first hurtles into Jane's consciousness in the dark, on a crashing great horse. The horse has slipped on the ice and his rider struggles to regain control. Jane, we are told, is 'mortally afraid' of the horse.[46]

There are echoes of Cinderella in *Jane Eyre*, but in more conventional versions of the fairy tale, the prince arrives less stormily, ready to rescue the heroine, mounted on a white horse. Rochester is all passion and turbulence, he's no Prince Charming. Heyer's *The Nonesuch* is a Cinderella story which draws also on *Jane Eyre*. The heroine Ancilla (the name means slave-girl) may work as a lowly governess, but she is distinguished by her innate breeding and refinement. In spite of her compromised social status she manages to attract the affections of Sir Waldo, who is of course both wealthy and charming. A turning point comes in the narrative when Ancilla is invited to a ball. She fears that propriety requires her to stay in the background, but longs to go to the ball. In the end her desire gets the better of her and she joins the festivities, hair loose in ringlets, arrayed in a low-cut, pale orange gown. She waltzes in Sir Waldo's arms. This attracts hostility from local matrons, who see Ancilla as getting above herself and are jealous for the opportunities of their own daughters.[47]

Walt Disney's animated cartoon version of *Cinderella* premiered in 1950 and was a resounding success, helping to restore the studio's fortunes after the difficult years of the Second World War. 'A dream is a wish your heart makes' sang Ilene Woods, in the title role. Dreams and hopes for a better future abounded in the 1950s and early 1960s. People were tired of austerity and deprivation. British pop star Billy Fury scored a hit with the song 'Once upon a Dream' in 1962. 'Dreams can come true, darling', he sang, in a tone of yearning sincerity that made girls ready to queue up to live with him in his dream castle for ever and ever.[48] The Cinderella story exerted a potent appeal in these years: a number of plays and films drew upon the fairy tale. MGM's musical adaptation, *The Glass Slipper*, starring Leslie Caron and Michael Wilding, appeared in 1955.[49] Leslie Caron's Cinderella is a petulant urchin with a smutty face and an hourglass figure, who irritates those around her by boasting that 'one day I'm going to live in the Palace'. Michael Wilding makes an awkward Prince Charming; he looks much older than her and is wooden in tights; though they both scrub up well enough for the ball. As 'Prince Charles', heir to an (unnamed) dukedom somewhere in the mountains, Wilding's wedding ensemble included white brocade, lashings of swansdown, and silver satin breeches.

In the United States, a romantic comic-book series appeared through the 1950s with the title *Cinderella Love*.[50] Cinderella-themed consumer goods were commonplace. This was partly Disney merchandising: a whole generation of little girls grew up reading the time from wristwatches with Disney's Cinderella pictured on the dial. You could also buy a clockwork Cinderella toy. Enamelled in forget-me-not blue, Cinderella clutched her prince, and when you wound them up they waltzed round and round, at least on a smooth surface. But it wasn't just Walt Disney: the cultural hold and the commercial potential of the Cinderella story were visible everywhere. In 1946, for instance, an advertisement for Shell petroleum showed a smart young girl in a boxy, fashionable suit stepping out of a pumpkin-shaped coach, while footmen bowed deferentially.[51] In the following year Revlon cosmetics introduced new lipstick and nail varnish colours in 'Cinderella's pumpkin' shade of orange,[52] and soon afterwards, Coty began to market its *L'Aimant* perfume in a faux glass slipper.[53] Girls and young women were bombarded with messages encouraging them to imagine themselves as Cinderella; to assume that all they needed was a prince, and that finding one would deliver everlasting joy.

Princes, princesses and royalty generally commanded a great deal of attention in these post-war years. In November 1947, the wedding of England's Princess Elizabeth to Philip Mountbatten, newly created Duke of Edinburgh, broadcast from the BBC to millions of people around the world. The Princess wore a dress designed by Norman Hartnell, said to have been inspired by Botticelli's *Primavera*, spattered with flowers.[54] It had a sweetheart neckline and was in a lustrous ivory satin, encrusted with sparkling crystal and seed pearls. Much was made of the fact that because wartime rationing remained in force, clothing coupons had to be amassed to purchase the fabric. Philip wore his naval officer's uniform and carried a sword, resplendent with tassels and braid. This was a gift from the king, suggestive of history and valour, and was used to cut the wedding cake.[55]

Contemporary diarist Sir Henry 'Chips' Channon noted that 'the Edinburghs' looked like a couple out of a fairy tale: Philip's charm 'is

**Figure 12.** *Cinderella Love*, Aug. 1954. Wealth versus sex appeal?

colossal, like all Mountbattens' he noted after a dance in 1948.[56] The young duke had been 'the success of the ball'. The magic intensified with the coronation in 1953. Chips commented that 'The fashionable complaint is now known as Coronation Thrombosis. People talk of nothing else...and prattle all day about places, tiaras, coaches, postilions, robes and coronets.'[57] Though hardly Cinderella, the queen nevertheless arrived at the abbey in a golden coach. The duke wore the dress uniform of an Admiral of the Fleet. His outfit was stiff with embroidery and braid, his gold epaulettes topped fetchingly with satin bows. Channon observed that he looked like a 'medieval knight'.[58] Philip was the first to pay homage to Her Majesty, swearing to serve as her 'liege man of life and limb, and of earthly worship'. Chips was not alone in marvelling at this as a wonderful day for England, and for 'the traditional forces of the world'.[59] Women's magazines were full of it.

Young girls' dreams of finding—or being found by—Prince Charming were magnified. Writing about her mother, historian Carolyn Steedman described a life of disappointment, of poignant and unrealized dreams. Her mother's imagination had been fired by fairy tale, Steedman observes, the make-belief that a king could fall in love with a goose-girl.[60] 'Born into the old working class, she had wanted: a New Look skirt, a timbered country cottage, to marry a prince.'[61] Magazines and newspapers around mid-century were full of stories about women from relatively 'ordinary' backgrounds who managed to attract princes, or at least men who laid claim to some kind of princely status, dubious though this might be.

In reality it helped if a girl—or woman—had money, of course. Highly successful cosmetics businesswomen Elizabeth Arden and Helena Rubinstein both managed to marry princes. Elizabeth Arden married Prince Michael Evlonoff in 1942, although the marriage didn't last long.[62] Her rival Helena Rubinstein's marriage, in 1938, to the genial Prince Artchil Gourielli-Tchkonia fared rather better. Though he was some twenty years younger than her, the marriage lasted until Artchil's death in 1955.[63] The prodigiously rich Barbara Hutton, heir to the Woolworth fortune, clocked up seven marriages in all, three of them to self-styled 'princes'.[64] In 1933 she married Prince Alexis Mdivani, one of three brothers often dubbed 'the marrying Mdivanis' on account of their success in wedding rich women. In 1947 Hutton married Prince Igor Troubetzkoy. Her final attachment, in 1964, was to 'Prince' Pierre Raymond Doan, vinh na Champassak.[65] The Champassaks were originally a royal family from Laos, with lands adjacent to the Mekong, but Hutton's biographer, C. David Heyman, alleged that it was Barbara's money that purchased Doan's rank and pedigree.[66] No wonder that when an ex-assistant of Barbara Hutton came to write about her employer's life she chose the title, In Search of a Prince (1988).[67] Reports of 'celebrity' weddings with princes featured large in women's magazines in Britain and North America. The marriage of film star Rita Hayworth to Prince Aly Khan in 1948 was described by Woman's Own as 'the fabulous story of a modern-day Cinderella who rose from obscurity to marry her millionaire Prince Charming'.[68] Again, in 1956, Grace Kelly's wedding to Prince Rainier of Monaco was represented as a real-life fairy tale.[69]

All this enthusiasm for Prince Charming in the 1950s fed into the popularity of one of the oddest celebrities of the decade, the American showman pianist, Wladziu Valentino Liberace. Liberace's mother named both of her sons after the heartthrob of her youth, Rudolph Valentino, but it was Wladziu (more familiarly, Walter or Lee) who was destined to pull heartstrings. His popularity among women was immense. Memorably described by historian Marjorie Garber as 'the crown prince of Mother's day', Liberace's fans included younger women as well as more maternal types.[70] Men found this hard to take. Their unease about his style permeated critical reviews on both sides of the Atlantic. In England, The Times, reporting on Liberace's first concert in London in 1956, was acid about his clothes, described as 'lurid in their opulence', and commented that 'a black suit of tails flecked with gold thread' that the star had worn for a television performance 'appeared to have been spun out of frogspawn'.[71] The auditorium at the Festival Hall was nevertheless 'thronged with girls and women of all ages, ready to squeal or swoon when they thought the occasion required it of them'.[72]

This *Times* review is interesting because the reviewer clearly *expected* to feel distaste and appeared somewhat surprised to find that the performer 'did not swank or slobber, or flash diamond rings shaped like grand pianos at his admirers'. Indeed, he was forced to admit that Liberace had 'a quiet sense of humour and is ready to laugh at himself'.[73] This attempt at fairness—or composure—was not always so evident. The virulence of loathing which Liberace could inspire in some men was most famously evident in two abusive articles written by William Connor ('Cassandra') and published in the *Daily Mirror* in 1956. Liberace sued for libel, won his case, and was awarded £8,000 in costs and damages.[74]

Figure 13. Liberace.

Returning to Connor's articles today, even granted that the writer seems to have got carried away by his own loquacity, it is difficult to credit the intensity of disgust that they embody. Liberace is described as 'a slag-heap of lilac coloured hokum', accused of 'slobbering over his mother', and of representing 'the biggest sentimental vomit of all time'. In the most quoted passages he is sneered at as a 'deadly, winking, sniggering, snuggling, chromium-plated, scent-impregnated, luminous, quivering, giggling, fruit-flavoured, mincing, ice-covered heap of mother love' who has 'had the biggest reception and impact on London' since Charlie Chaplin in 1921. Liberace, Connor opined, represented 'the summit of sex—Masculine, Feminine and Neuter. Everything that He, She and It can ever want'.[75]

One doesn't have to read much further to realize that this kind of abuse says more about the abuser than the abused. Just why (for instance) was a man's love for a mother deemed to be so degenerate? How was scent supposed to destroy masculinity? If Liberace's appeal was so widespread, why was Connor attacking him, rather than his admirers? Who was being seen as perverted here?

Connor got into even deeper water in the hearings in the High Court which followed. There were troublesome inquiries into the covert meanings of descriptions like 'fruit-flavoured' and 'fairy', and Connor had to wriggle out of a suggestion that his aversion to a particular breed of dogs (poodles) was because he associated them with certain kinds of sexual expression, or prostitutes.[76] There was a massive amount of circumlocution, a refusal to speak straight. Connor had written that 'There must be something wrong with us that our teenagers longing for sex and our middle aged matrons fed up with sex alike fall for such a sugary mountain of jingling claptrap' as Mr Liberace.[77] But Liberace repudiated any suggestion that his act was about sexuality. In his view, it was sentimental appeal, respect for his audience, and showmanship that kept his female audiences in thrall. And he was almost certainly right.

Looking back on the proceedings of this case today, what stands out most of all is the confusion. Several of the qualities which women found appealing in Liberace were precisely those qualities which led some men to impugn his masculinity. It wasn't clear, at the outset, that it was Liberace's own sexual affiliation that was on trial. When asked, early in the proceedings whether or not he was a homosexual, Liberace replied, 'No, sir.' Many have dismissed this as perjury. But as an insightful biographer, Darden Asbury Pyron, has shown, Liberace's repudiation of the homosexual label made perfect sense at the time.[78] The culture was one where homosexuality was defined as criminal, diseased, and revolting; Connor's articles, with their frequent reference to emetics and vomit, made this abundantly clear. Homosexuality was defined *in opposition* to manliness. If Liberace lived in a culture where homosexuals could not be seen as men, then the choice itself was meaningless and unacceptable. It was hardly hypocritical—and certainly safer—to stay in the closet.

It was prudent to keep the door shut on wardrobe excess while the hearings lasted, too, and Liberace appeared regularly at the High Court in understated suits. *The Times* had reported in 1956 that Liberace described himself as 'a glamourist', adding that he had explained that 'people expect it of me: otherwise I should dress much more soberly'.[79] During the court hearing in 1959, his defence counsel, Gilbert Beyfus, warned those present not to jeer at the American public for enjoying glamour, nor to assume that glamour made manliness impossible. After all, men in Regency Britain had liked to dress up, too. He reminded his listeners that contemporaries still enjoyed the spectacle of guards at Buckingham Palace, gartered knights, and even judges wearing wigs in the high court.[80]

Liberace's appearance in the 1950s wasn't as wildly flamboyant as it later became, anyway—he tended to turn out like an eighteenth-century gentleman, or a pantomime Prince Charming. There was a famous occasion in 1956 when he swapped clothes with Elvis.[81] The two men had something in common aside from their interest in music; both were rehearsing and performing a new, more opulent style of masculinity. Female fans appeared to revel in it. Liberace's extravagant brocades, furs, and twinkling gemstones brought forth sighs of appreciation and possibly a touch of envy in female audiences who had been glad to say goodbye to wartime rationing. When Liberace performed in Manchester and Sheffield he had been heckled by men shouting 'fairy' at him, and 'go home, queer'. But he took heart from his loyal female fan base, boasting that he was receiving some six to ten thousand letters a week, alongside a sizeable number of proposals of marriage and a veritable avalanche of Valentines.[82] The ladies liked his wit, his courtesy, and his obvious love and respect for his mother. Elvis adored his mother, too. Men like William Connor might have found this nauseating and unmanly but women had a different perspective.

There are parallels which can be drawn between Liberace and another cultural phenomenon of the time, the English romantic novelist Barbara Cartland. Cartland's books seem to have sold best from the 1960s to the 1980s, and her most flamboyant presentation of herself came towards the end of this period. But she had been writing steadily from the interwar years and remained prolific, even upping her output in old age, until her death at the end of the century.[83] Like Liberace she perfected an intensely gendered performance for the public: in Cartland's case this was a caked-on masquerade of femininity which belied her focused ambition and strong will. Highly attractive in her younger days, in her more mature years she became something of a self-parody. By this time her appearance had become outlandish and attracted a great deal of masculine derision: critics vied with each other to do justice to it in prose. The most succinct description came from Australian–British writer Clive James, who declared: 'Twin miracles of mascara, her eyes looked like the corpses of two small crows that had crashed into a chalk cliff.'[84] Cartland wore lush silk gowns designed by Norman Hartnell: sugary pink or delphinium blue. These were accessorized with extravagant hats and matching plumage.

Cartland, known as the 'Queen of Romance', published over 700 books and regularly appeared in the Guinness Book of Records for her productivity, which could reach the heights of two dozen books per year. Her books sold in thirty-six languages and were popular world-wide, although their appeal seems to have declined in Britain and North America after 1980. The Cartland formula for romance is well known. Her heroines—whom she referred to generically as her 'Cinderellas'—were innocent, pure, and lovely. They fell in love with dukes or princes who were handsome, rich, and worldly wise.[85] Love, for this writer, was spiritual and divine. Cartland claimed that her main inspiration, throughout her writing career, came from her youthful reading of the novels of Ethel M. Dell, from whom she had learned to believe in 'the gospel of love'.[86] She herself had always identified with the 'Cinderella figure of the pretty, all but penniless young virgin, dancing till dawn, dreaming about her unknown Prince'.[87] Although her own life had been fraught with vicissitudes and she had experienced many difficult and troubled relationships with men, Cartland still saw herself as an innocent, possessed of 'a sort of mental virginity'. 'I have always had this other image of myself as a sort of flower-like creature', she told biographer Henry Cloud, 'very delicate and feminine and always longing to be protected by a superior man'.[88]

Cartland, like Liberace, was a conundrum. Liberace, in his performance, and Cartland, in her romances, busied themselves in highly gendered representations that were oddly devoid of sexuality. Both were hanging on to—and propagating—an understanding of sexual difference that could reassure, as rooted in the rigid codes of the post-war world, where men were men and women were women and gender roles were seen as clearly demarcated. But at the same time their own personalities and experiences unsettled these assumptions and brought them into question. There was a great deal of denial. Publicly, Liberace denied his sexual attraction to men. Cartland, regularly challenged to explain how her heroes got their sexual experience in a world of virgins, simply retorted that the question 'wearied' her.[89] She had decided to set her romances in the past, she explained, precisely because she wanted to keep her heroines pure and innocent. Modern society was becoming far too permissive for her tastes.

By the 1970s Cartland's publishers were suggesting that her heroines were slightly dated, maybe too pure and ethereal for contemporary audiences. She would have none of this. Nor did her heroes change much over the years. For Cartland, manliness meant class, money, and a certain kind of distance from, and rigidity towards women. For all her exaltation of love as a spiritual commodity, her heroes needed wealth to be truly attractive. If not a palace, a country estate was a definite lure: she often spoke of a girl being fortunate enough 'to marry Park gates'.[90] Any suggestion from second-wave feminists that men should share tasks with women in the home was met with horror and incomprehension. 'Be men', she exhorted husbands in talks about her books, 'and refuse to do the washing-up.'[91] For Cartland, men who stood at the kitchen sink were emasculated, the products of a female—but wholly unfeminine—sadism.[92] Class was an integral part of this outlook. Lords and ladies had servants.

Cartland heroes were usually dukes or princes with titles such as the Duke of Buckminster (*Pride and the Poor Princess*, 1981), the dashing Duke of Darlington (*Afraid*, 1981), or the Earl of Rockbrook, who falls in love with Purilla, a simple country girl, in *The Lioness and the Lily* (1981); or they were heirs to kingdoms situated vaguely in middle or Eastern Europe, the Balkans, or Russia. Thus we have King Miklos of Karanya in *The Hellcat and the King*, 1977, Prince Ivan Volkonski (*The Passion and the Flower*, 1978), or King Maximilian of Valdastien (*A King in Love*, 1983). These princes load the heroines with expensive presents. The charming Prince Ivan, for instance, presents cash-strapped Lokita with white star-orchids and a diamond-encrusted butterfly brooch, nestling *en tremblant* in its white velvet jewel box.[93] Cartland liked to set her historical romances after the 1790s, when men stopped wearing wigs, because she confessed that she could 'never really believe that a man in a wig could be an attractive lover'.[94]

From the 1950s, cover illustrations by Francis Marshall added enormous appeal to Barbara Cartland's romances as published in paperback by the New English Library (NEL), Corgi, Bantam, and Pan.[95] Francis Marshall (1901–80) had earlier worked as an illustrator for

British *Vogue*. His cover art for Cartland romances shows inexhaustible flair in depicting saturnine princes, stiff with backbone, towering over fluffy and wilting Cinderellas. His design for *The Enchanted Waltz* (Arrow, 1955), for instance, had the happy couple swirling round a dance floor, the prince resplendent in blue–green tailcoat and white silk stockings. Twenty years later Marshall's princes have the same physiognomy: all jawbone and erect carriage. On the cover of *A Very Naughty Angel* (1975), the raven-haired prince sports a sable-trimmed cloak over scarlet silk sashes. He is booted and spurred, with a sword slanted at a suggestive angle, checked coyly by his lady-love's parasol.

Cinderella stories were wearing a little thin in some quarters by the last quarter of the twentieth century. Even before the advent of the women's liberation movement, dreams of being freed from domestic drudgery by a prince began to look unrealistic. After marriage, and outside the fairy tale, many women in the 1950s and 1960s struggled to balance housework with paid employment.[96] Domesticity wasn't all castles in the air, even for the better off: it could prove stultifying and oppressive. At a time when sexual activity before marriage was still fraught with risk, and frowned upon by many, writers such as Penelope Mortimer explored the ways in which men, marriage, and motherhood could entrap women.[97]

The title of Mortimer's most famous novel, *The Pumpkin Eater* (1961), refers to the nursery rhyme ('Peter, Peter, pumpkin eater/had a wife but couldn't keep her /He put her in a pumpkin shell/and there he kept her very well.') The reference is rich in meanings. Pumpkins are soft inside, fleshy, and full of seeds. The woman in the text is at the mercy of her body and her own fecundity. The suggestion is that men control women through sex and pregnancy. The pumpkin shell is no longer the golden coach which conveys Cinderella to the ball: it is her prison.

Second-wave feminists urged women to take control over their own bodies and sexuality and they inveighed against the passivity of women in fairy tales.[98] A number turned their energies to rewriting fairy stories generally, with feistier heroines who looked much more

**Figure 14.** Barbara Cartland book cover, design by Francis Marshall: *A Very Naughty Angel.*

critically at the charms of a prince.[99] 'Cinders jilts Prince Charming' announced the *Daily Mirror*, in 1987, reporting on how libraries were now looking for non-sexist children's books to promote equal opportunities and career opportunities for girls.[100] Cartland, of course, was horrified. 'These books are ghastly,' she told the reporter, 'girls should be soft, sweet and gentle—the opposite of men'.[101]

It wasn't just Cinderella who could look a bit wet in traditional interpretations. David Frost's production of the film *The Slipper and the Rose* in 1976 set out to beef up the characters of both Cinders and her prince in the fairy story. In this version, 'Prince Edward of Euphrania', played by Richard Chamberlain, is given to angst caused by pressure from his parents to make a politically prudent marriage. They organize a 'bride-finding ball'. Drawing on the language of women's liberation the prince complains of 'a cattle show', 'a sordid beauty contest' in which he himself will be commodified, reduced to the prize. Chamberlain certainly makes a gorgeous sex object, in a series of velvet frockcoats in varied hues of taupe, amber, and chartreuse. Less formally, he favours ruffled poet-shirts sprigged with delicate, embroidered flowers. He looked like the answer to a maiden's prayer, and the film did reasonably well in the UK. But it failed to impress in North America. 'Glass Slipper into Sow's Ear' declared the *New York Times*.[102] The paper's critic, Vincent Canby, thought it turned 'a prince into a frog', and that Cinderella and Prince Edward 'were less like characters in a fairy tale than pictures on a jar of peanut butter'.[103]

In Britain, *The Slipper and the Rose* was chosen for the Royal Command performance in 1976. The Queen Mother loved it.[104] Five years later, Lady Diana Spencer arrived at St Paul's Cathedral in a glass coach, arrayed in a huge puffball of ivory silk taffeta and antique lace. The 'fairy-tale' wedding of the shy, pretty young woman to Charles, Prince of Wales and heir to the throne was watched by an estimated television audience of some 750 million around the world. It certainly reactivated anachronisms, as many drooled anew over the details of tiaras, raiment, and precedence. Feminists worried that all this would have a distorting effect on girls' ambitions. *The Times* published an article, 'A-level or glass slipper?' written by Penny Perrick, who was concerned about Diana's suitability as a role model for girls: a pretty nursery assistant with no education to speak of who had captured the heart of a prince.[105] But the cracks in the royal marriage soon became apparent. A new scepticism about fairy tales was hard to avoid. Diana's—and the public's—investment in the happy-ever-after vision of the royal marriage was shown to have been a pipe dream. The prince had long been in love with someone else, it emerged, who happened to be a married woman. Hurt, unseemly confessions, and stabs at emotional revenge followed. None of this was contained within the private sphere, as similar goings-on sometimes had been in the past: all was played out loudly, in public, amplified by the world's press. Barbara Cartland—who just happened to be Diana's step-grandmother— sighed. She was quoted as having said that the only books that the young Diana had ever read had been hers, and she had to concede, now, that they hadn't been awfully good for her.[106]

**Figure 15.** Lady (later Princess) Diana reading Barbara Cartland.

A new kind of irony crept into representations of Cinderella's prince. In the year of the royal wedding, British pop star Adam Ant released the album *Prince Charming*: the title track became a number one hit.[107] Working with Malcolm McLaren, manager of the punk rock group the Sex Pistols, Adam Ant (born Stuart Leslie Goddard) exemplified what became known as 'the new romanticism'. His performances offered a smörgåsbord of masculinities. In the video version of *Prince Charming* he poses as a masculine Cinderella, vulnerable in a grubby singlet, transformed by a fairy godmother (buxom, ageing blonde bombshell Diana Dors) into a sexily trussed-up and dandified Hussar. He arrives at the ball in a sleek, low-bodied sports car. Swinging from a chandelier, he struts through the ballroom to a hypnotic drumbeat, wearing tight, silver leather breeches. He pointedly makes for his reflection in a large mirror, smashing it into smithereens. Shots of the star posing as Clint Eastwood, Alice Cooper, and Rudolph Valentino's Sheik represent the shards from which this multifaceted picture of desirable maleness has been composed. The performance unpicks cultural representations of gender. It shows masculinity as both cocky and vulnerable, as needing to overcome the possibility of ridicule, and as haunted by a fear of female voraciousness (the ugly sisters chomp on heart-shaped chocolates). It is oddly profound, and both men and women found it appealing.

Reinterpretations of the Cinderella story are unstoppable. Kenneth Branagh's adaptation of the story, in Walt Disney's (2015) live-action remake of the 1950s classic, though not without wit, stayed pretty close to type: a reviewer in *The Guardian* described it as a bit 'naff', 'a perky, pretty, lavender-scented cupcake' of a tale, charming on account of its old fashioned romanticism.[108] But Cinderella stories in recent decades have generally had more of an edge to them: they've been less likely to feature pretty princes rescuing hapless heroines and protecting, or propping, them up forever. Social changes since the 1970s—including the rise of feminism, more equal opportunities, and the advent of more efficient contraception—have made it possible for both women as well as men to experiment more with relationships, to think about what they might want in a partner, or indeed, to find out whether they want to settle down in a long-term relationship at all.[109] The idea of love at first sight seems naive. In a society where women are better educated, with more scope for self-support, there's usually an attempt to make Cinders or Sleeping Beauty feistier, and to look rather more sceptically at her dream of the prince.

Like the 1987 film version of *The Princess Bride*,[110] *Into the Woods* (2014), based on the Broadway musical of the same name, brings comedy into fairy tale.[111] There are two princes: one of them falls for Cinderella, the other, Rapunzel. Both are narcissistic, and primarily concerned with their own sufferings in love. A highlight of the film has them clambering over a waterfall ripping open their shirts to reveal toned and gorgeous torsos, while singing melodramatically and competitively about their angst: the song is entitled 'Agony'. Dreams of romance at first sight involving a lifetime's commitment are shown to be self-serving and hollow: there is no happy ever after. Cinderella's prince soon cheats on his lady-love. She protests, but he's not bothered. 'I was raised to be charming', he retorts, silkily, 'not sincere.'

# 5

# Dark Princes, Foreign Powers

## Desert Lovers, Outsiders, and Vampires

In 1959 Daphne du Maurier published a short story called 'The Menace'. It is about an ageing movie star. 'The Menace,' she explains, 'in movie language, and especially among women, means a heart-throb, a lover, someone with wide shoulders and no hips.'[1] Always fascinated by what women were drawn to in a man, du Maurier goes on to explore the style of masculinity which had made her fictional movie star, Barry Jeans, such a hot property. It had something to do with his personal appearance. 'Above all it was the mouth, firm and decisive above that square jaw, with the cleft in the chin that had maddened millions.'[2] Barry Jeans was terse and uncommunicative with women, given to pulling his trilby down over his eyes. There are shades of James Cagney, James Mason, and Humphrey Bogart here. Barry Jeans was a manly man, credited with an appetite for rare steak, sleeping in the nude, going out without a topcoat in a blizzard. Du Maurier's story focuses on unpicking or deconstructing this performance of masculine ruggedness. In 'real life', Barry has a strong-minded wife, who bosses him about and keeps a controlling eye on his timetables and regime. Why the vogue for these uncommunicative types of film star, between the wars, du Maurier wondered? Were men more comfortable keeping their distance from women, backing out of responsibility for all the bother and sentimentality of courtship? In her story, the advent of a new kind of cinema technology, 'the feelies', registers Barry as losing his vital force and sex appeal. His backers and publicity team panic, and try to prop him up with stimulants, none of which work. In the end, invigoration—a kind of mental Viagra—comes from an unlikely and homely source.

From her family background, closely linked with theatre as well as literature, Daphne du Maurier knew a great deal about masculine performance. The imagination of her grandfather, George du Maurier, had conjured up the unworldly and devoted lover, Peter Ibbetson. as well as the manipulative Svengali.[3] Her father, the actor–manager Gerald, had been notorious for his appeal to women.[4] The du Mauriers were a close-knit family with complicated emotional relationships and they often resorted to a private language studded with code. Margaret Forster, Daphne's biographer, tells us that the word 'menace' was always used by her subject to convey the idea of sexual attraction.[5] To speak of someone as 'a fearful menace' meant they were strongly and unsettlingly attractive.

Danger in a man could be sexy. Lady Caroline Lamb's famous description of Lord Byron has rattled down the centuries because it makes the point so succinctly. She was half crazed by her obsession with Byron not least because he was 'mad, bad and dangerous to know'.[6] The Byronic hero, brooding, saturnine, nursing injured sensitivities and dark passions, oozes testosterone and has had enduring appeal. There is Heathcliff, in Emily Brontë's *Wuthering Heights*, although he is imbued with too much menace in the literal sense of purely evil intent to be properly described as a hero. There is Charlotte Brontë's Mr Rochester, with his rakish past, in *Jane Eyre*. Rakes could be seen as manly men, desirable if only they could learn to control themselves to some degree and had the potential to be reformed. Every women dreams of reforming a rake, pontificated Barbara Cartland, 'every woman instinctively wants to tame a devil through the purity of her love'.[7] It was 'tall, dark and rather challenging men,' she confessed, that she herself found attractive.[8] The desire to reclaim, or to help to bring about reform in a rake had been the dream of Richardson's Clarissa, charmed by the unscrupulous Lovelace, but in women's romantic texts the dream is more likely to be realized. Here women inspire and manage men, propping them up where they see damage. This makes masculinity an achievement in which women share. As in du Maurier's short story 'The Menace', masculinity is at least partly understood as both a fiction and a joint project.

Georgette Heyer's novel about an irresistible rake, *The Devil's Cub*, was first published in 1932 and has not been out of print since then.[9] Many contemporary readers claim it as one of their favourite Heyer novels. It features Dominic, Marquis of Vidal, who is the son of the Duke of Avon and his wife, Léonie, characters in Heyer's earlier novel, *These Old Shades*. We're given to understand that Avon had been somewhat wild in his youth, but the young Vidal is worse. He's dissolute: a heavy drinker, a gambler, and a seducer; given to living fast and even faster driving. When we meet him in the first chapter his coach is attacked by highwaymen. He deftly plugs one of them in the head and nonchalantly abandons the corpse, brains spilling across the road, in order to get to a London party. Dominic is of course fearfully handsome. Raven-haired, with broad shoulders and legs so shapely that his stockings call for no padding, he is the joy of his tailor and valet, as well as of his fond Mamma.[10] In the course of the book his philandering is shown to be relatively harmless: that is, he only goes for loose-ish women of a lower social class. He meets his match in the form of the spirited Mary Challoner, who first tries to shoot him to protect her virtue, but subsequently learns how to love and manage him. In the course of a lively internet discussion between 2012 and 2014 about 'favourite Georgette Heyer heroes', several readers confessed their fondness for Vidal, in spite of, or because of, his recklessness and risk taking.[11] He's 'a hero that I really, really, really but really should not like' commented one reviewer, 'and yet I do!'[12]

In *Venetia*, first published in 1958, Heyer explored ideas about rakish heroes and the Byronic legacy further and in more detail. Her young heroine, Venetia, is introduced as someone who

> had never been in love; and at five-and-twenty her expectations were not high. Her only acquaintance with romance lay between the covers of the

books she had read; and if she had once awaited with confidence the arrival on her scene of a Sir Charles Grandison it had not been long before common sense banished such optimism.[13]

Readers in the 1950s would have had no trouble with this: it was a decade when the age of marriage was falling. Teenage marriages were not uncommon, and at twenty-five, girls worried about being 'left on the shelf'.[14] Venetia's social life is dull, and her only suitors are 'a rackety bunch' of impossibles. Two men seek her attention: Edward Yardley, a boring, steady type, and Oswald Denny, far too young, a boy whose head has been turned by Byron. Oswald combs his hair into wild curls, knots silk handkerchiefs around his neck, and broods over 'the dark passions in his soul'.[15] Both Venetia and the author regard him with amused tolerance. Then we learn about a third male, Lord Damerel, the owner of a nearby priory, where locals tell stories of lewd goings-on and vulgar romping. This is clearly an echo of the real Lord Byron's reputation for wild parties at Newstead Abbey in the early 1800s. Damerel bursts into Venetia's acquaintance when she is taking a country walk, enjoying a quiet spell of blackberrying. He's tall and loose-limbed, 'with a faint suggestion of swashbuckling arrogance', mounted on a handsome grey horse.[16] He has cynical eyes, and his lip—like that of Byron's Corsair—curls in a sneer. Venetia, accused of trespassing, is stand-offish, but her dog, Flurry, takes an instant liking to the man.[17] This is all code, of course: we're left in no doubt whatsoever that Damerel will turn out to be Venetia's Mr Right.

Heyer plays wittily with the conventions of romance and constructs an elegant comedy of manners. But she's also exploring styles of masculinity, and the appeal of the Byronic prototype, for men as well as for women. For Oswald, modelling himself on *The Corsair* is a pose, and he'll no doubt grow out of it. Damerel is closer to the original. Damerel's cousin and presumed heir Alfred, on the other hand, is a dyed-in-the-wool dandy, 'the pinkest of Pinks', who sports 'a buttonhole as large as a cabbage' and emits a strong aroma of Circassian hair oil.[18] Worse, his 'inexpressibles' (Regency slang for underpants) are 'of the most delicate shade of primrose'. Damerel's relatives, it seems, are faced with an unenviable choice between a 'fop' or a 'rip' as heir to the family fortunes.[19]

The narrative convention dictates that rakes should be reformed by pure-minded virgins, unlikely though this is. Georgette Heyer is more subtle. Venetia is shrewd. She ponders the double standard, reflecting on men's and women's different experiences of sexuality, but aware that some women could enjoy sexual dalliance and even look upon men as sexual objects. Her own mother turns out to have been a woman of the world, ignoring convention when it stood in the way of her own pleasure. Maybe chastity wasn't always a primary virtue?[20] Venetia's affection for Damerel is based on friendship and a shared sense of humour as well as on physical attraction. She's in no danger of seeing him through rose-tinted glasses. In any case, she has learned from Edward Yardley that too much worthiness can easily prove boring. But getting to know Damerel better, and falling in love, she finds that 'a well-informed mind and a great deal of kindness' count for much in a man.[21]

Byron's attraction, for his contemporaries, had been tinged with the lure of the exotic. His poetry is full of it. The well-known portraits by Thomas Phillips show him resplendent in Albanian dress, russet and gold, with a richly-hued silk turban wound around his head.[22] Byron had written to his mother, excited about his purchase of this costume, which he described as 'magnifique': he was acutely aware of his self-image and he knew that it made him look like a cross between a Barbary pirate and an Oriental potentate.[23]

Outsiders had glamour, hinting at different worlds: bygone days, the forbidden, and the exotic. There was the excitement of discovery and adventure in escaping imaginatively from the constraints of the everyday. As Britain's overseas empire expanded in the nineteenth century, the lure of the exotic was felt at all levels of society. After Prince Albert's death, Queen Victoria found herself attracted to the moody and exotic political figure, Benjamin Disraeli, an Anglican convert of Jewish parentage.[24] Both found their imagination fired by stories of the Ottoman Empire. Disraeli courted Victoria as his 'Faerie

Queen', flattered her with the title of 'Empress of India', and played the chivalric knight, while gambling on breathtaking adventures in foreign policy.[25] Victoria, beguiled, gave him primroses.[26] When Disraeli died in 1881 she sent a wreath of them, with a little note which read simply, 'His favourite flower'.[27] The lure of the Jewish exotic pervades George Eliot's novel, *Daniel Deronda* (1876). The young Deronda, represented as highly attractive, is given a mysterious past, exceptional sensitivity, and inexhaustible reserves of moral and spiritual integrity. He is both respectful of and protective towards women. Prominent male critics such as Henry James and F. R. Leavis were not impressed by him as a romantic hero.[28]

Queen Victoria was also close to Abdul Karim, a Muslim Indian servant who arrived at court in 1887. Aged twenty-four at the time, he was tall, slim, and strikingly handsome.[29] He bent down and kissed her feet. Victoria was smitten. Karim introduced the Queen to curry and gave her lessons in Urdu and Hindi. Victoria called him her 'Munshi' (teacher or secretary). She acquired an oil painting of Karim by Laurits Tuxen and commissioned portraits by the orientalist painter Rudolf Swoboda and Heinrich von Angeli.[30] This close relationship between the Queen and her Indian secretary provoked jealousy and racist comment for many years, but was highly valued by both parties. Victoria was generous to Karim, showering him with gifts and honours. When she died, Karim was allowed to join the Queen's funeral procession and to view her in her coffin, as she had directed, but Edward VII then stripped him of whatever personal letters and correspondence he could lay his hands on and sent him packing.[31]

At all levels of society, women hedged in by domesticity and boredom might hanker after a more colourful, exotic world. 'The Orient' represented fertile ground for Western imaginings, an exotic world where pleasurable dreams were rendered safe by distance. Queen Victoria never visited India, although she eagerly collected Indian artefacts and paintings, even constructing a 'Durbar Room', decorated by Punjabi architect Bhai Ram Singh, in Osborne House on the Isle of Wight. The idea of the Orient conjured up visions of luxuriant sensuality for both sexes: compliant *houris* and sex slaves on cushioned silk divans; hawk-browed desert tribesmen.

After Victoria's death, popular literature and the cinema amplified such visions and increased their currency. E. M. Hull's sheik became a cliché of popular culture in the 1920s and 1930s, seemingly without losing any of his potency. E. M. Hull followed up her own success with *The Sons of the Sheik* (1923), *The Desert Healer* (1925), and similar titles. Close on her heels, Louise Gerard produced *A Sultan's Slave* (1921) and *Son of the Sahara* (1924) for Mills and Boon. There was an avalanche of imitations by minor authors in cheaper magazines such as *Peg's Paper* over the next fifteen years or so. *Peg's Paper* advertised a 'thrilling new serial', *Call of the East*, for instance, in April 1939. *Bride of a Sheik*, featuring a doomed love affair between Joan and 'Ahmed Bur Din', had just concluded. The new story was advertised with an image of a commanding Arab figure towering over a slip of a girl, captive in chains. Her hair is fashionably Marcel-waved, and she's wearing a fetching little jersey number with matching high-heeled shoes. 'He was ruthless...he was fascinating', read the byline. 'She adored him. But he was a man of the East and she was an English girl.'[32] Berber and Arab costume came to signify virility: skilled horsemanship, of course, had always done so. Tents in the desert became fantasy locations where women imagined their senses awakening to thrilling new pleasures. That sheiks and princes were masterful, even to the point of forcing these new pleasures on them, was an important part of the narrative. Ladylike modesty had to be left behind, and if it wasn't your fault that you succumbed to pleasure then you could hardly be blamed for it. It mattered that women remained in control of this narrative; it was the product of their imaginings. Happy endings were often secured by giving the forceful tribesman European or even British ancestry of a kind, although this usually came to light only at the end of the book. Genuinely mixed-race love affairs might be titillating, but they were rarely consummated with happy endings. *Bride of a Sheik*, for example, has Ahmed stabbed by a jealous slave-girl, Shelula, while Joan goes off with Derek, an upright Englishman.[33]

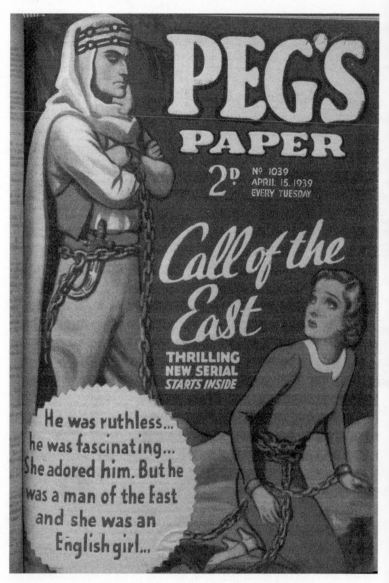

**Figure 16.** *Peg's Paper*, cover image: *Call of the East*, 15 Apr. 1939.

One of the characteristics of Orientalism involves the projection of desire on to non-white races, who are represented as 'the other', primitive or exotic. Since Edward Said published his classic work on the subject in 1978, scholars such as Billie Melman have questioned the ways in which Orientalism can carry different meanings for men and women.[34] Australian scholar Hsu-Ming Teo, has made a detailed study of the history of the oriental romance, tracing it back into medieval times: nineteenth-century colonialism provided new and fertile soil.[35] In the minds of women, the politics of the imagination were complex and might involve both critique and celebration of patriarchy. Western women might empathize with non-white women in zenanas or harems, for instance, or where women were the victims of practices like child marriage or sati. But the simple charge that Westerners were prone to depict brown-skinned men, or 'the other', as effeminate, is undermined when we distinguish between male and female perceptions. Through women's eyes, it was often the Western male, measured against an image of the sensuality or masterful virility of the desert lover, who could be found wanting.

Hsu Ming-Teo suggests that sheik novels had run out of steam in Western culture by the late 1930s but revived in the 1970s.[36] Post-war dreams of domesticity in Britain and America had their own potency, and following the disruptions of wartime, dreams of domestic harmony could in themselves seem like fantasies of escape. But desert lovers never wholly disappeared from the cultural imagination: they sometimes resurfaced in unlikely forms. In the 1965 film *Harum Scarum*, for instance, Elvis Presley swashbuckles around 'Babelstan' in a burnoose, side-burns fetchingly teased into kiss curls under a turban. He's Johnny Tyrone, a movie star, bent on rescuing Oriental-underdog stereotypes, introducing notch dancers to Las Vegas, and falling for the lovely Princess Shalimar.[37]

But in Britain, mass-market romance writers of the 1960s and 1970s faced a different public. Tourism had increased, and package holidays within Europe, at least, became widely available. In many ways, readers were more sophisticated. Dashing Italian and Spanish types

Figure 17. Elvis channelling Valentino in *Harum Scarum*.

began to compete with Arabs as imaginary foreign lovers. Violet Winspear, who became one of Mills and Boon's popular authors in the 1970s, published *Blue Jasmine* in 1969. One of her first novels, it depicts Lorna, the heroine, falling for 'Kasim ben Hussayn'. The text drew heavily on Winspear's reading of E. M. Hull. But in *Palace of the Peacocks*, another early success for Winspear, her horizons widened and the novel was set in Java.[38] In many of Winspear's later novels heroes are from European families (the Stephanos, Romanos, and Mavrakis family sagas). Interestingly, the author herself lived in Southend and never stepped foot outside Britain.[39]

There was however a marked resurgence of the desert romance in the 1980s and 1990s, particularly in America, and against a background of growing political turbulence in the Middle East, international tensions, and Western dependence on oil. Hsu-Ming Teo has shown how the novels of Barbara Faith (*Bedouin Bride* and *Desert Song* (1984), *Flower of the Desert* (1986), *Lion of the Desert* and *Desert Man* (1994)) recycled older narratives and projections of Orientalism, while challenging, at least to some extent, the idea of female powerlessness and portraying Muslim family values in a positive light.[40] She suggests that this kind of fiction played a part in tempering cruder American stereotypes which denigrated Muslim culture and portrayed Arabs as evil.[41]

Something similar might be said of British writer Penny Jordan's first offering from Mills and Boon, *Falcon's Prey* (1982).[42] Here the heroine Felicia gets involved with a comparatively Westernized Arab, Faisal, only to find herself falling for his much more traditional uncle, Sheik Raschid. There is a fair amount of exploration of different family structures, values, and cultural attitudes to women. Extended families in the Middle East are shown as offering protection, alongside control of women. In the end the clichés—arrogant, hyper-masculine Arab brought to heel by love for the comparatively innocent heroine—predominate. Raschid is described as 'sardonic'—perhaps the most over-used adjective in the whole lexicon of romance writers—some fifteen times in the course of the book. Shirley Conran's enormously successful *Lace* (1982) also features an Arab, 'Prince Abdullah of Sydon', depicted as rich and magnetically attractive but more than a little creepy, with an ingenious line in eroticism: his imagination and skills are perfectly honed to giving women pleasure.[43] But here myths are unpicked and there are no happy endings. *Lace* has been described as a 'feminist bonkbuster' for the way in which it charted women's painful achievement of sexual knowledge alongside autonomy and selfhood.[44]

Fantasies around dark-skinned, exotic lovers on the cinema screen or in romance fiction had their limits, not least because they were generally imagined as appealing mainly to white women; in Western culture, black or non-white women as sexual subjects rarely got a look in. Harlequin Enterprises set up Kimani Press in 2005, to feature 'sophisticated, soulful and sensual African-American and multicultural heroes and heroines', with a first launch of Kimani romance titles in 2006.[45] But for most of the twentieth century race and romance were brought together uneasily, and in highly stylized ways, even in the imagination. In the early 1900s, broodingly handsome Japanese–American film star Sessue Hayakawa became disillusioned by typecasting which relentlessly drove him into exotic villain or forbidden lover roles.[46] Bronzed or olive-skinned Arabs were regularly represented as glamorous, although in the first half of the century, at least, happy endings to stories of romance between these men and white heroines often depended on the chance discovery of hidden Western ancestry. E. M. Hull's sheik, we recall, turned out to be the 'lost' son of the English Lord Glencaryll.[47] Indian Princes and Rajahs were fine as romantic heroes if they were rich enough and shared something of the values of the British Empire. They might have been schooled at Eton, for instance, or have studied in Oxford or Cambridge.

A fascination with the lives of women whose appetite for adventure had led them into highly unconventional relationships was evident in the huge literary success of Lesley Blanch's book, *The Wilder Shores of Love*, in 1954.[48] This focused on the life histories and desires of four women: Isabel Burton, Jane Digby, Aimée Dubucq de Rivery, and Isabelle Eberhardt, all of whom had found passion and fulfilment in travel in North Africa and the Middle East. Jane Digby's life had been the incarnation of the desert romance. She had married into the English aristocracy, acquiring the title of Lady Ellenborough, in 1824. Her life had been sexually adventurous, to say the least: she had had many lovers, including King Ludwig I of Bavaria, and a bandit–hero of the Greek revolution. Aged forty-six, and still beautiful, she travelled to Syria, and fell in love with Sheik Abdul Medjuel el Mezrab. Though Medjuel was twenty years younger than Jane, the couple married. Much of the rest of her life was spent living in a villa which she built in Damascus, or in tents, with the nomadic Medjuel, in the desert. This was a love affair which had lasted some twenty-eight years, until Jane's death in 1881.[49]

If brown-skinned heroes could be seen as acceptable, black African masculinity appeared more threatening. Shades of non-whiteness mattered, and the exotic was often marked off from what was seen as primitive, or unacceptably primal. Edgar Rice Burroughs's phenomenally successful *Tarzan of the Apes* (1914, film version 1918) played with the idea of the white man raised by apes in the jungle—Tarzan is the lost son of Greystoke, an English Lord—who gains in virility from a knowledge of 'jungle ways'. His enemy is Terkoz, the black rebel ape who tries to abduct and rape the white-skinned Jane.[50] The rescue of a white woman from a black seducer is a common theme in pulp romance of this period. Book jacket illustrators sometimes went to town on this idea. An early edition of Louise Gerard's *Jungle Love*, for instance, has a naked-but-for-loincloth dark-skinned African looming over the swooning body of a pale-skinned English rose.[51] This kind of imagery shaded naturally into that of the film *King Kong* in 1933, for all that this film's setting is 'Skull Island' rather than darkest Africa.[52] Black masculine potency is represented as menacing, serving as both spectre and spectacle. Up until the 1950s and early 1960s even a bare mention of the Congo was likely to evoke images of drums, rubber plants, and sex.[53]

Evidence of white women finding black men attractive almost always provoked social unease, particularly in the first half of the twentieth century. Projections and prohibitions could of course reinforce each other, contributing to a steamy atmosphere of gossip and scandal. Rumours of affairs between rich—and sexually liberated—white society women and black celebrities circulated like wildfire. Singer Paul Robeson was plagued by rumours of liaisons with Nancy Cunard and Edwina Mountbatten.[54] Nancy Cunard, deeply involved with black American jazz musician Henry Crowder, published her essay *Black Man and White Ladyship* in 1931, attacking racist attitudes (and particularly those of her own mother).[55] Cabaret singer Leslie Hutchinson, born in Grenada and one of the biggest stars in Britain between the wars, was rumoured to have been involved with Edwina Mountbatten in the 1930s.[56] The stunningly handsome and debonair 'Hutch' was a massive heartthrob: for some men as well as for women. But the stakes in these relationships were high: desperate attempts to deny involvement, to cover up, and to bring libel actions were common.[57] Some high-profile love affairs, such as that between Seretse Kharma, son of the Chief of the Bamangwato people in what was then the British Protectorate of Bechuanaland, and the English girl Ruth Williams in the 1940s (they married in 1948), elicited international consternation and criticism.[58] More ordinary men and women, such as young white British women who fell in love with black American servicemen whom they met during the Second World War, had to contend with a great deal of hostility and disapproval. Some of these difficulties were reflected in contemporary films focusing on the problem of race relations, but they were on the whole too great to feed into contemporary romance, whether literary or on the cinema screen.[59]

Alongside foreign princes and desert tribesmen, dark strangers, outsiders, and outlaws had long been invested with romantic cachet. Pirates and highwaymen with an edge of menace in their make-up have featured regularly in popular romance. Byron's *Corsair* (1814) built on legends of Barbary pirate–adventurers from the sixteenth century and earlier. In the seventeenth and eighteenth centuries, piracy flourished in the West Indies, and stories of the exploits of 'Blackbeard' (Edward Teach) proliferated. Some descriptions have it that Blackbeard was tall, sported knee-length boots, and bright silk or velvet clothing. He wore his thick black beard long, bits of it plaited into tiny pigtails and tied with coloured ribbons. Conrad, Byron's Corsair, was blessed with 'sable curls in wild profusion', and a haughty expression about the lip. A great deal of him was attitude: 'There was a laughing Devil in his sneer.'[60] Errol Flynn's inimitable performance in *Captain Blood* (1935) set a new benchmark: irresistibly handsome, breathtakingly lithe, hair lustrous in the style of a page-boy bob rather like Garbo's. Flynn's Peter Blood was the perfect romantic hero, dash infused with decency and a firm grip on democratic values.[61] Daphne du Maurier's imaginary pirate–lover, Jean-Benoit Aubéry in *Frenchman's Creek* (1941), was another such paragon: courageous, dashing, and in his case brimming with cultural capital; Aubéry's tastes are refined and he draws exquisitely, making sensitive studies of wild birdlife.[62] Pirate heroes have continued to swagger, swashbuckle, and seduce through the centuries. The phenomenally successful performance of Johnny Depp in *Pirates of the Caribbean* (2003) and its sequels shows Captain Jack Sparrow camping it up with kohl'd eyes, gold teeth, and bits of reindeer shinbone in his hair. His performance draws on a number of legends. Depp has acknowledged that he gained inspiration from ageing rock star Keith Richards, of the Rolling Stones.[63] But there are touches of Blackbeard, too, in the braided chin-hair.[64]

Highwaymen had similar appeal. *The Newgate Calendar*, published in the nineteenth century as a work of improving literature, was packed with often salacious tales of both kinds of outlaw.[65] Prominent among the highwaymen was Claude du Vall, 'the Romantic Darling of the Ladies'. Du Vall or (Duval) was a Frenchman who, in the seventeenth century, had regularly robbed stagecoaches around London. The many stories and what we would now call 'urban myths' about his activities celebrate his exquisite manners alongside his thieving. When he was caught, sentenced to death, and hanged at Tyburn in 1670, women were said to have mourned in droves. His epitaph, carved into a white marble stone, read:

> Here lies Du Vall, reader if male thou art,
> Look to thy purse; if female, to thy heart.
> Much havoc hath he made of both; for all
> Men he made stand, and women he made fall
> The second conqueror of the Norman race
> Knights to his arms did yield, and ladies to his face.
> Old Tyburn's glory, England's bravest thief,
> Du Vall the ladies' joy! Du Vall the ladies' grief.[66]

A nineteen-year-old Georgette Heyer first tried her hand at a novel with *The Black Moth* (1921), which introduced Lord Jack Carstares, a young aristocrat who, having nobly shouldered the blame for his cheating younger brother, is driven into exile and becomes a dashing highwayman.[67]

The 1940s were a something of a golden age for highwaymen in the cultural imagination. Kathleen Winsor's *Forever Amber* (1944) featured Black Jack Mallard, who rescues Amber from Newgate prison. Jack is a highwayman with a physique and dress sense reminiscent of pirate

**Figure 18.** Douglas Fairbanks in *The Black Pirate*, 1926.

Figure 19. William Powell Frith painting of Claude du Vall.

Blackbeard. He's huge, with muscular calves and long black wavy hair. His blue velvet suit covers slightly grubby white linen and lace, the whole outfit being set off with bunches of garnet-coloured satin ribbons at waist, sleeves, and shoulders. Gold rings in each ear don't make him look foppish, we're assured: the jewellery simply accentuates 'his almost threatening masculinity'.[68] The following year saw James Mason as the suave, sardonic highwayman, Captain Jerry Jackson, in *The Wicked Lady* (1945), the film version of Magdalen King-Hall's novel, *The Wicked Lady Skelton*.[69] Jackson looked handsome in a hat of dark beaver-felt crowned with flamboyant plumes: his voice added a memorable tone of silky menace to the part. A film version of *Forever Amber* soon followed (in 1947) with John Russell cutting a dash as Black Jack Mallard.[70] Curling locks, twirled mustachios, and a manly torso tightly contoured in velvet, buttons, and lace completed the picture.

Some forty years later the image was still recognizable. Actor Hugh Grant starred in Gainsborough Pictures' 1989 television offering, *The Lady and the Highwayman*, which was based on Barbara Cartland's romance, *Cupid Rides Pillion*.[71] Grant, posh-voiced and blessed with an eighties mullet-style hairdo, lacked the sardonic touch as Lucius Vyne, even if he looked good in silver lace. Truer to type, the stereotype was reinvigorated—if bashed out of shape a little—by Adam Ant, cavorting with a hand mirror as the dandy highwayman in his song 'Stand and Deliver' (1981).

Highwaymen (even Hugh Grant as Lucius Vyne) charmed with displays of chivalry on the gallows, and showed no trace of fear. They are represented as gallant and reckless: as objects of desire and also as models for emulation. As readers or viewers women might identify with both positions. Stories of women pirates and highwaymen could stir the blood of female audiences in a society where femininity was often constrained and defined in terms of passivity and meekness.[72] But maybe such stories were particularly inspiring in wartime, when women were called upon to act differently, and to draw upon all their reserves of resourcefulness and courage. Barbara

**Figure 20.** Adam Ant posing as dandy highwayman, 1980s.

Skelton in *The Wicked Lady* masquerades as a highwayman, preying on travellers in the dead of night. She defies the conventions of femininity at every turn. *The Spanish Main* (1945) was a pirate adventure film that paid homage to Anne Bonney, legendary seventeenth-century female pirate whose name is often coupled with that of another cross-dressing pirate, her friend Mary Read.[73] The lure of literature and films about resilient, courageous men and women, defying conventional expectations and living against the grain is easy to understand, given the horrors of the early 1940s.

The world of vampire fiction, more other-worldly than mere outlaws or the exotic, has offered a special slant on Princes of Darkness, or sexy Princes of the Blood. These days, vampires can be blond and Nordic-looking, but still thrillingly in possession of dark powers. Vampire fiction has a number of roots, going back to the folk tales of Serbia and central Europe. Byron, Percy and Mary Shelley, and John William Polidori famously amused each other with scary stories of the supernatural while holidaying in the summer of 1816 at the Villa Diodati, on the shore of Lake Geneva.[74] Bram Stoker's *Dracula* (1897) added more to the brew of ghosts, ghastliness, and Gothic references which bubbled away fairly predictably until the second half of the last century, when the formula began to change.[75] New writers—Anne Rice, 'Marilyn Ross', Charlaine Harris, and Stephenie Meyer—had an enormous impact, boosting the popularity of the genre in the process: 'paranormal romance' is now one of the most flourishing branches of popular fiction.[76]

Anne Rice's work established vampires as 'elegant, tragic and sensitive' people who agonize over the nature of good and evil. They look good and dress well. Vampires become glamorous, moving towards the status of superheroes—albeit with poetic souls. Rice's Lestat de Lioncourt transmutes from roistering aristocrat into rock star.[77] Barnabas Collins, vampire hero of the American soap opera series *Dark Shadows* (1966–71), was capable of selfless heroism. Textual and film reinterpretations made him sexier: in the 2012 screen version of *Dark Shadows*, Collins was played by Johnny Depp, whose box-office appeal as a teenage heartthrob had reached such heights that he was twice heralded by *People* magazine as 'the sexiest man alive'.[78] Teenage girls have shown an insatiable appetite for vampire fiction.[79] But older women are by no means immune. Vampire Edward Cullen, played by Robert Pattinson in the film version of Stephenie Meyer's *Twilight* saga, had women of all ages weak with longing.[80]

What is all this about? The physical charms of a Tom Cruise, Johnny Depp, or Robert Pattinson clearly have something to answer for, but the matter goes far deeper. Trying to explain the appeal of vampire Cullen, British journalist Tanya Gold commented that he represents 'the lover that the young girl desires and fears', but also wants to rescue, a kind of 'Edward Rochester with fangs'.[81] American horror writer Stephen King's suggestion, cited earlier in this book, is that stories such as the *Twilight* series aren't really about vampires and werewolves at all; 'they're about how the love of a girl can turn a bad boy good'.[82] There is a lot in this. But at the same time, a young girl fantasizing about becoming a vampire is also fantasizing about power, and power is something that many teenage girls and women can still feel desperately removed from. A vampire lover in the shape of an ardent young male with supernatural powers *who is wholly and completely obsessed with you* offers a great deal. Power *and* protection, riches, beauty, excitement, enduring youth, love and devotion... for ever and ever... what more could a girl ask for?

# 6

# Soulmates

*Intimacy, Integrity, Trust*

Imagined intimacy with a vampire might provide a fantasy route to power and protection for young women. But the very idea of intimacy is in itself potent; the word itself has a history of serving as a euphemism for sexual intercourse. Historian Claire Langhamer has argued that over the first half of the last century in Britain, 'emotional intimacy' came increasingly to be seen as the core of 'true love'.[1] Up to that time, she suggests, a fair amount of pragmatism had characterized women's—and men's—search for partners in marriage. But somewhat relentlessly, ideas of true love became inflated to include passion and self-fulfilment, as well as companionship and mutual support.[2] Some women started to look for everything in a partner: they set out to find their 'soulmate'. Such idealism can be seen as having put severe strain on actual relationships: how would a young woman recognize her soulmate? A belief that you could fall in love instantly, with someone who would look into the depths of your soul and recognize that this was a perfect union, wasn't always good preparation for the lifetime of practical challenges that long-term relationships bring.

According to the Oxford English Dictionary, the term 'soulmate' was first used by romantic poet Samuel Taylor Coleridge, to suggest a union based on much more than practicalities: 'You must have a soulmate as well as a House or Yoke-mate,' he wrote in a letter dated 1822.[3] An ideal of the perfect pair-bond, of two souls twinned forever in harmony, goes back much further than this, to classical times.[4] It was an ideal that inspired both 'high' and 'low' culture in the Victorian and Edwardian years, George Eliot as much as Marie Corelli. 'What greater thing is there for two human souls, than to feel that they are joined for life', Eliot asked in *Adam Bede*, to work and minister to each other and 'to be one with each other in silent unspeakable memories at the moment of the last parting?'[5] Marie Corelli's novels, massively popular in her day, often focused on the quest for ideal love or a soulmate, a sentimental journey which might involve other-worldly, astral or transcendental dimensions.

Two recent studies of Corelli, by Annette Federico and Teresa Ransom, have begun to explore some of the reasons why this 'Queen of Victorian Bestsellers' fell so suddenly out of favour after her death, in 1924, with a public who had previously idolized her.[6] Corelli was a celebrity in her day, with a carefully constructed image. Born Mary MacKay, the name 'Corelli' was invented to make her sound more romantic, like an Italian countess. Royalty cheques allowed her to live in some style in Stratford-on-Avon, where she was fond of swanning up and down the River Avon in a gondola imported from Venice.[7] Like several of the writers of romance referred to in Chapter 1 (this volume), Corelli had been almost universally damned by the critics, even though her novels—especially *A Romance of Two Worlds* (1886) and *The Sorrows of Satan* (1895)—were enjoyed by prominent figures including Queen Victoria, the Prince of Wales, and William Gladstone, as well as having set new records in the sale of popular fiction.[8] Federico has pointed out that it was the emotional-ism in Corelli's writing that came to be regarded as embarrassing, her sentimentality that was increasingly seen as obscene or degenerate.[9] Historians of the emotions need to be attentive to such shifts.

Novels which had mass appeal in their day can give us valuable insights into changing sensibilities and values. Two texts which helped shape romantic conceptions about soulmates before and after the First World War were George du Maurier's novel *Peter Ibbetson* (1891), and Margaret Kennedy's *The Constant Nymph* (1924). *Peter Ibbetson* is a story about a pair of lovers who have been childhood sweethearts during idyllic years in Paris, but from there have gone their separate ways. Each of them has endured unhappiness and misfortune. When they meet again in mid-life they realize that their attraction to each other is still extraordinarily powerful. But tragedy strikes: the man, Peter, gets involved in a struggle with a wicked uncle who has insulted his mother and compromised a woman friend: the uncle dies and Peter is tried for murder. Though the verdict is 'not guilty', he is sentenced to confinement in a lunatic asylum. This confinement is for life, but in the novel, this is where Peter's real life and happiness begins. He establishes a kind of shared, dream life with his lover, Mary (Mimsie): she is the good fairy of her childhood reading; he is her 'Prince Charmant'.[10] The pair enjoy a rich imaginative life with each other, they travel and explore the world together and go back in time to their happy childhood years and even centuries before this, visiting the lives and experiences of ancestors. 'This long sweet life of make-believe, so much more real than reality' comforts both lovers until Mary's real death, in an accident, some years later. Coming to the end of his life, Peter records in a mystical vein that 'All I know is this: That all will be well for us all and of such a kind that those who do not sigh for the moon will be well content.'[11] Preposterous though all this inevitably sounds to the modern reader, *Peter Ibbetson* has a haunting quality, and undeniable poignancy. It rambles through a whole world of romantic dreams, soul entwinement, and the agony of loss, ending on a note of solace.

Margaret Kennedy's *The Constant Nymph* was also about star-crossed soulmates.[12] This was the story of an adolescent girl, Tessa, and her love for a much older musician, Lewis Dodd. Dodd marries Tessa's cousin but the marriage isn't happy: Dodd is 'bohemian', his wife a *bourgeoise*. Tessa's freshness and innocence inspire and move the older man and the pair run off with each other. To the relief of many readers, both in the 1920s and today, Tessa dies before the relationship gets physical. It's something of a let-out clause, morally. But the intimacy of soulmates represented is such that the text could be read as rising above any impulse of the flesh, or bodily concerns.

*Peter Ibbetson* was refashioned as a Broadway play in 1917, starring John and Lionel Barrymore and Constance Collier. John Barrymore hated playing Ibbetson, which he described as a 'pansy role', though his public loved him in it.[13] Two screen versions of the story followed, *Forever* in 1921, starring matinée idol and screen heartthrob Wallace Reid, and the film *Peter Ibbetson* of 1935, starring Gary Cooper.[14] *The Constant Nymph* was adapted for the London stage in 1926, and there were film versions in 1928, 1933, and 1943.[15] Both stories resonated with a public many of whom had lost loved ones during wartime; melancholy stories of lovers doomed by life's events, their passions unconsummated but somehow transcendent, had particular appeal in the interwar years. They offered a kind of spiritual consolation.

The melancholy beauty of matinée idol Ivor Novello made him ideal for the role of Lewis Dodd.[16] Novello had excelled himself as the tortured male sex object/victim in three earlier films. In Adrian Brunel's *The Man without Desire* (1923), he played Count Vittorio Dandolo, lovelorn for the death of his lady, Leonora.[17] The grieving Dandolo enters a state of suspended animation rather than death, waking two hundred years later to rediscover love with Ginevra, a descendant of Leonora who looks identical to his eighteenth-century soulmate. But where Leonora had asked for a friend, not a lover, Ginevra is a modern girl, and altogether more physical. Dandolo, tragically, finds himself impotent. Novello exudes a similar kind of helpless, passive eroticism in Hitchcock's two films, *Downhill* and *The Lodger*, in 1927.[18] In *Downhill* he plays Roddy Berwick, a paragon of a public schoolboy, falsely accused of sexual harassment by Mabel, a saucy, working-class waitress who runs the local sweetshop. Roddy's gentlemanly code of honour won't allow him to inform on anyone, so although it was actually his best mate who misbehaved with Mabel in 'Ye Old Bunne Shoppe', he holds his tongue. He's expelled, heartbroken at the prospect of never being able to play for the old boys' rugby team. From then on, as the film's title implies, it's downhill all the way for Roddy, brought low by alcohol, listlessness, and women's wiles. Novello's role as the mysterious, troubled Adonis wrongly suspected of sexual violence in *The Lodger* had also been well received, and he was the natural choice for Adrian Brunel's version of *The Constant Nymph* in 1928. No-one played other-worldly sensitivity and suffering quite like Novello, those dark, soulful eyes intense against his camellia-white skin.

In the 1920s, Novello's popularity among women was such that in Britain at least he came a close second to Valentino in the heartthrob stakes.[19] His performance as Parisian bad-boy Pierre Boucheron in *The Rat* (1925) had a dark eroticism about it and his image was artfully constructed in the media, playing on his understanding of women and camouflaging his homosexuality.[20] In 1925, for instance, *The Daily Mirror* carried an advertisement for a new girls' magazine, 'A weekly paper of love and laughter' to be called *Joy*, and published by the Amalgamated Press.[21] An introductory offer involved readers sending in their photographs for Ivor Novello to comment on their attractiveness. Every submission would earn a certificate signed by Ivor Novello telling the competitor 'to which type of beauty she belonged', there would be cash prizes, and the 300 lucky girls judged nearest to Ivor's ideal of each type of beauty would receive special sets of silk lingerie. Readers were assured that *all* age groups were eligible. An illustration showed an oddly disembodied head of Ivor, circled by girlish arms, all outstretched and yearning.[22]

Gary Cooper, in Paramount's film version of *Peter Ibbetson*, directed by Henry Hathaway, required more props to suggest soulfulness and eternal love than any performance by Ivor Novello. He was less cut out to pose as an icon of suffering, or *homme fatal*. Where Novello's eyes pooled soulfully and his body could melt and wilt, helpless in the hands of destiny, Cooper had a physique imbued with a more robust, easy grace. It is said that he considered himself miscast as Peter Ibbetson, but the performance is still successful, propped by clever cinematography.[23] The film opens with titles rolling against images of limpid pools and weeping willow trees. Gardens and light-filled mountain meadows suggest soul and spirituality. The pairing of the debonair Cooper with Ann Harding as Mary, self-possessed in spite of

Figure 21. Ivor Novello, advert for *Joy, Daily Mirror*, 10 Feb. 1925.

her ribbons, ringlets, and crystal sparkles, actually works. The love and dreams that the couple share in the face of cruel fate and all worldly odds is both touching and haunting: many found it so in the 1930s and comments posted on the internet testify to this still being the case today.[24] Faith in the idea of the soul living on after death and love as everlasting can be deeply consoling.

Next best to an actual soulmate was the idea of intimacy with someone who could really understand you by looking into your soul. Opportunities for sharing deep discussions about the meaning of life with a father-confessor or priest-like figure, sincere in his sympathy with you and your predicament, have inspired romantic illusions in generations of girls. This was no doubt particularly the case for girls immured in rural villages where there were few young men with any education apart from the local curate. Women's secrets might be confided to a priest in the intimate setting of the confession. A priest or clergyman's calling suggested honour and safety, as well as knowledge of the soul: these were important qualities for young women; it meant that they could *trust* a man.

Vows of celibacy might stoke rather than stifle fantasies of transgression, of course. Australian writer Colleen McCullough's bestselling novel, *The Thorn Birds* (1977), centres on the lifelong passion which Meggie Cleary has for a handsome priest, Ralph de Bricassart.[25] In the text, Ralph is introduced as a 'beautiful' man with fine, 'aristocratic' features, his hair in loose black curls. He's 'a charmer', thinks rich widow Mary Carson, who desperately fancies him but knows she's too old. She flirts with him, nonetheless: 'Curious', Mary thought, 'how many priests were handsome as Adonis, had the sexual magnetism of Don Juan. Did they espouse celibacy as a refuge from the consequences?'[26] But Ralph is clever, too, with an equally subtle mind. He knows that 'any priest under fifty is a target for lovesick girls', but he certainly feels secure with a widow in her sixties.

Ralph's attraction to Meggie Cleary starts when she's a little girl; he thinks it 'safe' for the very reason of her youth. Mary Carson's not so sure, particularly as Meggie, approaching adolescence, develops a crush on the priest. Their intimacy grows. When Meggie begins to menstruate she's fearful, ignorant of what is happening to her body. It is Ralph who reassures her, and begins to explain the facts of life.[27] Things get stickier and stickier. McCullough knew what she was doing in creating Ralph de Bricassart as the stuff of female fantasy. He's terrific to look at, dashing in highly polished knee boots, tanned and lithe in shorts, and completely stunning in ecclesiastical vestments: white, purple, or cardinal's red. He rides like a dream, and when not prancing about on horseback he has a penchant for roaring up the miles in fancy red and silver sports cars. Ralph's sensitive, soul-obsessed but sharply stylish masculinity marks him out as an altogether different species from the farmers and stockbreeders of the Outback: hard men who, we're told, would sleep on the floor rather than in beds soft enough to endanger their masculinity.[28] Ralph fights 'a gruelling battle to retain his soul's integrity, the long pressing down of will upon desire'.[29] This frees Mary to express her own sexual need, though not to have it met on any regular basis, since Ralph is always bent on getting back to his high-ranking career in the Vatican.

*The Thorn Birds* sold more than thirty million copies worldwide. It was adapted for a television mini-series in 1983 starring Richard Chamberlain and Rachel Ward: this, again, was a huge success. Richard Chamberlain was one of the biggest celebrity heartthrobs of the 1970s and 1980s in both Britain and America: he excelled himself in playing leading male roles which suggested understanding, soulful-ness, and sensitivity. Chamberlain's own homosexuality was kept a close secret, until he 'came out' many years later. In his autobio-graphical *Shattered Love* (2003), Chamberlain explained that he had considered his work as a 'leading man' had required living this kind of lie, and described how difficult this had been for him.[30] This confession itself was another kind of soul-baring, testimony to the real man's capacity for intimacy and integrity. It did little to harm Chamberlain's popularity.

Before Richard Chamberlain, Dirk Bogarde and Montgomery Clift had starred in roles projecting a capacity for sensitive understanding and integrity. These qualities were often conveyed through the role of psychiatrists, 'mind doctors' who like priests, were assumed to be conversant with the soul; or doctors of medicine, with their assumed familiarity with both mind and body. Men in these professional roles could signify both intimacy and high moral standards as advisors or counsellors to women. For example in *Suddenly, Last Summer* (1959), a film based on a play by Tennessee Williams, Montgomery Clift plays a gifted young neurosurgeon, John Cukrowicz, who has a particular bent for understanding the female psyche.[31] The psyche in question belongs to young Catherine (Elizabeth Taylor), who is exhibiting troubled behaviour through memory lapses, and also through being victimized by her wealthy, ageing-harpy aunt, Violet (Katharine Hepburn). The sinister Violet wants poor Catherine lobotomized so that she'll shut up about the horrible circumstances which resulted in the death of Violet's homosexual son, Sebastian. She attempts to bribe her way to this end, offering the hospital big donations if they play ball. Cukrowicz manfully resists, exhibiting sensitivity and profound understanding of Catherine's plight. He's the soul of integrity. 'Trust me', he murmurs to Catherine, searching deep into her eyes while injecting her with 'truth serum' so she'll recover her repressed memories. She does trust him, of course, and the film ends with them walking hand in hand towards love and new beginnings. Three years later Montgomery Clift played soul doctor once more, this time in the role of Sigmund Freud, in John Huston's semi-biographical film, *Freud: The Secret Passion* (1962).[32] Here he sets about sorting through the mental agonies and sexual confusion of 'Cecily Koertner', played by the glamorous Susannah York, a kind of amalgam of some of Freud's real patients such as Dora and Anna O. Clift's dark, slightly scary eyes bore into the predicament of Cecily, a lush confection of tumbled blonde hair, lacy peignoir, and father complexes. For all the film's intelligence (the original screenplay was by Jean-Paul Sartre), it's hard not to think of Brigitte Bardot being doctored by Svengali.

Doctors came to occupy a prominent place in twentieth-century romance. On the cinema screen, a reference to medical training often served to compound other kinds of attraction. Film audiences enjoying *Captain Blood* in 1935 understood the dashing pirate figure played by Errol Flynn to be a man of integrity because the narrative informed them that he had earlier practised as a doctor, 'a healer not a slayer', a man of selfless kindness who was driven to the high seas only when falsely accused of high treason.[33] In the *The Rains Came*, a 1939 film by 20th Century Fox, Tyrone Power starred as Major Rama Safti, a devastatingly handsome doctor and major in the army who just happened to be an Indian prince.[34] With the help of lots of bronze make-up, he serves as love interest for the privileged but bored English beauty Lady Edwina Esketh (played by Myrna Loy), who is immediately attracted to this 'pale copper Apollo'. Edwina is drawn by Safti's social and spiritual values—he's something of a poet as well as a social missionary. The fictional 'Ranchipur', in which the film is set, suffers earthquakes, floods, and plague. There's a terrific scene expressive of these end-of-empire tribulations in which a monster statue of Queen Victoria is submerged up to her neck in raging torrents. In the face of all this, the lovesick Edwina turns selfless nurse to Safti's doctoring, but then herself sickens with the plague and dies, neatly sidestepping a few of the problems of interracial romance. It's Tyrone Power who carries the film, a vision of gorgeous masculinity in the guise of bronzed Apollo, army hero, selfless surgeon, spiritual counsellor, and jewel-bedecked Indian Prince. He's little more than the ultimate fantasy male: an overdetermined sex object.

By the 1950s doctors had established themselves as well-heeled professionals in Western societies. Their lengthy education and training were expensive but brought rewards in terms of salaries, status, and security.[35] In the UK, the post-war expansion of the newly established National Health Service contributed to this development. In a society where women's opportunities for higher education and economic autonomy were still so limited, marrying a doctor could look like a good bet for a girl with ambitions for a secure home and family life, a safe respectability. There was an explosion of interest in 'medical romance'. In Britain, film producer Betty Box had an immediate

**Figure 22.** Tyrone Power as Indian Prince, still from *The Rains Came*, 1939.

success with the comedy film *Doctor in the House* in 1954, starring Dirk Bogarde as handsome young medical student Simon Sparrow.[36] The film made Bogarde an instant celebrity, 'the idol of the Odeons', and a new kind of romantic hero.[37] Consultants might be a bit scary and up themselves, but junior doctors could exhibit endearing flashes of vulnerability or high spirits. They could be dreamed about as excellent marriage material. In the film, the somewhat gauche Sparrow becomes an obvious target for the amorous ambitions of his land-lady's boldly flirtatious daughter. He's embarrassed and not interested. She's the wrong social class, anyway. But capturing a junior doctor became seen as a canny investment: women knew from their BBC accents that they were on to the right thing.

The popularity of *Doctor in the House* led to sequels and to associated television and radio series.[38] Many more television series and soaps have capitalized on the popularity of the medical setting. In the United States, fictional character Dr James Kildare first appeared in a novel of the 1930s by 'Max Brand' (Frederick Schiller Faust).[39] The Kildare figure inspired several films as well as magazine stories and further novels. He featured in a radio series of the 1950s, and most memorably the television series of the 1960s, as well as comic books through from the 1960s to the 1980s. It was Richard Chamberlain's performance as Kildare that made the actor such a heartthrob in 1960s Britain.[40] Also popular at this time was the British television series *Emergency Ward Ten* (1957–67).[41] The hospital setting lost nothing of its popularity in the later twentieth century, generating new, highly successful television series such as *Casualty* and *Holby City* in Britain, and NBC's drama series of 1994–2009, originally starring George Clooney as Dr Doug Ross, *ER*.[42] All of these programmes have dramatized courtship between doctors, nurses, and other hospital staff, alongside their regular treatment of the human dramas of illness, accident, and death.

Doctor types, especially those with psychological insight and a sensitivity towards women and children, were credited with powerful allure. The 1950s and 1960s witnessed some extreme cultural representations of this. *Magnificent Obsession* (1954) was Douglas Sirk's remake of an earlier film version of a best-selling novel by Lloyd Douglas. The earlier version, in 1935, had helped to establish actor Robert Taylor as a star.[43] The 1954 version did much the same for Rock Hudson, who plays the part of super-rich, super-handsome but socially irresponsible playboy Bob Merrick, who is brought to realize the error of his ways. Merrick transforms himself into a gifted neurosurgeon with a massive social conscience, capable of effecting social and medical miracles. He acts as a male fairy godfather to the woman he loves and feels responsible for; showering her with gifts, armfuls of lilac, and marriage proposals. But she's unnerved by all this devotion and fears that Merrick's love has to do with pity, since she was blinded in an accident in which he was tangentially involved. Disappearing for a while, she falls seriously ill. Merrick flies to her sickbed and performs an emergency operation so successful that not only does he save her life but he manages to restore her sight at the same time.

Good-looking doctors with soul, social conscience, and near-magical powers were so fashionable that even Elvis Presley had a go at playing the part. In *Change of Habit* (1969), he's a doctor with a Christian mission, the appropriately named John Carpenter, committed to bettering the lives of the poor in an urban ghetto.[44] Three Catholic nuns decide to help him out. They decide that they'll be more accepted if they wear ordinary clothes, so they ditch their habits in favour of miniskirts. Carpenter sings, plays guitar, and runs music groups with the local youth. Everyone adores him, especially the girls. He forms a close relationship with one of the nuns, Michelle, played by Mary Tyler Moore. Although she's a trained speech therapist, Michelle is stumped by the problems presented by a small, mute, autistic girl. Brushing Michelle's skills aside, Carpenter steps in manfully with a new kind of 'rage reduction therapy'. This involves imprisoning the struggling child in his arms and telling her over and again that he loves her until she gives in. Little wonder that the scene has proved lastingly controversial among those concerned with paediatrics and child psychology.[45] In the film, it works, of course: Carpenter has performed a miracle. Michelle falls for him, and she's completely smitten. For a while she and Carpenter play at being Mummy and Daddy to the little girl, taking her on outings to fairgrounds and so forth. Carpenter is demonstrably good husband material. But Michelle is horribly torn between God, her vows, and the Messianic heartthrob Carpenter. In the final scenes we see her in church, listening to a smartly dressed Carpenter belting out the gospel song, 'Let us Pray Together'. Her eyes swivel, desperately, between Elvis and a Crucifix.

Hospitals were represented as hotbeds of romance, hunting grounds for young women with marital ambitions. *Romeo* magazine, for instance, began a serial story in 1957 with the promising title *Nurse Janet and the Forty Bachelors*.[46] According to Jay Dixon's history of the romantic fiction published by Mills and Boon, the company published its first 'medical romance', Louise Gerard's *Days of Probation*, in 1917.[47] The genre burgeoned around mid-century, becoming a distinct 'line' on the publisher's list by the 1970s. Mid-century authors with a talent for medical romance included Caroline Trench, Elizabeth Gilzean, Alex Stuart, and Peggy Dern; there were many, many more. Historian Joseph McAleer has shown how in the 1950s, publisher Alan Boon tried to persuade some of his most successful authors into turning their hand to hospital romance, owing to the huge demand for such titles.[48] By 1957 he estimated that around one quarter of the romance novels published by Mills and Boon were Doctor–Nurse Romances. It is scarcely surprising that for those growing up in the 1950s and 1960s, 'playing doctors and nurses' became shorthand for children's sex–play.

Women who had trained and worked in medical settings before taking up romance writing were in a strong position, because their knowledge and skills helped them to avoid unfortunate gaffes and to get the medical details right. One of the most enduringly popular writers of medical romance was Betty Neels (1909–2001), a trained nurse and midwife who worked for many years in hospitals in Britain and the Netherlands and who only took up writing after her retirement.[49] Neels's first book, *Sister Peters in Amsterdam*, was published in 1969: she wrote prolifically through the 1970s and 1980s, but her books retained a pronounced 'feel' for the 1950s.[50] She has a strong following today, with most of her fans waxing lyrical over this characteristic 'vintage' appeal.[51]

Neels's heroines tend to be honest, hard-working Cinderella types, who have fallen on hard times. Unlike Cinderella, they're represented as quite ordinary-looking, making it easier for readers to identify with them. They are seldom slim: the author introduces many of her female protagonists as tall, big-boned, and buxom. Their figures are often described as 'splendid'. One of Neels's early novels bore the title *Amazon in an Apron* (1969), although it was later retitled *Nurse in Holland*: maybe the publisher thought the earlier version off-putting.[52] Neels's hero-figures are very stereotyped. They are wealthy, powerful yet intuitive doctors or surgeons, usually Dutchmen. Fans of Neels refer to them as 'RDDs' (rich Dutch doctors).[53] These rejoice in wildly improbable posh names and titles. Some of the more delightful examples include 'Baron Professor Coenraad Blankenaar van Essen' in *Sister Peters in Amsterdam*; 'Baron Adam de Wolff van Ozinga' (*Cruise to a Wedding*, 1974); 'Professor Eduard van Draak te Solendik' (*Grasp a Nettle*, 1977); and 'Professor Jake Luitingh van Thien' (*Britannia all at Sea*, 1978). These guys have class. And big expensive cars. They are prone to drive sleek Rolls-Royces which purr up the gravel drives of their big, imposing houses. Some drive a Bentley or, even more exotic, a Panther De Ville. Their big houses are staffed by servants, a house-keeper at least, and often a butler or old family retainer.

Neels's books envisaged a world which was rapidly vanishing. Women read them in the last decades of the twentieth century as they read them now, for escape and solace. They serve as a kind of comfort food, and it isn't surprising to find that descriptions of real food loom large in Neels's writing. The heroines are always downing 'sustaining soups', roasts and treacle puddings with 'lashings of cream'. In a patriarchal world, Neels's rich Dutch doctors offer protection and class privilege to heroines whose working lives have been anything but glamorous: these girls have often been toiling away in dismal care homes or working on night shifts in geriatric wards. Marriage to a rich, distinguished man offers them an opportunity both to escape, and also to demonstrate their frustrated good taste as consumers. Neels often endows her fictional heroines with cultural capital by describing them as having learned about antiques or fine art from knowledgeable but impoverished and deceased fathers and uncles in bookselling or the antiques trade. When these heroines are safely installed as the love interest of the rich doctors, these protectors hand them credit cards to Harrods or Harvey Nichols.

Integrity and trust are important in Neels's medical romances but these qualities tend to be guaranteed by social class and professional-ism. Her heroines aren't after soulmates, and the relationships that make them happy aren't really based on intimacy. There's too much social distance between heroine and hero for this. Given the author's values and the time she was writing, it's hardly surprising that there's next to no physical sex in her books. The men—as medics—have a capacity for intuition, though, and often understand what's going on in the heroine's mind. Neels's ideal of a romance depended squarely on separate gender roles and shared values: the values of hearth and home and family life—in a highly privileged form. Her heroes clinch their courtship activities with lines like 'I should like to wrap you in furs, my darling.'[54] For women battling away in dogsbody jobs with no prospects in the middle or even the later decades of the last century, this carried distinct appeal.

Shared values as a basis for intimacy, trust, and nest-building emerge as a strong theme in the popular culture of the post-war world. Betty Neels's heroines recognize the dependability of their heroes when they find themselves working together, often in crisis situations, caring for small children, sick people, and lonely widows. In Georgette Heyer's Regency romances of the 1950s and 1960s, heroes show what they are made of when the heroine's family fortunes are endangered by gambling, dare-devil or spendthrift behaviour on the part of younger brothers. Older and wiser, the hero figures act wisely and with generosity to younger men, rarely confronting them, but rather exhibiting a tolerant and effective sexual authority. This quasi fatherly–brotherly authority is represented as bound up with respect for the extended family and ties of kinship. In *Venetia* (1958), for example, Lord Damerel shows sensitivity and understanding for Venetia's disabled and bookish brother, Aubrey.[55] In *Cotillion* (1953), the heroine, Kitty, forms a strong, brotherly relationship with Freddy, who she exploits, relying on him for his kindness and practical support.[56] Kitty is powerfully attracted to Cousin Jack, a handsome rake. She takes it for granted that the foppish Freddy is uninterested in women: he openly confesses that he's 'not in the petticoat line'. But Kitty gradually comes to realize that the rake is a self-centred opportunist while good-hearted Freddy is worth his weight in gold; someone on whom she can wholly depend.

Heyer's judicious exploration of the values of trust and mutual dependency which might underpin comfortable family lives was taken even further in A *Civil Contract* (1961), where the hero, a gentleman fallen on hard times, marries the physically unattractive daughter of an extremely rich and vulgar businessman in order to restore his family fortunes.[57] Notwithstanding such an inauspicious beginning, the young couple manage to forge a mutually respectful and caring relationship allowing for a great deal of domestic harmony. The family takes precedence over individual needs and attractions.

A great deal has been written about domesticity in the 1950s. The appeal of living in a comfortable 'modern' home was a powerful aspiration for many women, exhausted by wartime austerities, housing shortages, and hard work.[58] In Britain, the *Daily Mail's* Ideal Home Exhibition proved massively popular, attracting some 1.5 million visitors in 1957.[59] There weren't many high-paying jobs for women around, and the shrewd bet for securing an ideal home and starting a family was to marry a man who could provide. Professional men—doctors, lawyers, and 'city men' with integrity and family values, men women could trust and depend upon—were seen as the best 'husband material'. Many of the popular male film stars of this period became heartthrobs through playing roles which conveyed these qualities. Examples included Rock Hudson, James Stewart, Henry Fonda, and Gregory Peck.

Domesticity could mean difficult adjustments for men who had fought in the war. Competing ideals of masculinity, painful memories of combat, and the difficulties of submitting to a nine-to-five existence were all themes explored in the film *The Man in the Grey Flannel Suit* (1956), which starred Gregory Peck as a troubled paterfamilias who eventually learns to 'worship' his forgiving, devoted wife.[60] But domesticity was double-edged for women, too, both refuge and prison for wives in the post-war world. In Britain, Penelope Mortimer's novels *Daddy's Gone A-Hunting* (1958) and *The Pumpkin Eater* (1962) dramatized the plight of the middle-class housebound wife, with no real autonomy or avenue to healthy self-expression, verging on nervous breakdown caused by loneliness and depression.[61] For women in these novels, husbands and doctors collude in attitudes and forms of betrayal which drive women mad. In the United States, Betty Friedan's research into the dissatisfactions of her housewife contemporaries led to the publication of her groundbreaking feminist study, *The Feminine Mystique*, in 1963.[62] The dream of suburban happy coupledom was revealed as a sham, associated with high costs for women. In another key text, Germaine Greer's *The Female Eunuch* (1970), the housebound mother is represented as 'the dead heart of the family', stuck at home while her husband and children escape to live the best part of their lives outside of its confines.[63] These books were extraordinarily influential, helping to shape the rise of second-wave feminism on both sides of the Atlantic. Breadwinner husbands and men generally started to be seen in a different light.

Historians now see the 1950s as a decade of instability, though tensions were often concealed beneath a profound social desire to build a better and more secure world after the war.[64] There was never any doubt about the period that followed: the 1960s were years of fast-paced social change. But the turbulence of the 1960s—the civil rights movement, the teenage revolution, the manifestations of a 'counter-culture', and the rise of feminism—can all be traced back into the previous decade. Women's lives, in particular, were changing fast, especially those of younger women. In Britain, the 1944 Butler Education Act ushered in secondary education for all. By the 1960s and 1970s more and more girls were going into higher education of some kind, and these girls began to live lives that differed from those of their mothers.[65] As young women, they began to have different ambitions, expectations, and fantasies about men and marriage, and were often drawn to new models of desirable masculinity: the rock star, the rebel, and the revolutionary.

Outlaws had long possessed allure, but outsiders seen to possess integrity alongside social vision could be even more appealing. Serious-minded young people of both sexes have ever felt the pull of Robin Hood, bandits with social conscience, or charismatic revolutionaries.

The image of Argentinian Marxist guerrilla Che Guevara inspired a whole generation. There was the virile romance of his motorcycle journeys, his radicalism, bravery, and uncompromising opposition to exploitation and capitalism. And it helped, of course, that he looked so dashing. Alberto Korda's photograph of Che Guevera, described as the most famous—and most reproduced—photograph in the world, became a cultural icon.[66] It has adorned mugs and posters in countless student lodgings and bedrooms across the world, as well as all those t-shirts.

The 1950s and 1960s were characterized by a burgeoning teenage revolution and the rise of new forms of 'permissiveness': disillusion with an older generation and what looked like peremptory and out-worn forms of authority coloured the outlooks of young people of both sexes. Marlon Brando's performances in *The Wild One* (1953) and *On the Waterfront* (1954) modelled a sultry rebelliousness and struggles with conscience. In *Viva Zapata* (1952), Brando gave a memorable performance as the 'Robin Hood of Mexico,' Emiliano Zapata, depicted somewhat romantically as an incorruptible rebel leader bent on restoring land to disinherited peasants. Brando made motor-bikes, blue jeans, and leather jackets iconic even before James Dean's performance as a moody, angst-ridden youth in the 1955 film *Rebel without a Cause*. James Dean's ambivalent sexuality exerted a strong appeal for both women and men, and indeed, continues to do so. *Rebel without a Cause* was released shortly after Dean's death, when his Porsche 550 Spyder crashed on the highway near Salinas: he was only twenty-four years old. Today his official website, instructing fans to 'dream as if you'll live for ever, live as if you'll die today', is available in eleven different languages.[67]

In the 1960s many male performers sought some aura of revolution, even if only by singing of it. According to the Lennon–McCartney song, 'Revolution', we all wanted to change the world. The Rolling Stones' song 'Street Fighting Man' was said to be inspired by British Pakistani left-wing commentator Tariq Ali, anti-war demonstrations, and student protests on the Left Bank in Paris.[68] Radical chic was in the air, even if there was unease about violence. In Hollywood, a number of stars aligned themselves with the civil rights movement and opposed the war in Vietnam. Heartthrob Paul Newman came out in support of Eugene McCarthy in 1968, stood against war, and expressed his support for environmentalism.[69] The appeal of 'Flower Power' was associated with expressions of a new kind of masculinity: uncompromising in challenging old hypocrisies, but rejecting war and conflict. Young men could question gender stereotypes, grow their hair, and show their sensitive, feminine side. Beatnik-y men could work alongside women for a new social order: John Lennon showed one way of advertising his commitment to such, in coupledom and performance art with Yoko Ono.[70]

But transitions in cultural history are rarely abrupt or total. Many of the male singers and performers of the post-war years became or continued to be popular not least because they seemed to exemplify family values, integrity, and dependability: Pat Boone, for instance, or Perry Como, or Cliff Richard. Perry Como had been voted 'Crooner of the Year' by *Life* magazine in 1943: a former barber, his hair was neat and sleek and he wore cardigans. He was the epitome of 'Mr Nice Guy'.[71] Polls among young women in America in the late 1950s sometimes ranked Perry Como ahead of Elvis Presley in the popularity stakes, and particularly when voters were asked who they would choose as good husband material.[72] In Britain, the new magazine *Boyfriend* singled out Perry Como as readers' 'dreamboat' in 1959— the magazine was aimed at teenagers, and Como was forty-seven years old at the time.[73] Girls' magazines such as *Boyfriend*, *Romeo*, and *Valentine* helped to promote the fan base for the new pop singers and heartthrobs. Strong affirmations of love for mothers and sisters, satisfaction in home-cooked food, and delight in hand-knitted sweaters were obviously calculated to increase these stars' appeal.

Back in the early years of the twentieth century, girls had devoured popular magazines such as *Peg's Paper*, *Oracle*, and *Red Star Weekly*, most of which featured serial stories with titles such as 'A Man's Plaything', 'Wife in Name Only', or 'Dangerous Love'. This kind of fiction, full of dastardly seducers and schemers out to trap innocent women and do them wrong, is usually dismissed as cheap sensationalism. But we shouldn't forget that courtship and sexual relations could indeed be full of dangers for young women. Even fifty years later, the advantages of the 'permissive society', with its more relaxed attitudes to sexual experimentation and freedoms, could be double-edged for girls. Feminists have been quick to emphasize that the persistence of sexual double standards has meant that girls have tended to benefit less from sexual freedoms than boys. Unwanted pregnancies, traumatic abortions, and a reputation for easy morals can have heavy and damaging consequences for young women. In societies which combine relaxed morals with double standards, sexuality is still an area of danger. It is important for girls to know who they can *trust*: integrity, honesty, and dependability matter a great deal. The continuing appeal of boy bands made up of young, non-threatening boy-next-door types can be understood at least partly in this light. Girls can express desire and devotion and let themselves go freely in contexts when they feel safe.

Equally, the romance attaching to men of vision, rebels, and revolutionaries has a long history. Young women in the nineteenth century could feel powerless. They were, after all, literally disenfranchised, often cut off from politics and effective social action. Yet many nursed a youthful idealism and were passionately interested in social reform. The idea of joining forces with a young man who was fired with similar reforming zeal could be irresistible. In part, the idea allowed girls a kind of vicarious satisfaction that was consonant with conventional feminine ideas of self-sacrifice. You could devote yourself to a good man *and* his cause. Others dreamed about a more egalitarian and intimate relationship: two comrades, working together for a better world. The first generation of women to gain access to university education in late Victorian times produced a crop of now forgotten novels featuring romance between earnest young women and budding political visionaries, or men working in missions and settlements in the slummier districts of the East End of London.[74] And well into the following century, the appeal of becoming a doctor's or a vicar's wife was often enhanced by the idea of the heroine being able to share in his work, functioning as his (unpaid) helpmeet.

But romantic visions of this kind don't easily accommodate happy endings. Rebels and revolutionaries with a strong sense of mission may be too driven and self-absorbed for intimacy, too restless to settle for love and domesticity. Something of a warning along these lines was spelled out in Warren Beatty's 1981 production of the film *Reds*. Based on *Ten Days that Shook the World*, journalist John Reed's novel about the Russian Revolution, the film featured Beatty, already a major heartthrob, in the role of Reed, whose political commitment continually threatens his emotional commitment and availability to his wife and colleague, Louise Bryant.[75] Cowboy heroes had long posed something of the same problem: their integrity bound up with 'loner' status and defiance of convention. Even though a generation of women swooned over Clint Eastwood in *Rawhide*, or Robert Horton as Flint McCullough in *Wagon Train*, it was not easy to incorporate these qualities into traditional narratives of romance.[76] Cowboy loners might stand for freedom and ethical purity, but they weren't easy to domesticate. But off-screen, and outside the pages of romance, many male actors and celebrities found their images enhanced by a reputation for political integrity and philanthropy. Marlon Brando was known for taking a strong stand on civil rights; Clint Eastwood was for a long while critical of American foreign policy and US interventions in Korea, Vietnam, and Afghanistan.[77] More recently, George Clooney's reputation for humanitarian work and his rights activism have added another dimension to his appeal.[78]

The writer Jane Miller reflected on some of the differences between men's and women's ideas of a hero in a book entitled *Women Writing about Men*, published by Virago Press in 1986.[79] Discussing the reasons why so many male critics have been dismissive of women writers' attempts to depict male heroes, she suggested that for men, a hero's life is a quest, 'an exceptional life, garlanded with achievements'.[80] For a woman writer of romance, a hero is someone much more ordinary, who, once committed to the heroine, gives shape to her life and makes it meaningful. *Her* quest is to find a man whom she can marry, who will make her life imaginable.[81]

Popular romances written in the middle of the last century amplify this vision. In Betty Neels's *The End of the Rainbow* (1974), for instance, we're told that the heroine, Olympia, in training as a hospital nurse, dreamed of meeting a young man who would want to marry her 'and thus solve the future for her'.[82] A rich Dutch doctor, Waldo van der Graaf, duly rides in to the rescue, and all ends happily ever after. But readers of Neels today are more critical than those of half a century ago, and their expectations of intimacy and mutual respect are greater. They tend to find a fantasy figure such as Waldo too patrician, too up-himself for true love. Comments on the reader-review site Goodreads. com include a complaint that 'she (Olympia) was more his housewife and nanny than his wife', and 'I just saw a lifetime of servitude in front of her'.[83] As the twentieth century drew to its close, women wanted more from their ideal men than integrity, breadwinning, and credit cards: they wanted equality, partnership, and communication.

# 7

# Power

*Protection, Transformative Magic, and Patriarchy*

Some thinkers regard patriarchy as biologically given: the social outcome of evolutionary design. Most cultural theorists—and feminists—reject this line of argument. Argument over the issue of whether women are fundamentally and essentially drawn to favour strong and powerful males has a long history. Back in the nineteenth century, social-Darwinist thinkers Patrick Geddes and J. Arthur Thomson published *The Evolution of Sex* (1889), in which they maintained that biology determined gender.[1] Male cells were *katabolic*, full of energy and go, whereas their female equivalents were *anabolic*, energy-conserving and passive. They suggested that this explained why men were eager and rational, keen to take the initiative in life, while women were more intuitive, couch-potato-like, and restrained. There was only so much social and political tinkering could do to change this. 'What was decided among the prehistoric Protozoa' they intoned portentously, 'cannot be annulled by Act of Parliament.'[2]

This kind of argument was often used in an attempt to derail feminists. Victorian philosopher Herbert Spencer added his two penn'orth to the social evolutionists by suggesting that 'real' women blossomed under the protection of patriarchy.[3] In his view, social progress came about through the rise of men to power positions that enabled them to protect women. Women's demands for economic independence were heard only when there weren't enough men to go round, Spencer averred.[4] Feminists had it all wrong.

Controversies over the 'modern woman' in the early decades of the twentieth century often got bogged down in this kind of biological essentialism.[5] In his controversial novel, *Ann Veronica: A Modern Love Story* (1909), for instance, H. G. Wells saw himself as defending the freedoms of the modern girl. The subtext was a fantasy about the married Wells's own relationship with the young Amber Pember-Reeves.[6] Ann Veronica is based on Amber. Wells depicts her as having strong, independent desires, but in the pillow talk between them, described in the novel, he makes her confess to her lover, Capes (a thinly disguised version of H. G.), that far from being modern, she wants to be as 'primordial as chipped flint'.[7]

The cultural history of the 1920s and 1930s is shot through by a fascination with the power of the primitive and the primordial. This had roots in both Darwinism and empire. Texts such as Jack London's *The Call of the Wild* (1903), Edgar Rice Burrough's *Tarzan of the Apes* (1912), and the original 1933 film *King Kong* had huge appeal and impact.[8] In *The Call of the Wild* a pet dog goes back to nature, discovering long-lost instincts and reinvigorated when no longer stultified by domestication. Burrough's Tarzan is the perfect man: forged in the jungle but with aristocratic genes, a fusion of primitive virility with gentlemanly manners. Kong is a terrifying vision of potency, but when he rescues Ann (Faye Wray) he cradles her gently in the palm of his hand. What power! What protectiveness! Wasn't this what all women really wanted?

Google N-grams, which chart the frequency of use of words and phrases in printed sources through time, can be a helpful tool for the historian. A search shows the use of the term 'cave-man' rising to an impressive, parabolic peak in the printed sources of the twenties and thirties, when there was a great deal of discussion about whether most women found the 'cave-man' type irresistible.[9] In Aldous Huxley's novel, *Point Counter Point* (1928), for instance, the cerebral–intellectual Philip Quarles is compared with 'cave-man' types whose passion and capacity for violence, he ruefully considers, seem to appeal to women.[10] And indeed there was evidence which seemed to confirm this. Alongside images of sheiks carrying women off on horseback, cover designs and illustrations in popular romances of the time began to feature lipsticked heroines swooning against the manly chests of heroes tricked out in fetching bits of leopard skin, fashioned into tunics and loincloths, while lions (or dark-skinned natives) loomed in the jungle beyond. Sylvia Sark's *Take Me! Break Me!*, published by Mills and Boon in 1938, is one such example.[11]

**Figure 23.** Cover illustration and spine of Mills and Boon volume, Sylvia Sark's *Take Me! Break Me!*, 1938.

Popular magazines were awash with this stuff. But use of the term 'cave-man' gradually tailed off after the Second World War. It was gradually replaced by references to the 'alpha male', a term originally used by zoologists to convey dominance among primates. In the 1970s, the use of this term to describe patterns of human behaviour rose rapidly, and it continued to do so until the end of the century. Ubiquitous in pop-psychology, the description 'alpha male' could sometimes be used disparagingly, in connection with male carousing, boorishness, and bad behaviour. Film stars Oliver Reed, Richard Harris, and Russell Crowe, for instance, or Jeremy Clarkson, famed for having presented BBC Television's motoring epic *Top Gear* until he was sacked for allegedly assaulting a colleague, have all earned notoriety for their uncontrolled or roistering behaviour.[12] Levels of tolerance for such behaviour—often described as 'testosterone-fuelled outbursts'—have varied widely. Some are reluctant to condemn what they see as the mark of red-blooded masculinity. The term alpha male can also carry positive associations with leadership and courage. And on the internet there are many companies which advertise sprays, colognes, and deodorants containing 'alpha' pheromones. With names such as 'Maschio', 'Trust and Respect', or 'Power and Awe', these claim to draw upon sexual chemistry to produce products which will magnify male sexual attractiveness and pulling power.[13]

We have seen that alpha males have no monopoly in female fantasy. Nevertheless, the appeal of the powerful male remains strong, particularly in wartime, and has persisted through modern history. Male power can take a variety of forms. There is physical strength and courage, and the technical competence associated with driving, riding, or flying planes. The fearless pilots of the RAF, silver wings on blue-grey uniforms, epitomized glamour for many in the 1940s: one thinks of Stewart Granger manfully striding off to defend his country and his sweetheart in Gainsborough's hugely popular 1944 film, *Love Story*.[14] Soldiers, rally drivers, skilled horsemen, and airmen have long featured in the annals of romance. Then there is economic clout, which in its turn can be based on a variety of resources: land, monetary wealth, investment capital, houses, furniture, paintings, or other works of art. And there are many varieties of social and political power: inherited status, cultural capital, physical skill, and so forth. The attractiveness of particular resources and skills has varied, to some extent, through time. Not all men possess these resources, nor do all women lack them. However, historically women have been much less likely to have command over such assets than men.

Attachment to a rich and powerful man could offer protection to women. It might seem to offer the promise of a life transformed: comfort, luxury, new horizons, and a new social world. The dominating importance of marriage in romance fiction is bound up with the promise of transformation. The heroine's life is brightened and settled by it—at least in her dreams.

This explains something of the lure of patriarchy for women, and it has been strong, both historically and at the level of fantasy. Popular romance is full of it. In the stories of writers such as Barbara Cartland, Georgette Heyer, and Betty Neels, heroes exude manliness essentially based on power. They are almost always very rich, with 'old' money more in evidence than new-found wealth, since this confers status and cultural cachet. Barbara Cartland referred to women who married into wealthy, landed families as 'marrying park gates': park gates, of course, stand at the entrance to a luxurious world. Heroes are further likely to be physically impressive, risk takers, and proud defenders of aristocratic lineage.

Betty Neels's romances celebrated a world that was disappearing even as she wrote in the 1970s. Her stories suggested a pattern of courtship and family life resonant of the 1950s, a world in which a clear demarcation of men's and women's roles reflected deeply entrenched gender divisions in the world of work. Hers was a world which was based on class privilege as well as patriarchy. There is an assumption, in Neels's romances, that domestic service in the home would make life comfortable for well-off wives and mothers. Some of her heroes still rejoiced in the service of butler-cum-valet types, even in mid-twentieth-century Britain. Neels's heroes are moneyed, with aristocratic and imposing titles, and they further cement their alpha male status with high professional achievement, usually as senior consultants, doctors, and surgeons. Georgette Heyer's and Barbara Cartland's novels are mostly set in the more distant past, and their heroes inhabit settings so privileged as almost to exclude the world of work altogether, at least for the main characters. Flunkies hover everywhere, eager to shoot off to do their masters' bidding.

'Masterful' men are presented as irresistibly attractive within these texts: the heroines eventually (if not at the beginning) look up to them adoringly and address them as 'Sir' or 'My Lord'. Georgette Heyer's remarkably successful novel *These Old Shades* was first published in 1926, the year of the General Strike.[15] It offers an interesting representation of powerful masculinity in the shape of Justin Alastair, Duke of Avon, whose characterization was discussed in Chapter 4 (this volume). Justin is in a class of his own. He is a man with a reputation for rakishness who manages to combine his appetite for risk taking with family values, his physical courage with a dandified dress sense and exquisite manners. Like so many romantic heroes, he is haughty, sardonic, and elegant. Women sigh over him, but he remains aloof. The story begins when this paragon rescues a nineteen-year-old, Léon, who becomes his page. Léon is in fact Léonie, a girl of noble birth who dresses as a boy. She has been rejected by her father, the evil Compte de Saint-Vire, at birth. There is much play on the eroticism of sexual ambiguity in the text, but little doubt about who is dominant. Léonie falls for her rescuer, whom she calls 'Monseigneur', losing no opportunity to fall at his feet, kiss his hand, and do his every bidding. Dismantling her disguise, Justin sets about feminizing his young charge, who (for all her nineteen years) he refers to as his 'babe', 'child', or 'infant'. Eventually, of course, he falls for her, and after a complex sequence of unravellings and unmaskings they marry. Heyer shows how Avon's masculinity is buttressed and smoothed by Léonie's adoration. She reflects him at twice his natural size, and insists on making him her hero. Even though Léonie is spirited and has a mind of her own, she is wholly smitten with the duke. He himself mildly objects to this idealization, but she will have it no other way.

Women collude with patriarchy, in Heyer's world, because for many of them it's a kind of protection racket. And this protection is represented, on the whole, as benign. Most of Georgette Heyer's novels paint an affectionate picture of both masculinity and patriarchy: brothers are good-hearted and fun to be with, uncles are kind, and heroes, of course, are paragons or enlightened despots. You do get the odd villain, like the Compte de Saint-Vire, but the decent fellows make short work of them. The injuries of patriarchy—girl children unable to inherit, sexual double standards, and the constraints of femininity—are brushed aside, ignored, or quickly forgotten.

British academic and journalist Rosalind Coward published a book entitled *Female Desire* in 1984.[16] She deftly dissected some of the ways in which patriarchal societies make it complicated for women to experience and express desire. Women rarely act openly on their own desires, she argued: they tend to focus on looking and behaving in a way that they hope will be attractive to men.[17] In effect, they make someone else responsible for their own desire. It isn't difficult to find examples of this. Sylvia Plath's diaries from the 1950s provide sharp insights alongside instances of what Coward describes.[18] As a young woman about to leave home for Wellesley College, Plath clearly spent a great deal of time thinking about sex and wrestling with the 'problem' of desire. Her frustration caused her to envy boys, whom she imagined as being able to 'dispel sexual hunger freely, without misgiving, and be whole', while her own femininity reduced her to dragging out 'from date to date in soggy desire, always unfulfilled'.[19]

Plath's frustration with social expectations around femaleness and how she would negotiate love and sex and creative ambition would continue to obsess her through her years as a student. At one point in the early 1950s she confessed in her journal that she would like to 'get in a car and be driven off into the mountains to a cabin on a wind-howling hill and be raped in a huge lust like a cave-woman, fighting, screaming and biting in a ferocious ecstasy of orgasm'.[20] Immediately checking her own daydream, she wryly admitted that this didn't sound 'very nice, delicate or feminine'. It isn't difficult to read this entry as a fantasy fuelled by frustration, where the writer's own pent-up energy has to be projected on to an imaginary, powerful male. Plath's journals are threaded through with references to her desire for a powerful, dominant male. How do I like men? she asked herself at one point. Money would help, she confessed: this ruled out teachers, in the main. But most of all she craved a giant, a superman, 'a demigod of a man'. In more sober moments she admitted that what she really wanted was 'a non-existent romantic hero'.[21]

Some ten years earlier, albeit with much less literary skill, Sylvia Sark's heroine, Sanchia, in *Take Me! Break Me!* had expressed very similar longings. Sanchia dreams of being taken and broken, of surrender as a quintessentially feminine route to fulfilment. She is turned on when she meets a lion tamer, Leo, an example of 'superb virility', 'pagan beauty', and 'proud mastery'. Belying the assumption that all Mills and Boon publications rigidly avoided 'immorality', the text does allow the married Sanchia a fling with her masterful lion-tamer, though chastened, she returns to her reliable husband Julian at the end.[22] Stories in popular magazine fiction in the 1930s and 1940s teemed with haughty, boastful, sardonic, bullying males who magically turned into loving husband material when they encountered pure-minded heroines. The first issue of *Glamour*, for instance, in March 1938, offered a serial by Anita Russell called 'Island of Desire'.[23] It was described as 'A pulsating long complete novel of a man who scorned and hated women—but was tempted by the lure of soft lips ... "No girl will ever get me" was his arrogant boast, "I am girl proof. I make women obey me as I make the natives on this my island obey me, without question."'[24] Readers were expected to 'quiver' and to 'thrill' to this kind of offering.

Assumptions about power games and male brutishness as somehow sexy reached new heights in the romance literature of the 1960s and 1970s.[25] These were years which saw the rebirth of feminism, and the rise of what was often dubbed the women's liberation movement. They were also years in which sales of popular romance rocketed. How we are to best understand any connections between these trends is complicated. Was this some kind of cultural lag, or a backlash against change? Those who have tried to make sense of what was going on, both contemporaries and cultural historians, have often found themselves deeply embroiled in controversies about feminism, the new sexual freedoms associated with 'permissiveness', social class, and women's imaginative pleasures.

About a new trend from the 1960s onwards towards explicitness in writing about sexuality, there can be no doubt. The demand for such came from a variety of sources. Young people were keen to learn and to experiment, and informative books on the subject sold well. For women, a landmark text was *Our Bodies, Ourselves*, originally published in America by the Boston Women's Health Collective in 1971. The book quickly established itself as a bible of second-wave feminism. A British edition, edited by Angela Phillips and Jill Rakusen, was published by Penguin in 1978 and reprinted in 1980, 1983, 1984, and 1986. It was a groundbreaking compendium of straightforward, non-judgemental information for women on subjects relating to health, reproduction, and sexual choice.[26]

The following year Alex Comfort's phenomenally successful *The Joy of Sex* (1972) shot to fame, a 'gourmet guide to lovemaking' which was to stay on the *New York Times* best-seller list for a decade and eventually to sell some twelve million copies.[27] Comfort saw himself as striking a blow for erotic freedom for women, as well as men, and inserted what he described as a feminine viewpoint in the text ('Women (by her for him)'), but which of course he helpfully wrote for them. The book contained quite a lot that made women uneasy. The vagina, for instance, is described as looking scary to many men: 'like a castrating wound' which 'bleeds regularly, it swallows the penis and regurgitates it limp, it can probably bite and so on'. A rear-entry sex position was offensively dubbed sex 'à la Négresse', and as the writer Ariel Levy has pointed out, the original text reads a little like 'a penis propaganda pamphlet'.[28] Vibrators are no substitute for a penis, we're firmly told, size is relatively unimportant, and the penis has more symbolic importance than any other human organ. The illustrations were unforgettable. The male lover depicted in the artwork was a large, hairy, caveman type. To quote Ariel Levy again, he looked like 'a werewolf with a hangover'. The original illustrations made her think of Beauty being pawed by the Beast.[29]

Books about female sexuality and female fantasy sold extremely well. Erica Jong's *Fear of Flying* (1973), which introduced the term 'zipless fuck'—to refer to sexual pleasure for its own sake without forethought, recrimination, or power games—was a massive hit, as were texts such as Nancy Friday's *My Secret Garden: Women's Sexual Fantasies* (1973), followed up a couple of years later with the same author's *Forbidden Flowers: More Women's Sexual Fantasies* (1975).[30] Shere Hite's *The Hite Report on Female Sexuality* (1976) broke new ground, adding critical perspectives from women's experience to the earlier sexological investigations of Kinsey and Masters and Johnson.[31] It was as if the lid had come off Pandora's box: many in an earlier generation had inclined to the view that women didn't have sexual fantasies: at least, 'nice' women didn't go in for this kind of thing. Writing two decades later, in the 1990s, Nancy Friday remembered that even in 1973, as her first book came out, respected American psychologist Alan Fromme was asserting in *Cosmopolitan* magazine that most women were 'destitute of sexual fantasy' because their upbringing hadn't allowed it.[32]

Amid a ferment of unisex, flower power, and free love, the old-fashioned romances of Barbara Cartland and Betty Neels began to look a bit faded. Cartland moaned continually that her publishers wanted her to update her heroines: she wanted to keep them 'pure' and retorted that if virginity was now unfashionable she'd give up writing about the contemporary world altogether and set all her romances in the past.[33] Neels, as we have seen, kept to her formula and never wholly lost her devotees. But other writers adapted to the new era; and writers new to the field were often more forthright about sexual desire than their predecessors.

In North America, Avon Books published Kathleen Woodiwiss's debut novel *The Flame and the Flower* in 1972, which proved a huge success on account of its frank descriptions of sexual experience and pleasure.[34] *The Flame and the Flower* begins with what has often been described as a rape scene, when the hero mistakes the heroine for a woman of easy virtue. She becomes pregnant, he marries her, and the novel from then on develops into a love story. The book reverses many of the conventions of romance literature in that it begins with, rather than ending in marriage; its heroine is intelligent and wilful, and the couple have to work out their individual emotions in a difficult relationship. Even so, the hero, Captain Brandon Birmingham, draws on all the clichés of the genre: he's hugely rich and eligible, dark, handsome, 'with the look of a pirate about him', wears spotless white ruffled shirts and tight-fitting fawn breeches, etc. He just happens to be a practised and brilliant lover to boot, and Woodiwiss helpfully details some of his erotic skills for the reader.

One of the most successful of Mills and Boon's new writers in Britain in the late 1960s was Violet Winspear.[35] Winspear's writing was racy compared with most of her predecessors, but less explicit than that of Woodiwiss. 'I believe that sex is a smouldering thing,' she explained, 'not a neon light.'[36] She held fast to many of the conventions of the genre (freely admitting, for instance, that she drew inspiration from E. M. Hull and Ethel Dell) but she turned up the *brio*. Her men, particularly, became larger than life; their backgrounds more exotic, their jaws firmer, their determination darker and more elemental. These heroes were in no way 'new men': they were powerful forces of nature, likely to address the heroine as 'little fool' and to sort out her life for her. Winspear was fond of foreign settings and she had a liking for heroes in the guise of Greek shipping magnates or Italian or Portuguese noblemen with imposing names such as 'Don Raul Cesar de Romanos'.[37] Their tendency to act as control freaks and to overpower her somewhat pallid heroines was for her, an essential part of their charm.

In Britain, the rising sales of romance literature, at a time when many feminists were increasingly vocal in deploring it, generated sufficient interest to inspire several radio and television programmes.

For instance, a number of women readers and writers were interviewed by Benedict Nightingale for a BBC Radio 4 programme in 1971, which asked 'Why is the Romantic Novel so Popular?'[38] The voluble Winspear, who could be relied on to speak entertainingly about her craft, might have seemed a good choice of interviewee. But in July 1970 her agreement to appear on the BBC's current affairs television programme, *Man Alive*, had got Winspear into deep water. The *Radio Times* published an account of her interview with journalist Molly Parkin alongside an unflattering, full-page colour photograph of a bespectacled Violet at her typewriter.[39] Inset into the photograph was a little heart-shaped cut-out framing Violet's words, 'All my heroes must be capable of rape'. The feature made Violet look a trifle unbalanced. She was described as being 'mad on men' and suffering from 'man mania' as well as having an insatiable desire for 'little iced cakes, and hot tea with lots of sugar'. It was a cruel piece of journalism. Winspear blamed Parkin, and never forgave her for it.[40]

What Violet was reported as having actually said about the men in her books is worth quoting in full. She explained:

> I get my heroes so that they're lean and hard-muscled and mocking and sardonic and tough and tigerish and single, of course. Oh and they've got to be rich and then I make it that they're only cynical and smooth on the surface. But underneath they're well, you know, sort of lost and lonely. In need of love, but when roused, capable of breathtaking passion and potency. Most of my heroes, well all of them really, are like that. They frighten but fascinate. They must be the sort of men who are capable of rape: men it's dangerous to be alone in the room with.[41]

Unfortunately, these words would come back to haunt her. One of the non-negotiable tenets of second-wave feminism was that women should have control over their own bodies and sexuality: men had no entitlement to any sexual 'rights' over women, even within marriage, hence the popular mantra 'yes means yes and no means no'. There were active campaigns against sexual abuse and domestic violence, and individuals and groups all over the country busied themselves setting up refuges for battered wives and rape counselling centres. Winspear's suggestion that women were drawn to potential rapists didn't go down well.

Winspear read the article in the *Radio Times* as a betrayal: full of contempt for her lack of sophistication, and a sneer on her spinster-hood. She hadn't had an easy life. A working-class woman, she had grown up in the East End of London during the war. In her own words, she had had to fight 'fang and claw' for survival.[42] She had left school at fourteen and worked at a variety of jobs in small-scale factories, such as sewing book covers, machining the 'cake-frills' which were fashionable at the time, and making artificial flowers. Her father had died when she was still a child, and she had come to assume sole support for her invalid mother. As a young girl Violet found solace and escape in going to the cinema:

> that big, warm, human-scented haven from all cares and hungers...with The Charge of the Light Brigade up there on that magical screen, and Errol Flynn the prince of hearts with a sword in his hand. In those days of course, it cost very little to go to the pictures and Mum would take us about twice a week, for in the long run it saved on the coal if you sat in the warm cinema until it was time to go to bed.[43]

Violet had kept herself sane by reading and writing, 'filling up exercise books with my dream people'. She was over the moon when Mills and Boon accepted her first book, although she had to endure a great deal of teasing from friends at work who were incredulous 'that a Cockney factory girl had dared to write a flaming love-story...well, many were the comments'.[44]

Violet Winspear went on to earn a considerable amount of money from her books, but her ambitions remained modest. In spite of finding it impossible, as a single woman, to get a mortgage, she managed to amass the capital to buy a modest bungalow by the sea for herself and her mother.[45] Although many of her novels were set in European resorts and in tropical climes, she never went abroad. For her, Southend was as good as the Cote d'Azur. Throughout her life, reading, and the books she wrote, were her escape: 'I think I always saw romance as a colourful means of escape from the cold and the hurts of life,' she confessed, some years later.[46]

We know a great deal about Violet and her attitudes to writing on account of her voluminous correspondence with her publisher, the always sympathetic and gentlemanly Alan Boon, in the early 1970s. Violet had few illusions about herself or her writing, and knew only too well that many saw her as a bit of a joke, a bespectacled, cat-loving, 'scatty old maid' who had never had sex or travelled, and who comforted herself and her readers by spinning dreams. Highly intelligent, with a good sense of humour, she regularly poked fun at herself, but was resentful of what she saw as the class condescension of commentators such as Molly Parkin or of middle-class feminists who she thought sneered at the pleasures of working-class women.[47]

Violet never for a moment doubted that the heroes in her books were pure fantasy. She thought that most women 'dream of a caveman', and that they wanted someone 'in command' but who was also warm and loving.[48] An edge of danger could be arousing, she explained to Alan Boon: men shouldn't be too nice, too bland, or too perfect. She had learned from Elinor Glyn in this respect, and was confident that her heroes appealed to her readers because they wrote appreciative letters: early in 1972 she was tickled by a letter from a woman who had enjoyed *The Bride of Lucifer* on account of 'that beautiful man': 'did such men really exist?' the reader had inquired, and did Violet know any of them?[49] Women had dreams of what they'd like—one woman had recently written to say she thought Omar Sharif 'the perfect dreamboat'. 'My heroines are always working class,' Violet explained further to Boon: 'the heroes offer them a better life. They are always dominant men, based on my favourite film stars, Humphrey Bogart and Sean Connery.' She also confessed to a weakness for Yul Brynner.[50] Violet may have come to regret using the phrase 'capable of rape' in her interview with Parkin, but she repeatedly tried to explain in her correspondence that she had meant only to suggest masterful heroes, fantasy figures through and through, who would fall uncontrollably for her heroines, would brush aside their hesitation, sweep them off their feet, and—ultimately—would love and cherish them forever.[51] This for her was what romance was all about: a dream of consolation, 'a dream world for women only. An escape from the ironing board and the frying pan.'[52]

This was a dream world in which, however powerful and 'commanding' the man might be, women retained *ultimate* power, through the very act of their imagining. But since the 1970s, fantasy scenarios where heroes 'overcome' women's resistance have raised anxieties about 'rape' for feminists. The use of the word itself isn't always helpful. As the cultural historian Molly Haskell pointed out in an important essay written as early as 1976, rape is properly defined as an act of aggression and hostility, 'to which the only possible response is horror and fear':

> For a woman to fantasize rape in the correct sense of the term would be to fantasize not love or lust but mutilation, and no sane women—and very few insane ones—express such a desire, even unconsciously.[53]

If women admitted to 'rape fantasies' then this was something altogether different, not remotely like the idea of 'a stranger holding a knife at your throat in a dark alley'. 'A rape fantasy', as one of Haskell's friends emphasized,

> has nothing to do with having a couple of teeth knocked out. It's when Robert Redford won't take no for an answer. It's a tribute to the woman's desirability, and the man acts for your pleasure.[54]

To understand 'rape fantasies' in novels for and by women writers in the 1960s and 1970s the cultural historian needs to look closely at the writing. Books by women tended to invest the male hero with dominance and represent women as relatively passive because this accorded with the gender expectations of the time. As Tanya Modleski emphasized in her pioneering study of Harlequin romances in 1982, the hero might be an adventurer, but the heroine must at all costs avoid looking like adventuress.[55] A happy ending would see her secure in the love and protected by the wealth and power of a rich man, but she couldn't be seen to be seeking this. It was a classic double bind. This often leads to a certain instability or oddness in the writing style, involving phrases such as 'ravished gaze' or 'unbridled charms', where who is actually doing what to whom isn't clear.

Scenes where women are overpowered often serve as plot device, in order for the narrative to move on. In Georgette Heyer's early novel, *The Transformation of Philip Jettan*, the plot reaches a stalemate two-thirds of the way through.[56] The heroine is too feminine and too proud to confess her love, the hero too proud and frustrated by her seeming indifference. The author makes an older woman, the heroine's aunt, advise Philip that women long to be mastered by men, and she suggests he be 'brutal' and take control of the situation. This novel was written when Heyer was only twenty years old. There's no suggestion of any physical overpowering or violence. Even so, the suggestion of mastery, and that women don't know what they really want, makes many modern readers uneasy. This is in part a measure of how assumptions about gender have changed since Heyer was writing. The overpowering of reluctant heroines by dominant, but decidedly eligible, males remains as one of the key conventions of romance, and the outcome is wholly predictable. The story centres on the transformation of rampant hero into loving husband: love softens male brutishness, and ultimately it empowers women. Once married to the hero, the heroine gains access to his wealth and can hope to rest secure in his protection.

Plot conventions whereby heroines in romance gained power relative to dominant males also included more brutal imaginings, whereby heroes were maimed, crippled, or blinded. This kind of levelling down in power through imaginary violence to the hero is a theme with a long history in romance. In *Jane Eyre*, Mr Rochester loses his sight when his mad wife burns his house down: this gets rid of the wife, and thus chastened and brought down to size through suffering, he's a much more deserving candidate for Jane's devotion. Nick Ratcliffe, in Ethel M. Dell's *The Way of an Eagle*, loses an arm in his

long-drawn-out courtship of the elusive Muriel.[57] In Florence
L. Barclay's The Rosary, a New York Times best-seller of 1909, the heroine,
a plain woman, falls in love with a male aesthete, Garth Dalmain
(a natty dresser with a penchant for pale-violet shirts and scarlet silk
socks).[58] Florence fears she's too old and not good-looking enough for
Garth, but when he's blinded in an accident she nurses him and their
love blossoms. At another level, investing the hero with a hidden
history of hurt, of crediting him with having endured a miserable
childhood of abuse, or the trauma of an exploitative relationship, can
serve the same function: an excuse for the rougher edges of potency.
In this scenario, the heroine's function is to understand—her infinite
resources of feminine understanding and compassion will ensure that
she captures the heart—and the hand—of the hero. In E. L. James's
recent blockbuster, Fifty Shades of Grey, handsome control-freak
billionaire Christian Grey gets excused for his sadism because he's
represented as damaged emotionally, through having suffered from
deprivation and bad mothering in the past.[59]

It might seem that a more obvious—and less troubling—way of
evening out the power imbalances between hero and heroine in
fiction would be to make the women stronger. Would conventional
romance survive stronger women? This was a question which was
sometimes approached by women writers who had little truck with
feeble heroines. The answers weren't always reassuring. After all, Rhett
had walked out on the indomitable Scarlett, and Kathleen Winsor's
resourceful and determined Amber failed to secure the man she really
wanted. Too much agency just didn't look feminine. Kathleen Winsor
followed up her hugely successful Forever Amber with an interesting
novel which failed to engage the public imagination of her day, Star
Money (1950).[60] The story was loosely autobiographical, in that it
centred on the life and relationships of an attractive young woman
whose first novel had been a spectacular success, earning her large
amounts of money. A hot property in the literary world, the heroine's
relationships with men suffer, not least because she's too rich and too
powerful in relation to them. Her success is shown as undermining the

male ego. 'Don't ever forget there's an equation in the masculine mind between money and virility' warns her (female) literary agent in this novel.[61] Probably one of the reasons why the book sank without trace was because the predicaments of powerful femininity were not widely experienced among women in the 1950s.

The late 1960s and 1970s were a turning point in the history of women. In Britain, the first generation of women to have benefited from secondary education as a right had higher aspirations than their predecessors: in tertiary education and employment they were strafing against inequality and gender discrimination.[62] Widening use of the contraceptive pill revolutionized attitudes to sexuality, making it possible for women to experiment with relationships without the terror of unwanted pregnancy that had haunted them in the past.

Up until this time, the age of marriage among women had been falling. Teenage marriages had been common, and girls had begun to worry about being 'left on the shelf' if they hadn't bagged a husband by their early twenties. But the early 1970s saw a dramatic reversal of this trend to marry young.[63] Girls' magazines of the 1950s and 1960s had tapped into widespread anxiety about the need to get a man. 'Don't show too much independence', *Petticoat* magazine had warned its readers in 1966, 'let him admire you for your total femininity', 'let him take full control'.[64] But there were signs that things were beginning to change. In another magazine, *Honey*, a young Cilla Black reflected on how her career as a singer was altering the way she saw the world. As a schoolgirl she'd feared that if she wasn't married by the age of eighteen she'd kill herself, she remembered: now she thought she'd be mad to marry before the age of thirty-five. 'Money changes a girl's attitude to romance, I can tell you,' she wryly admitted.[65]

This was in 1970. Twenty years later, the image of girls as powerless and hopelessly frail had been eroded by popular cultural representations such as *Buffy the Vampire Slayer*.[66] It might be stretching a point to see girl power as having mounted a threat to patriarchy, but insofar as girls could be persuaded out of passivity and victimhood it was a move in the right direction. In what has become a cult coming-of-age film, Jim Henson's *Labyrinth* (1986), the fifteen-year-old heroine, Sarah, embarks on a dangerous journey to rescue her baby half-brother, who has been carried off by the goblin king.[67] The part of Jareth, the goblin king, was played by David Bowie. Dressed fetchingly in ruffles, spangled leather, and breathtakingly tight trousers, Bowie oozes sexual allure. He's a bad-boy Prince of Darkness with biker chic and supernatural overtones. Carried away in his arms on the dance floor, Sarah hovers on the brink of sensual meltdown. 'Fear me, love me, do as I say and I shall be your slave' imprecates this fluffy-haired, silver-tongued answer to a maiden's imaginings. But the girl galvanizes herself. 'My will is as strong as yours', Sarah counters, 'and my kingdom as great. *You have no power over me.*' For many young women this scene was an inspiration.[68]

Older women were becoming less likely to stay in marriages which had gone stale: the rate of divorce rose significantly between 1971 and 1985.[69] The sense of frustration and powerlessness, of suffering as a hapless victim of male philandering and exploitation which had permeated novels such as Penelope Mortimer's in the 1950s, was less in evidence twenty years later.[70] Jackie Collins's novel *The World is Full of Married Men* had a sensational impact when it was first published in 1968.[71] It lobbed bricks at the double standard: the women in the novel are strong characters who refuse to become victims, and they turn the tables on David, a weak and selfish man incapable of fidelity to wife or mistress. Roundly denounced by many as 'filth' and 'sleaze', it sold well in Britain and America but was banned in Australia and South Africa.

Collins's later books turned up the volume to delineate women who went much further, making short work of men who strained their commitment or stood in their way. Comments in the press showed that male journalists could find it hard to know what to make of her writing. In the *Daily Mirror*, Christopher Ward summarized Collins's *Lovehead*, in 1974, as 'a pleasant little story, full of four letter words, some of them rude, about three hookers who set about emasculating and then murdering a few men who rub them up the wrong way'. 'I'll say this for women, they're thorough when they're not doing the washing-up,' Ward added, ruefully.[72]

The *Daily Mirror* juxtaposed features on Jackie Collins with articles on rising rates of marriage break-up: it was *wives* who were pressing for divorce, journalist George Fallows reported in 1977, his copy squeezed into a space next to a big shot of a bare-chested, 'rugged superstud', Oliver Tobias, who was to star in the film version of Collins's 1969 erotic novel, *The Stud*, along with her sister, Joan.[73] But however much critics dismissed Collins as 'the Queen of Sleaze' she was on to a new trend.[74] The strong woman with ambitions and desires of her own was starting to appear in a whole crop of new novels by women writers in the late 1970s and 1980s.

Barbara Taylor Bradford's *A Woman of Substance* (1979) was a spectacularly successful epic account of the life of Emma Harte, a quick-witted, resourceful girl born into a poor family in Yorkshire.[75] Socially and sexually exploited as a kitchen maid, Emma becomes pregnant by the son of her employer. Let down by this scared and callow youth, she determines to somehow shift for herself. Over the years Emma develops into a formidably competent businesswoman. Her love life is rocky and varied. Men fail her in different ways, and further, as her brother explains to a man who does become a great love, 'most men can't cope with an independent and brilliant woman'.[76] The men in Emma's life come and go, but the form of the novel is not dictated by any conventional romance plot. Emma herself is powerful, and an adventuress, and no less admirable or attractive for it.

Novels by Shirley Conran and Judith Krantz also broke new ground in exploring adventures in women's working and sexual lives, along with their friendships with other women and their more chequered relationships with men. Conran's best-seller, *Lace*, first published in 1982, focused on the lives of a group of women who first met when they found themselves schoolgirls together at a finishing school in Europe.[77] Towards the close of the book, the friends reflect upon what life has taught them and discuss what they wish they had known much earlier in their lives. They all regretted having been taught that it was somehow unfeminine to be independent. It hadn't been helpful to have picked up 'the idea that you were a failure if you didn't have a man, because then you would be without status and protection'.[78]

Krantz's heroines, like Barbara Taylor Bradford's and Shirley Conran's, find power and strength in work, even if they come from wealthy backgrounds. They use their strength as a basis for relationships, rather than seeking relationships with men as a substitute for autonomy and independence. Heroines get tougher. The lure of powerful men is still in evidence, but not exclusively so. In Judith Krantz's *I'll Take Manhattan* (1986), Maxi's first husband, the hardworking Rocco Cipriano, is disgusted and undermined by his wife's inherited wealth and sense of entitlement.[79] Rocco, we're told, is gorgeous, boasting 'an indecent chaos of black curls' and 'the nose of a Medici Prince'.[80] Maxi drifts through a series of men who loosely accord with her fantasy heroes: 'bad Dennis', stylish and congenial, but an inveterate gambler; Laddie Kirkgordon, a Scottish laird who had 'all the best points of King Arthur, Tarzan and Warren Beatty' and was an earl to boot, living in a draughty castle.[81] But in the end she discovers her true strength and purpose in working as a magazine editor. This transforms her from an idle parasite into a woman of strength and substance. Maxi earns a new respect in the eyes of Rocco Cipriano, who falls in love with her all over again.

Novels about groups of women who first met in college, or who befriended each other as room-mates or in house-shares in the city, have a history going back at least to the 1950s. Most of these have explored women's choices—or the lack of them—in relation to 'eligible' men. In Rona Jaffe's *The Best of Everything* (1958), the characters have to face up to the impossibilities of having everything, and in particular to the non-existence of the ideal man, a message the author spelled out again in a later collection of short stories entitled *Mr Right is Dead* (1965).[82] Mary McCarthy's *The Group* (1963) conveyed a similar message: candid about sex (Norman Mailer sneered at what he dismissed as 'a trivial lady writer's novel' emitting a 'communal odour' reminiscent of 'a cross between *Ma Griffe* and contraceptive jelly'), *The Group* warned female readers about the dangers of over-dependency on men.[83] Candace Bushnell's *Sex and the City* sits in the same tradition: its female characters bond closely while relationships with men often disappoint, and Mr Right (or Carrie Bradshaw's 'Big') proves as elusive as ever.[84]

Many of these novels, and soaps such as the television series based on Candace Bushnell's novel, have been denigrated for their celebration of materialism and shallow commercial values.[85] The characters are sometimes represented as desiring brand-labelled luxury goods as much as relationships with the opposite sex. With the availability of contraception now taken for granted, perhaps we have become more blasé about the idea of women shopping around for men.[86] But at least women in the modern novel have choices. Less depends on netting and domesticating a powerful man, and on the fantasy of transforming him in order to transform your own life chances. Women can be economically self-supporting, and free to make mistakes, break relationships, and to start afresh.

There have been sea changes in women's social and economic position since the 1970s, and imaginative literature both reflects these, and appeals to a new audience less likely to be beguiled by older narratives of romance in which heroines simply sat still and hoped, or suffered in silence. In these late twentieth-century texts, patriarchal structures remain in place but women aren't daunted: they work around them and find loopholes. Power relationships don't always accord with stereotyped assumptions about gender, either. The novels suggest new forms of desirable masculinity, men whose attractiveness stems in part from their sensitivity to women's needs for independence, men who are themselves attracted to competence and ambition in women. Women in these novels learn that work, and friendships with other women, can matter as much as their relationships with men. Women can be rich and powerful in their own right, and sometimes—just sometimes—they come to learn about their own desires, and to work out what they want.

# 8

# Sighing for the Moon?

What does it mean to dream of a lover? Victorian girls were regularly upbraided for daydreaming, for being fanciful, for losing themselves in worlds of their imagination. This was nothing new. There was a centuries-old tradition of criticizing the female sex for soft-headedness and gullibility in relation to romance. Indeed, the gendered nature of this criticism helped to reshape understandings of the very word 'romance', with its complicated evolution from the French vernacular and medieval chivalry through to more recent ideas about soggy escapism and second-rate fiction.[1]

Phyllis Bentley, a popular British writer of the 1930s, grew up in the West Riding of Yorkshire in the early years of the twentieth century. In her autobiography, written in the 1960s, she devoted a whole chapter to the daydreams which had haunted her youth.[2] Her tone was defensive: she clearly felt a need to apologize, in some way, for the 'inveterate' daydreams and imaginary tales which had begun to possess her well before she was eight years old. Her solitariness was one of the excuses she made for the way in which she had been totally carried away by dream-stories of herself as a kind of Cinderella figure.[3] The dream-heroines of her stories had all married young, she tells us, for love. They had fallen for striking and unusual heroes, 'outwardly rather difficult and dominant, inwardly very loving and protective'.[4] She was well aware that this had been a kind of wish-fulfilment, suggesting from the stance of adulthood 'that these dreams were fantasies in the Freudian sense; they never dealt with ambitions which I hoped would be realised; on the contrary they released precisely those desires which I consciously knew I should not fulfil.'[5] Later in life Phyllis Bentley had been reassured by learning about the Brontë family, and the way in which, as children, Charlotte, Emily, and Anne had immersed themselves in the imaginary worlds of Angria and Gondal. She must have realized by then just how much the craft of the novelist depended upon richness of imagination, upon the ability to daydream. But somehow the guilt hadn't totally evaporated. She recalled that although she'd managed to hide the content of her early daydreams from her family, her mother had become alarmed by the extent to which her daughter's capacity for making up stories had taken a hold on her mind. On the advice of the family doctor, it had been decided to pack her off to nursery school. This may have encouraged a little more sociability, but Phyllis continued to daydream. She read copious amounts of fiction, which further fuelled her imagination. Her mother had been mildly worried about the impact of *Jane Eyre*, Phyllis recalled. And indeed, it had been from Mr Rochester that she had 'derived my difficult but darling daydream heroes'.[6]

Phyllis never married. As a young woman she had to wear unbecoming steel spectacles, and was sadly beset by a lack of confidence in her own desirability. She found few opportunities to meet boys anyway, and was all too aware that her stories, 'strongly plotted' and with historical settings, served, like her daydreams, to satisfy vague stirrings of sexual interest.[7] Later, as a young woman, she remembered one particular Saturday night dance when she had met with a stranger in uniform to whom she had taken an immediate fancy. He had been intelligent, kind, and a book-reader. But this man turned out to have been in love with someone else, a girl with whom Phyllis had been friendly since her schooldays. None of this should—or would—have mattered, except for the fact that Phyllis confessed, with painful honesty, 'that the man in question (modified suitably) descended into my daydream world and played the hero's part for years'.[8]

The passions of our younger selves often linger, and may shape our choices later on in life. American writer Joan Didion confessed that from an early age, the sexual authority emanated by John Wayne shaped her ideas about what a man could and should be. 'When John Wayne rode through my childhood, and perhaps through yours,' she wrote, 'he determined for ever the shape of certain of our dreams'.[9] Prolific British diarist Jean Lucey Pratt, who wrote fully and frankly about her disappointments in love in her diaries of the 1940s and 1950s, was aware of being 'drawn to pirate types'. Though desperate for marriage, she couldn't summon interest in the nicer and more dependable men who approached her. Even so, Jean felt a lot more in touch with reality than her friend Josephine, who had hero-worshipped the actor Leslie Howard for years, and after Howard's death, became utterly convinced of sustaining a ghost or spirit relationship with him.[10]

Imaginative worlds can be extraordinarily rich and powerful. In Rachel Ferguson's strangely compelling novel, The Brontës Went to Woolworths (1931), three sisters construct a dreamworld in which they lose themselves to the point where it becomes difficult—not least for the reader—to know where fantasy ends and reality begins to intrude.[11] The story is narrated by Deirdre, all too conscious of literary precedents, who ruefully confesses that her imagination may have damaged her ability to make sensible choices about her life. She tells us that a while ago a man had proposed marriage to her, but much as she liked the person in question, she could not accept him because she was in love with Sherlock Holmes: 'For Holmes and his personality and brain I had a force of feeling which, for the time, converted living men to shadows'.[12] Wasn't this what love was about, she asked herself, 'the worship of an idea or an illusion' with 'flesh and blood the least part of the business'?

For many of the girls who grew up after the Second World War, youthful fantasies of love were as likely to flower around a pop idol or member of a boy band as a literary figure or a cinema star. What did it mean to be in love with a Beatle, with David Cassidy, Donny Osmond, or, more recently, to be obsessed by one of the members of One Direction? Academics now study fandom as cultural history, and there has been a long debate about whether girls are powerful or passive consumers of popular culture.[13] As consumers they have always exercised some clout. Young women in the 1920s and 1930s bought novels and film magazines and trooped into cinemas and dance halls. In the 1950s they spent their pocket money on fan magazines, coffee pots, cosmetics, ballerina pumps, and circle skirts. In the 1960s, sales of records, record players, and clothes designed specifically with teenagers in mind had begun to boom.[14] Some social theorists—the feminist writer Barbara Ehrenreich, for instance—identified Beatlemania as a form of libidinal self-expression for girls who had long been expected to keep a lid on their passions and to be demure.[15] Back in the 1970s Angela McRobbie and Jenny Garber drew attention to the importance of girls' bedrooms as cultural spaces: areas where female friendships could flourish alongside activities like listening to records, trying on make-up, and endless discussions about boys.[16]

We now have literary and autobiographical studies of fandom, alongside studies by sociologists and pop historians. The more personal accounts support the idea of the pop idol as a kind of transitional object in the emotional development of young girls; the worship of the teen heartthrob as a kind of 'dress rehearsal for love'. In Allison Pearson's novel I Think I Love You (2010), Petra and her friend Sharon spend hours in Sharon's room, stapling bits of a poster of David Cassidy together before sticking it to the wall, face at mouth-height, so that Sharon can implant a fervent kiss on his lips every bedtime.[17] Sharon constructs a shrine to David Cassidy in her bedroom. Together, the girls make a special study of every aspect of David's personality that it's possible to latch on to—most of it completely invented by his publicity machine. The highlight of their young lives is a visit to the Cassidy concert at London's White City Stadium in 1974: a real-life event at which many fans were crushed and trampled over, and one fourteen-year-old girl actually died from her injuries.[18] Pearson's novel shows adolescent girls in love with the idea of love, anxious about their own desirability, competitive, and vulnerable. It then switches in time to the girls as grown-ups, and to a process of disillusion and loss. Not all is lost, because some of the friendships endure, and the women have acquired understanding and tolerance of their younger selves. Pearson argues through her characters that teen heartthrobs change through time—the adult Petra's daughter in the novel is obsessed with the actor Leonardo DiCaprio—but that the need that they fulfil, the need to try out feelings about love and one's own desirability, is there through the generations.

**Figure 24.** David Cassidy at the Empire Pool, Wembley, 1973.

Cassidy was adored by incalculable numbers of young girls in the 1970s not least because he was so pretty and unthreatening. Sneered at by men who derided him as a girly-boy, with Bambi-like looks and a penchant for tank tops worn over flowery cheesecloth shirts, girls saw him, almost, as one of themselves and had no difficulty in imagining a special bond. Many women attest to having fantasized about this 'special relationship'. Journalist Liz Jones recalled that for her Cassidy was 'the perfect boy'. She put him on the cover of a magazine called 'Trendy', which she wrote and illustrated herself, and her adoration reached new heights at White City when he performed in an 'all-in-one jumpsuit scattered with rhinestones' and she could scarcely believe that they breathed the same air.[19] Writer Emma Freud confessed that at the age of thirteen David Cassidy was her 'total and complete No 1 love-boat'.[20] Nina Myskow, editor of *Jackie* magazine in the early 1970s, remembered Cassidy as by far the most popular of the boy pin-ups of the day.[21] He was *nice*, had a sweet smile, and felt *safe*. Among the mountain of Cassidy-themed memorabilia of the day was a white fluffy teddy bear, with a red satin bow and 'I think I love you' inscribed on its vest.

Donny Osmond and Marc Bolan also had their following. Bolan fans were likely to regard Osmond as too wholesome. Bolan, with his top hats and glittery eye make-up, could look like an evil cherub.[22] Any tendency towards the diabolic was balanced by his prettiness, though: his feather boas and his girly Mary-Jane shoes. Musician Viviane Albertine, one-time guitarist for the punk band The Slits, confessed that for a year in her teens, Marc Bolan had been 'the most important man in her life'.[23] What had appealed most was his prettiness in combination with an overt, but non-threatening, sexiness: 'pouting and licking and throwing his hips forward'. Marc had been safe to fantasize about, sexually: 'he wasn't the kind of guy who would jump on you or hurt you'.[24] There were other male musicians, more overtly sexual, that she remembered feeling intimidated by: Jimi Hendrix, for instance, whereas 'Marc was almost a girl.' Bolan's polymorphous appeal could offer young people a way of imagining

**Figure 25.** David Cassidy fan wearing huge rosette.

identities outside the gendered templates of the time. Viv Albertine's account of the passions of her youth is fascinating because of the way she weaves them into a coming-of-age story, her search for purpose and identity. The male musicians she fantasized about as desirable (Donovan, Lennon) also inspired her as musicians: at first she would study record covers for details about their girlfriends and wives, looking for the kind of clues that would enable her to enter their world.[25] What kind of woman did she have to become if she wanted to attract singers and poets? It was much harder to even begin to imagine herself as an independently sexual individual, a performer and a player in her own right.

Liz Jones once declared that as a young girl her adoration for David Cassidy ruined her life, because nothing or no-one afterwards ever quite measured up to the intensity of the experience.[26] But most accounts of teenage pop idolatry—or teen heartthrobs—are about how the subject or narrator moved on, into an adult awareness or towards a more dispassionate viewpoint. This often involved the facing of truths: the idolized one was only human, with human failings, his image carefully crafted by marketing and publicity machines. Not least, there's a coming to terms with ageing, both of the self and of the one-time hero. These themes, delicately dissected in Allison Pearson's *I Think I Love You*, are of course the stuff of many people's lives.

'Who was your first heartthrob?' someone asked a few years ago on Gransnet.com, 'an internet forum for grandparents'.[27] A lively discussion followed. For the post-war generation, Elvis and Richard Chamberlain loomed large. Photos of Elvis had adorned many bedroom walls as well as having been regularly Sellotaped under classroom desk-lids. Cowboys had also been popular. Clint Eastwood as Rowdy Yates in *Rawhide*, and Robert Horton as Flint McCulloch in *Wagon Train* were fondly remembered for their good looks and creaky leather cowboy gear by this first television-watching generation. One respondent reminisced:

> Adam Faith and Billy J Kramer were plastered all over my walls, along with most of the cast of Bonanza: I liked them all. Richard Chamberlain as Dr Kildare. I love the voice of Billy Fury but he was a bit daring for my mum to allow me to have his pic on my wall. I have two signed pictures of Billy Fury in a suitcase still and would not part with them for the world. Such memories.[28]

Another remembered swooning over:

> Dr Kildare, George Harrison, Eric Clapton, Mr Rochester and a rather glam boy at confirmation class . . .[29]

One woman confessed that she had so adored Donny Osmond that not only was her room covered in posters of him but that she 'used to "snog" his cushion every night before I fell into a blissful "Donny" dream'.[30] A handful of respondents remembered falling first for other women: whereas one confessed that her/his first passion had been for Champion the Wonder Horse.[31]

For most people this was pure reminiscence: their ardour for such heartthrobs had cooled with age. They were ready to smile, tolerantly, at their younger selves. One woman admitted that before she was old enough to know better she had dreamed of marrying 'a poet with sharp elbows and a guitar . . . No such luck . . . thank goodness!' Maybe she found someone more solid and well-upholstered, able to offer comfortable support. A number of women emphasized that their tastes had changed with the years. They cringed at the thought of having once swooned over Tommy Steele singing 'Little White Bull' and were all too glad to confess that nowadays they much preferred the more mature charms of George Clooney.[32]

But not everyone moved on: some kept faith with their idols. In June 2010 British newspaper the *Daily Mail* published a feature on Brenda Kirby and Carol Barton, two women then in their sixties who had been to see Cliff Richard perform some 8,000 times.[33] One of them calculated that they had travelled the equivalent in miles of going round the world almost five times to see and hear him sing. Sir Cliff hit seventy in 2010. A few years previously, a writer in *The Guardian* somewhat cruelly reported that Cliff Richard records were now so uncool that they were being used as a form of 'sonic warfare' to deal with anti-social youth; playing 'The Young Ones' had proved an efficient way of dispersing unruly teenagers at funfairs.[34]

Extreme forms of devotion to male heartthrobs have typically provoked a variety of responses, from contempt, sheer incomprehension, through amused tolerance, to genuine pity. In 2013 for instance, Lauren Adkins, then a twenty-four-year-old masters student at the University of Nevada in Las Vegas, attracted a great deal of often incredulous media attention when she went through a 'marriage ceremony' with a life-size cardboard cut-out image of Robert Pattinson as Edward Cullen from *Twilight*.[35] This was a piece of performance art which Adkins submitted as part of her thesis, *Love is Overtaking Me*, in which she explored fantasies of 'true love' and ideas about female fandom in the context of the wedding industry and highly commercial setting of Las Vegas. Adkins was subjected to considerable online abuse when accounts of her 'wedding' went live. Many journalists went for the bizarre elements of the 'story', omitting any mention of the thesis and ignoring Adkins's educational and scholarly purpose.[36]

'All young females are romantic novelists, feverishly plotting their own futures' suggested Allison Pearson, reflecting on her own youthful ideas about men.[37] As a bookish and 'agonisingly self-conscious' teenager she hadn't been too tempted by the spotty adolescent boys she met in the local Wimpy bar. David Cassidy had featured in her own courtship fantasies until she came across the lure of Fitzwilliam Darcy in *Pride and Prejudice*.[38] In a companion article to Pearson's piece, literary critic John Carey observed astringently that he'd never met a man who liked Mr Darcy, although most women seemed to.[39] Novelist Adam Foulds confirmed this.[40] As a schoolboy, Darcy had struck him as 'something of a cipher, composed for the fulfilment of a fantasy' that the girls in his class seemed to relate to, but that certainly wasn't his. These remarks are comparatively gentle in their dismissiveness, but this impatience with women who are accused of living in a world of fantasy, populated by unsatisfactory or less than convincing men, has long infused male literary criticism. We can trace this in the critical response to writers of the stature of Jane Austen or George Eliot, which was discussed in Chapter 3. But as we have seen, much of a huge corpus of popular literature by women writers over the last century and more has been dismissed as 'pulp romance' and ignored altogether by the critics.

The women who consume romance have sometimes rated even lower on critics' scales of respect than those who produce this literature. It is only comparatively recently that cultural and social historians have begun to ask questions about the social significance and meanings of this reading matter for generations of women. Even the chivalrous publisher Alan Boon once referred to the books his firm published as a drug, a form of Valium for women.[41] Does popular romance function like bromide, dulling discontents? The idea that women dope themselves is given credence by stories of addicts consuming a dozen romances per week or more, often forgetting what they've read. Older, ex-library copies of Mills and Boon romances sometimes have lists of initials pencilled inside the back cover— readers would jot down their initials so that they wouldn't find themselves reading the same story twice.[42] But as early as 1971, even before feminist critics such as Tania Modleski and Janice Radway started to ask more searching questions about how women read and responded to romance, journalist and critic Benedict Nightingale pointed out forcefully that the fantasies embodied in women's romance fiction weren't just fantasies: they were actually complaints about men.[43]

'When I read for Entertainment, I had much rather view the Characters of Life as I would wish they *were* than as they *are*' wrote playwright Richard Brinsley Sheridan to Thomas Grenville in 1772, explaining that 'therefore I hate Novels and love Romances'.[44] An element of wish-fulfilment was important to the women who enjoyed reading romances studied by Janice Radway in the 1980s. These women were nonetheless intelligent and self-aware about their reading.[45] Tania Modleski used psychoanalytic insights to show how the narratives of romance could be satisfying for women at a symbolic or fantasy level, allowing women to revenge themselves on unsympathetic men, reducing men to fealty, turning them into nurturers attentive to a woman's every need. In short, romance could transform a helpless woman, at an imaginative level, into the powerful centre of a masculine world.[46]

Some of the complexities of women's relationship to romantic fiction, both as writers and as readers, were sensitively dissected in a documentary film made by director and producer George Csicsery and first released in 1987. This film, *Where the Heart Roams,* focused on a project dreamed up by Chelley Kitzmiller, a then (1983) unpublished fan of romance fiction living in California.[47] Keen to attend a Romantic Booklovers' Conference in New York City, Kitzmiller hit on the idea of organizing a special train ('The Love Train') which would ferry a party of romance enthusiasts across to the East Coast. The idea caught the public imagination: big receptions were organized at each end, there was lively press coverage, and the affair turned into a joyous, six-day party. Csicsery's film allowed the women, both writers and readers, to speak for themselves: there is no editorial comment and the result is non-judgemental and often very revealing.

Several of those who appeared in the film were (or still are) successful writers: Janet Dailey, for instance, Jude Devereux, and Rebecca Brandewyne. Barbara Cartland makes a couple of arrestingly queenly appearances in trademark cornflower and sugar-pink tulle: 'I give women beauty and love,' she trills, suggesting that, these days, women have lost (she pronounced the word as 'lorst') 'the mystique' of femininity. A wife's job, she insists, is to make her husband's 'prison,' that is, his home, so attractive that he'll never want to leave her. The women discuss heroes, ambition, love, and life. No-nonsense journalist E. Jean Carroll delivers some sharp observations on the nature of romance fiction: men who want better relationships should read these books, she recommends, to find out what women really want. Csicsery said later that he'd intended to make a sociological film, but had instead become absorbed by the issue of fantasy, which he saw as one way in which people addressed loneliness and succeeded in making reality much more bearable.[48] What many of the women participants took away from the experience of travelling on 'The Love Train' and attending the conference in New York was very different. They had delighted in the camaraderie, the enthusiasm, and the friendships forged on the journey. For some women, the experience served to boost confidence in themselves and their social skills. Chelley Kitzmiller went on to write. Writer Kathryn Falk emphasized that the experience had enhanced women's entrepreneurial skills: it had felt as if 'we were starting a business', she recorded.[49]

Kathryn Falk, a sponsor of the Love Train, had founded a newsletter, *Romantic Times Magazine*, in 1981, and published a book, *Love's Leading Ladies*, in 1982. The book offered profiles and interviews with sixty-five leading writers of romance.[50] *Romantic Times Magazine* eventually became *RT Book Reviews Magazine*, with its own website.[51] By the end of the century, the world of the romantic novel had been completely transformed by the internet and the growth of the World Wide Web. A growing number of websites now allow women to share views on the writing and reading of romance. Examples include: http://teachmetonight.blogspot.co.uk/, 'Musings on romance fiction from an academic perspective'; http://romancenovelsforfeminists.blogspot.co.uk/, http://smartbitchestrashybooks.com/, and several more. There are also specialist journals such as the *Journal of Popular Romance Studies*.[52]

At both an academic and a popular level, what Falk identified as the 'business', the enterprise of writing romance for and by women, has grown in a way that its early exponents would have found hard to recognize. There are infinitely more ways of testing perceptions, sharpening critical edge, and sharing fantasy in this arena than ever before. Communities of women readers review and reflect on their response to romance fiction and how this may have changed over time. A site such as Goodreads, for instance, provides insights into the ways in which women often reconsider their youthful enthusiasm for romantic novels which featured dominating male heroes. 'Leona', for example, posted in 2012 on her changing response to Violet Winspear's *The Honey is Bitter* (1967). Leona remembered this as a particular favourite when she first encountered it as a young woman in the 1970s, but by 2012 she found the book disappointing. From the point of view of an adult, forty years later, the heroine's 'woe is me' attitude seemed tiring and her personality superficial and narcissistic.[53] Another reader ruefully noted that she should stop rereading her 'teen keepers' because they rarely stood the test of time. From a more mature perspective she couldn't stand books with a cruel hero and a doormat heroine.[54] It was like running into a childhood friend years later and realizing that you had nothing in common with them any more.

Both personal experience and changing social norms play their part in these reassessments. The Goodreads site allows the historian to explore the impact of social change through the changing reader reactions to classic texts. Kathleen E. Woodiwiss's *The Flame and the Flower* is a good example, since many younger women readers react with revulsion to the early chapters. 'Beth F.', for instance, posting in March 2011, was by no means alone in finding her 'modern sensibilities' deeply offended by 'this classic 1970s romance'.[55]

Several of the social historians who have studied women's lives in Britain between the wars have emphasized the pragmatism which working-class women of that era brought to marriage and family life. On the basis of her interviews with women, Judy Giles, for example, has argued that considerations of respectability ranked high in the choice of a husband.[56] Women wanted a good provider and a respectable home, and were often determined to renounce any passionate relationship which might drive them off course in their pursuit of such goals. Many women scoffed at romanticism, which they saw as 'silliness', and as contravening prudence and realism. To be 'swept off your feet' was too much of a risk for those who sought to build a solid, secure family life. In their study of love and marriage in early twentieth-century Britain, *Sex before the Sexual Revolution* (2010), historians Simon Szreter and Kate Fisher similarly emphasize the practical, 'down to earth' pragmatism of many working-class couples.[57] Their interviewees, they found, had little truck with the stories of romance and heady passion which they saw in the cinema—at least as a guide to shaping their own lives and loves. Romance was seen as the stuff of fantasy—'real' life just wasn't like that.[58] But we know that cinema-going, particularly among women, and the reading of popular romance, burgeoned during the interwar years. To dismiss both as simply 'escapism' would be to overlook the role that popular culture played in shaping fantasy and imagination.

In spite of the emphasis of Giles, Szreter, and Fisher on sober realism, their interviews sometimes allowed a glimpse of something different. One of Giles's interviewees, Gertie, castigated herself for 'silliness' and for 'living in a cloud' as a girl; she had been 'carried away' by the glamour and romance of the dance hall. Gertie had fallen for a younger man, who was a marvellous dancer, and—as it turned out—an attractive but feckless charmer. Rejecting her regular boyfriend, she had married this new flame, against the wishes of her parents.[59] The marriage had not been happy. Szreter and Fisher concede that some of their respondents appeared 'to lament the gulf between their own experiences of love and the fictional romances they encountered'. One such example was their interviewee Agatha, who had married in 1940. Agatha spoke wistfully about how men in real life had differed from those she had encountered in her reading of love stories, but her comment was tentative and half-embarrassed in tone: 'you think oh dear if only my hubby had been like that, sort of thing...did everything for them and shared everything...I mean they did everything to make them 'appy in their sex-life, sort of thing.'[60] Such desires weren't easy to put into words.

The social and technological changes of the late twentieth and early twenty-first centuries have reconfigured territories of intimacy, fantasy, and desire. In terms of social change, the 1970s were a turning point in women's history. In the West, control over fertility achieved largely through the adoption of the contraceptive pill facilitated the separation of sexual activity from reproduction.[61] Many at the time heralded this as 'liberating', allowing women to experiment with sexual pleasure freed from the anxiety and shaming social consequences of unwanted pregnancy which had blighted the 1950s. Others were more circumspect, fearing that opportunities for recreational sex or sex without commitment would benefit men more than women. But there can be few feminists who would want to return to the climate of continual worry and occasional panic which haunted sexually active women in the 1950s, however much the persistence of sexual double standards continues to undermine contemporary complacency about 'progress'.[62] Since the 1970s, young women in the West have experienced more opportunities for economic independence, personal freedom, and sexual self-expression than ever before.

The shape of women's lives has changed radically. In the 1950s and 1960s, many married very young. Marriage between teenagers was increasingly common: a trend which some contemporary observers fretted about, but saw as there to stay, a fact of modern life. Scarcely anyone predicted what actually came about: that the tendency to early marriage would go into sharp reverse after 1970.[63] From the last decades of the twentieth century, young people chose increasingly to postpone getting married until what would have been considered middle age in previous generations. Some couples gave up on marriage altogether, opting for cohabitation or serial relationships. Increasingly well-educated young women were reluctant to waste skills and training, preferring to establish themselves in employment before committing to parenthood, or deciding to forego motherhood. Such decisions weren't always a reflection of choice. Expensive childcare and the sharply rising cost of housing played an important part. Moreover, some women found it hard to find acceptable partners: were men becoming increasingly reluctant to commit? Were women themselves becoming too choosy? These were questions explored time and again in some of the popular cultural productions of the 1990s.

In her recent book, *Unmastered: A Book on Desire, Most Difficult to Tell* (2012), Katherine Angel, an academic and creative writer with an interest in the history of sexuality, explores some of the reasons why women can still find it difficult to understand and to come to terms with issues around sexual desire and gender, feminism, and a wish to have children.[64] Her account is highly personal and the book's style is idiosyncratic, consisting of fragmentary perceptions interspersed with blank pages and the suggestion of silences, of the story being 'difficult to tell'. We have seen that there was a something of an explosion of books addressing the subject of female sexual pleasure in the 1970s and 1980s. Nonetheless, as writer Olivia Laing commented, reviewing Katherine Angel's book in *The Guardian*, it can still be risky for women to write in a personal vein about desire: 'Desire, after all, is a form of hunger,' Laing reminds us 'and as such, incompatible with the notions of abstemiousness and passivity that continue to burden the female mind'.[65] Progress in these areas is never wholly secure, and it can seem as if each generation has to fight to reclaim ground.

The rise of digital technology and the internet, and the expansion of the World Wide Web and the ubiquity of smartphones have massively expanded both the possibilities of, and the potential for sharing, desire, and fantasy. This has been reflected in the rising popularity of fanfiction and slash fiction; in blogging, social media, and the proliferation of internet dating and hook-up sites. We are only just beginning to make sense of the social implications and effects of all this new technology, which many would see as completely transforming our intimate lives. In concern over the proliferation of easily accessible internet pornography, women have often been represented as victims. We hear less, perhaps, about the many ways in which digital technologies have widened opportunities for women's self-expression and their sense of having access to supportive communities, online. The feminists of the 1970s worked hard at what they called 'consciousness-raising', the formation of discussion and support groups which would help individual women to gain confidence and to understand that they weren't alone in feeling like social misfits. These groups would offer an informal education, helping their members to move towards a social and political understanding of the society in which they lived. Today, the internet offers similar spaces for the sharing of experiences as well as educative possibilities on an unprecedented scale.

Digital technologies have impacted on relationships in myriad ways, most obviously, perhaps, in expanding individual choice. At the beginning of the 1990s, sociologist Anthony Giddens suggested that there had been a late twentieth-century 'transformation of intimacy' in that men and women, more equal than ever before, were increasingly able to pursue 'pure' relationships based on mutual self-disclosure and trust.[66] Many people now select partners online, and a bewildering variety of websites and smartphone applications seek to widen and facilitate their choices. Statistics suggest that around a third of all marriages in the US and the UK are now contracted between couples who first met online.[67] There is undoubtedly something of the shopping catalogue about this, although it should be remembered that a proportion of such meetings will have come about through the sharing of interests and use of online discussion forums, rather than from the use of specific dating websites. People searching for a soulmate online don't always know exactly what they want, or whether they can trust the descriptions of those who advertise themselves as available. Indeed, authenticity is a major concern, with frequent horror stories about the sexual exploitation of young people, or of lonely, trusting women falling victim to the wiles of serial philanderers and predatory types. The compilation of a profile for a dating site or application allows for a great deal of fantasy: indeed, fantasy and imagination are *prerequisites* of this kind of activity.[68]

Writing about romance in the 1990s, Lynne Pearce and Jackie Stacey suggested that romance was best understood as 'a *quest* for love; a quest for another about whom the subject has very definite fantasies, investments and beliefs'.[69] They observed that against all the odds—the rise of feminism, for instance, and mounting rates of marital breakdown—the desire for romance, at the end of the twentieth century, was as strong as it had ever been.[70] Perplexed to explain this survival of idealism in the face of so much evidence to undermine it, they suggested that most people continued to enjoy the pleasures associated with romance even while they might view these pleasures with a certain critical irony. There is nothing new about this dualism, or ambivalence. Historian Stephen Brooke, thinking about love and romance in popular culture in mid twentieth-century Britain, contends that the emotional lives of ordinary people were shaped by *both* popular culture and by pragmatism. 'It is entirely possible to be an idealist and a realist at the same moment, to live in both dreamworlds and the real world,' Brooke reminds us.[71]

A similar combination of idealism and realism can inform women's expressions of desire for a romantic hero. A few years before Pearce and Stacey published *Romance Revisited*, Welsh singer Bonnie Tyler recorded a song, 'Holding Out for a Hero', originally for the soundtrack to the film *Footloose* (1984). Written by Jim Steinman and Dean Pitchford, the song was included in Tyler's album *Secret Dreams and Forbidden Fire* in 1986. The music video, produced by Jeffrey Abelson, has since attracted something of a cult following. It features a passionate Tyler bellowing out her desire for a superman, a white knight/cowboy hero, 'fresh from the fight', a 'larger-than-life' rescuer. Her need is hormonally driven, raw: she pitches herself against the elements, dragging herself on her knees from a burning house to a rock in the Arizona desert. There are no problems with woman as a desiring subject here, no inhibitions. But the girl is urgently demanding what she *knows* to be a dream man, a product of her wildest fantasy. The wonderful potency of this performance—shot through with rage and inevitably, frustration—have contributed to its lasting popularity.[72]

As well as being larger than life, heroes and heartthrobs of the imagination are usually characterized by another kind of 'unreality' in that they are perceived as composites of ostensibly contradictory qualities. The most commonly desired qualities include a mixture of power *and* vulnerability, for instance, brute strength and courage combined with an empathetic or even a poetic form of sensitivity. The more enduring masculine stars of the cinema screen demonstrated different characteristics through different performances. The film legacy of Rudolph Valentino, for example, shows his extraordinary versatility in performing as sensitive ladies' man and adoring son, graceful dancer and aesthete, forceful tribesman, fearless matador, and courageous war hero. Lord Nelson appeared both hero—intrepid protector of his country, and fragile—an injured man, in need of nurturance and feminine sympathy.[73] The enduring potency of Lord Byron as a kind of archetype has a great deal to do with the ways in which his particular style of masculinity seemed to bring together opposing qualities: he was courageous and bold but fussed about his diet and appearance; disconcertingly handsome but disarmingly insecure about being podgy and lame. Women were won over by this amalgam of strength and vulnerability, together with the subtle suggestion of androgyny.

Writers of fiction work hard to imagine and to represent heroes who similarly combine opposing qualities. English literary historian Mary Cadogan, whose study of romance fiction *And Then Their Hearts Stood Still* was published in 1994, concluded that the requirements of romance had remained pretty constant over the years.[74] In her view the formula demanded a hero 'with rugged-rather-than-chocolate-boxy looks' and 'a kind of sexy arrogance' which might border on savagery at times, but would nevertheless conceal 'a soft centre'.[75] This scar tissue would probably have come about because of 'some deep hurt or humiliation inflicted by women in his past'. The soft spot would only become apparent when the hero met the right girl and was sure of her love. The hero had to be rich, and he had to prove himself a suitable subject for domestication.[76] As Cadogan's language suggests ('chocolate boxy', 'soft centre'), she tended to regard romance reading in a fairly benign way: confectionery for the sweet-toothed, rather than a source of damaging delusions.

In addition to describing the narrative structure of countless romance novels, Cadogan's formula accounts for at least the outlines of the story in E. L. James's *Fifty Shades of Grey* series, published some twenty years later. E. L. James labours to explain the psychology of her billionaire, control-freak 'hero', Christian Grey.[77] She draws upon well-established conventions when she represents him as having suffered abuse (at the hands of women) in his childhood. Christian is presented as desirable. We're told that he looks good, smells good, and dresses with impeccable style. He's mega-rich, priapic, and cool. The boyish, self-made mogul of an international business empire, he's a philanthropist and skilled lover to boot. *And* he's loaded with desirable property, with a personal manservant and a private helicopter at his command. But there's a hitch: Christian is excited by the idea of hitting and hurting women. The narrative of transformation whereby he is emotionally reclaimed for love has strained the credulity of many critics, for whom he is simply too creepy and manipulative. The image of this cultural sophisticate kitted out in his ripped-denim 'dom. Jeans' for an afternoon in his private BDSM playroom (the 'Red Room of Pain') has provoked laughter and exuberant satire as well as lust. Bryony Gordon's review of *Grey* in *The Telegraph* was memorably entitled 'Mr Darcy with nipple-clamps'.[78]

It is hard not to see Christian as standing in the tradition of Richardson's Lovelace, or Emily Brontë's Heathcliff, as much as Darcy. He's less well-drawn and emotionally convincing, perhaps, but the continuities are there. There are important differences, too: neither Lovelace nor Heathcliff were ultimately saved by love. Is the idea that Christian can be reclaimed by the love of a good woman unconvincing and even dangerous? Novelist Jenny Colgan, writing in *The Guardian*, insisted that it was 'almost impossible to read *Grey* and not assume the narrator is going to end up in jail'.[79] If her own daughter wished to read the book, Colgan insisted, 'I'd make sure she knows that if anyone ever treats her like this, she should run like the wind'.

E. L. James herself repeatedly reminds us that her books should be read as *fantasy*. She has been reported as having suggested—somewhat tongue-in-cheek, no doubt—that what women really want in a man is not some Christian Grey-type figure, but a partner who will help them with everyday chores such as doing the washing-up.[80] Fantasies of romance have often had their dangerous edge, playing upon what is forbidden, the lure of transgression, and the power of the taboo. There can be danger in fantasy when it distorts, or has damaging implications in 'real' life. As Colgan reminds us, we live in a world where countless women still suffer from sexual abuse.[81] Too many women stay in abusive relationships, deluded into thinking that love and understanding will eventually transform their oppressors. But the hazard lies not in the text itself, but in how it is read or interpreted. 'The desert romance' has been with us for well over a century now, and the fantasy of the virile Arab warrior on horseback is well-engrained in Western romantic culture. Few women set out to be seduced by the reality. Even so, similar fantasies may have touched the imagination of those teenage girls who have deserted families in the West to travel to Syria, bent on becoming jihadi brides.[82]

Only time will tell whether Christian Grey lives on as a kind of fantasy-hero of the twenty-first century, or whether the texts in which he appears are remembered mainly as a publishing phenomenon, showing that books can successfully be marketed to audiences not normally in the habit of book-buying. The *Shades of Grey* volumes, crossing romance with soft porn, have been readily available in supermarkets, where they can easily be tossed into shopping trolleys alongside the week's supply of frozen fish fingers and family-sized tubs of ice cream.

This book has shown that fantasies are enmeshed in history and that the cultural historian can highlight both continuities and change through time. The heroes and heartthrobs—the icons of masculinity whom women have in part created and swooned over in the last hundred and fifty years—have all been, in their way, 'fictions'. Some of these figures, Fitzwilliam Darcy for instance, were born in a writer's imagination and took shape in the pages of a book, but may have drawn on real-life figures and were given new life and shape through cultural reinterpretation. Other legendary heartthrobs, actors such as Rudolph Valentino, Clark Gable, Richard Chamberlain, or George Clooney; singers such as Elvis or the Beatles, acquired reputation through performance. Their public images—often deftly honed and managed by publicity machines—offered templates of idealized masculinity which might at times be very remote from these actors' or performers' real lives. On screen, male leads have been carefully chosen to play the role of heroes and heartthrobs in literature or in the past, sometimes channelling earlier performances and often adding new layers of mythology. Richard Chamberlain was picked for a clutch of heartthrob roles, including Byron, Dr Kildare, and Ralph de Bricassart, for instance; Laurence Olivier played both a debonair version of Heathcliff *and* an urbane Mr Darcy. In the film *Harum Scarum*, Elvis channelled Rudolph Valentino as *The Sheik*.[83] Cultural interpretations can seem like halls of mirrors, with endless reinterpretations, layers, and revisioning. And certain forms and embodiments of masculinity—handsome princes, dashing soldiers and cavaliers, highwaymen and pirates—are lodged deep in our gendered imagination, exerting enduring appeal.

But there have been marked discontinuities, too. New templates of desirable masculinity have appeared at times of social, political, and technological change. The stiff-upper-lipped imperial adventurers of the 1890s and 1900s gave way to the lost boys and soulful poets of the First World War, to the exotic sheikhs and tribesmen and the debonair dancers and ladies' men of the 1920s. The possibilities of air travel and combat in the skies fostered adulation of the glamorous pilots of the RAF. Family men with secure professional status peopled many of the romances of the 1950s, a decade when doctors, particularly, featured large in many women's dreams. At the same time, the increasing purchasing power of young people, and particularly that of teenage girls, helped to fuel the popular success of crooners, and successive generations of rock stars and boy bands. Wider opportunities for women's economic independence meant that a man need no longer be seen primarily as a meal ticket. The more independent women of the 1980s and 1990s were sometimes represented in fiction, at least, as bold individuals: more go-getting, sexually; as likely to be attracted to good-looking, sympathetic, and often much younger men as to nurse a penchant for wealthy international businessmen. There was often misogyny in the way such relationships were portrayed or interpreted, with sexually active women depicted as 'cougars' prowling after 'toy-boys'. But showing women as active sexual beings with desires of their own was at least a step forward.

Women as consumers have played an important part in shaping the cultural history of masculinity and gendered performance, though their contribution and their tastes have been much reviled. Where critics in the 1900s expressed contempt for shop-girl romances, their equivalents in the 1980s sneered about 'chicklit', and more recently, we have heard dismissals of 'clitlit' or 'Mummyporn'. But in terms of numbers and economics, female consumers have proved a force to be reckoned with. The rules and expectations governing courtship and romance have changed dramatically, and digital technologies have opened up new worlds for the expression of choice. Women's fantasies, desires, and preferences are more visible than ever before. The impact of this, in cultural terms, can be measured not only through the growth and proliferation of new genres and forms of literature but through the ways in which digital social media and social networking can bring about celebrity. The phenomenal rise of stars such as Justin Bieber or boy band One Direction, for instance, has been highly dependent on Twitter. An article in the *Wall Street Journal*, published in 2012, speculated on the possibility of 'Bieber fever' (and other forms of fandom) being fuelled by neurotransmitters such as dopamine, but more pertinent, perhaps was the comment on Bieber's internet fan base, with (at that time) 44 million friends on Facebook and 23 million followers on Twitter.[84]

We now enjoy and consume both text and images in different ways. Where once it was helpful to think about cultural performance in terms of halls of mirrors, kaleidoscopes, and reflections, things are now more complex. Twitter's co-founders in 2006 are said to have settled on the idea of the 'tweet' as describing a short burst of communication, suggestive of a bird chirping. The network itself, now immense, with its constant refigurings, and evanescent patterns of fragmentary thoughts, communications, and 'trending topics' brings to mind the murmurations of bees or starlings. Understanding these new patterns, forms, and drifting enthusiasms will take time. What the digital revolution appears to have brought to us is a massive expansion of possibilities, and gendered performances are part of this. We are drawn into a world where we are confronted by a proliferation of different models of gender, a multitude of different ways of being male or female. The internet allows us all to explore history and cultural change. It can be fascinating to watch vintage film footage on YouTube or Internet Archive, for instance, and to observe how contemporary viewers post comments which continually reassess the performances of screen lovers of the 1920s, or pop legends of the 1960s and 1970s. Countless sites offer lists, polls, and rankings: the top twenty heroes of 1940s cinema, the twenty-five most popular literary vampires, and so forth. We can see how historical performances of masculinity—as well as femininity—are endlessly reshuffled, judged, and reassessed. Amid swirling currents of sexual preference, the past is continually raided to enrich and to inform the imagination of the present.

The proliferation of choice brings its own problems, in relationships as in other things. How do we know when to stop searching for a companion, let alone a soulmate? Does a relentless pursuit of happiness undermine our chances of actually finding it?[85] When it comes to gendered versions of the self, it seems that hegemonic masculinities—or femininities—may be harder to sustain today than in the past, which is in itself liberating. More space for women's voices and women's choices makes it clearer than ever how the history of gender has shaped the lives of both men and women. Feminists have long argued that social change empowering women frees up men's lives and choices, too. Maybe we can look forward now to a future in which men and women see each other less as gendered objects onto which they project their own desires and longings, and instead, strive to relate to each other respectfully, as individuals and human beings.

# NOTES

## Introduction

1. Jones, Ernest, *Sigmund Freud, Life and Work: Vol. 2, Years of Maturity, 1901–1919* (London: Hogarth Press, 1955), 468.
2. The term 'poodle-faker' seems to have been first used in the 1900s. The *Oxford English Dictionary* defines a poodle-faker as 'a man who cultivates female society, especially for the purpose of professional advancement; a ladies' man'.
3. Gullace, Nicoletta F., 'White Feathers and Wounded Men: Female Patriotism and the Memory of the Great War', *Journal of British Studies* 36 (April 1997): 178–206.
4. http://mydaguerreotypeboyfriend.tumblr.com, accessed 23 July 2015.
5. Lise Shapiro Sanders explores the social and cultural significance of the London shopgirl in her study, *Consuming Fantasies: Labor, Leisure and the London Shopgirl, 1880–1920* (Columbus, OH: Ohio State University Press, 2006), see esp. 129, 133, and *passim*.
6. See, for instance, Langhamer, C., *Women's Leisure in England, 1920–1960* (Manchester: Manchester University Press, 2000), esp. 58 ff.
7. Jephcott, A.P., *Rising Twenty: Notes on Some Ordinary Girls* (London: Faber & Faber, 1948), 111–13 and *passim*.
8. For young women's work and wages see Todd, S., *Young Women, Work and Family in England 1918–1950* (Oxford: Oxford University Press, 2005).
9. An early analysis of this trend which has become something of a classic was Mark Abrams, *The Teenage Consumer* (London: Press Exchange, 1959).
10. Friedan, B., *The Feminine Mystique* (London: Gollancz, 1963); Metzl, Jonathan, '"Mother's Little Helper": The Crisis of Psychoanalysis and the Miltown Resolution', *Gender and History* 15/2 (August 2003): 240–67.
11. Metzl, '"Mother's Little Helper"', 241.
12. See, for instance, Nelson, Jennifer, *More than Medicine: A History of the Feminist Women's Health Movement* (New York, NY and London: New York University Press, 2015).
13. More reliable sources, including Gloria Steinem herself, credit Australian journalist Irina Dunn, then a student at the University of Sydney, with the aphorism.
14. Greer, G., *The Female Eunuch* (London: Paladin, 1971), 178, 188.

15. McRobbie's later book, *Feminism and Youth Culture: From Jackie to Just Seventeen* (Basingstoke: Macmillan Education, 1991).

16. Heaf, J., 'This One Direction Interview Got us Death Threats' *GQ*, 23 July 2014, http://www.gq-magazine.co.uk/entertainment/articles/2013-07/29/one-direction-gq-covers-interview, accessed 22 July 2015. See also Burrell, I., 'All publicity is good publicity, except where GQ and One Direction Fans are concerned' *The Independent*, 31 July 2013, http://www.independent.co.uk/voices/comment/all-publicity-is-good-publicity-except-where-gq-and-one-direction-fans-are-concerned-8739859.html, accessed 22 July 2015. A not dissimilar outburst of fury among One Directioners followed the airing of film-maker Daisy Asquith's documentary, *Crazy about One Direction*, which was shown on British television (Channel 4) in August 2013, even though this aimed to give a voice to fans, and treated the subject of fandom sympathetically.

17. For a viewpoint more sympathetic to the fans' objections see http://www.fuse.tv/2013/08/one-direction-gq-story-fans-right, accessed 22 July 2015.

18. There are endless examples, but see, for instance, the list ranking vampires on the television screen compiled by Chelsea Mueller for the website 'Heroes and Heartbreakers.com', http://www.heroesandheartbreakers.com/blogs/2012/06/tvs-top-5-sexiest-vampires-eric-northman-damon-salvatore-and-more, accessed 22 July 2015.

19. Stephen King, interview with Emma Brockes published in *The Guardian*, 21 September 2013, http://www.theguardian.com/books/2013/sep/21/stephen-king-shining-sequel-interview, accessed 3 August 2016.

20. James, E. L. (Erika Leonard/Mitchell), James's blockbusting *Fifty Shades of Grey* began life as *Twilight* fanfiction with the author calling herself 'Snowqueen's Icedragon'. At the time of writing there are four books in the series: *Fifty Shades of Grey* (2011), *Fifty Shades Darker* (2012), *Fifty Shades Freed* (2012), and *Grey* (2015). All now published London: Arrow Books.

21. Berger, John, *Ways of Seeing* (London: Penguin, 1972).

22. Ibid., 47.

## Chapter 1

1. Mansfield, K., *Collected Stories of Katherine Mansfield* (London: Penguin, 2007). Also available at http://www.katherinemansfieldsociety.org/assets/KM-Stories/THE-TIREDNESS-OF-ROSABEL1908.pdf, accessed 2 August 2016.

2. Dyhouse, C., *Girls Growing Up in Late Victorian and Edwardian England* (London: Routledge & Kegan Paul, 1981), see esp. chap. 1.

3. Dyhouse, C., *Girl Trouble, Panic and Progress in the History of Young Women* (London: Zed Books, 2013), esp. 28–34. Coventry Patmore's narrative poem, *The Angel in the House*, was published in instalments between 1854 and 1862; John Ruskin's lectures on masculinity and femininity, *Sesame and Lilies*, first appeared in print in 1865.

4. Lewis, J. (ed.), *Labour and Love: Women's Experience of Home and Family 1850–1914* (Oxford: Blackwell, 1986). See also Dyhouse, C., *Feminism and the Family in England, 1880–1939* (Oxford: Blackwell, 1989), chap. 1.

5. There was a notable rise in the use of matrimonial advertising, marriage agencies, and marriage bureaux between 1870 and 1914. See Phegley, J., *Courtship and Marriage in Victorian England* (Praeger, an imprint of ABC–CLIO, LLC, 2012). See also Cocks, H., 'The Cost of Marriage and the Matrimonial Agency in late Victorian Britain', *Social History* (38/1 (March 2013): 66–88.

6. See Dyhouse, *Girl Trouble*, esp. chap. 2.

7. For the US and Canada see, for instance, England, K. and Boyer, K., 'Women's Work: The Feminisation and Shifting Meanings of Clerical Work', *Journal of Social History* 43/2 (Winter 2009): 307–40; for UK see Zimmeck, M., 'Jobs for the Girls: The Experience of Clerical Work for Women, 1850–1914', in John, Angela V. (ed.), *Unequal Opportunities: Women's Employment in England 1800–1918* (Oxford: Blackwell, 1986); Anderson, G., *The White Blouse Revolution: Female Office Workers Since 1870* (Manchester: Manchester University Press, 1988); Todd, S., *Young Women, Work and Family in England 1918–1950* (Oxford: Oxford University Press, 2005).

8. Nicholson, V., *Singled Out: How Two Million Women Survived Without Men after the First World War* (London: Viking, 2007); Holden, K., *The Shadow of Marriage: Singleness in England 1914–1960* (Manchester: Manchester University Press, 2007).

9. Thompson, T. (ed.), *Dear Girl: The Diaries and Letters of Two Working Women, 1897–1917* (London: The Women's Press, 1987).

10. Extract from Ruth's diary entry, 28 May 1908, in Thompson, *op. cit.*, 117.

11. Schreiner, O., *The Story of an African Farm: A Novel* (London: Hutchinson, 1883); Carpenter, E., *Love's Coming of Age: A Series of Papers on the Relations of the Sexes* (Manchester: Labour Press, 1896). Both of these texts went through a number of editions. For Ruth and Eva's response to them see Thompson, *Dear Girl*, 117, 118, 151, 246. For a recent analysis of the impact of Carpenter on his times see Rowbotham, S., *Edward Carpenter: A Life of Liberty and Love* (London: Verso, 2008).

12. Ruth, diary entry 23 June 2008, Thompson, 119.

13. Ruth, diary entry 19 August 1908, Thompson, 127.

14. Ruth, diary entry 21 March 1916, Thompson, 299.

15. Ruth, diary entry 17 July 1908, Thompson, 125.

16. Eva, diary entry 10 September 1913, Thompson, 182.

17. Ruth on Eva, diary entry for 26 January 1907, Thompson, 98.

18. Eva, diary entries 2 July 1913; 22 February 1914, Thompson, 176, 199.

19. Eva, diary entry 1 May 1913, Thompson, 166.

20. Ruth, letter to Eva, 17 May 1914, Thompson, 217–19.

21. Eva, diary entry 28 June 1913, Thompson, 175.

22. Ibid.

23. Eva, diary entry 4 July 1914, Thompson, 228.

24. Eva, diary entry 4 June 1913, Thompson, 171.

25. Eva, diary entry 19 June 1913, Thompson, 174.

26. Flint, K., *The Woman Reader, 1837–1914* (Oxford: Clarendon Press, 1993); Leavis, Q.D., *Fiction and the Reading Public* (first published 1939; this edn London: Penguin, 1979), 26, 153.

27. Jacobs, E., 'Circulating Libraries' in Kastan, Davis Scott, (ed.), *The Oxford Encyclopedia of British Literature* (Oxford: Oxford University Press, 2006), 5–10; Flint, *The Woman Reader*.

28. Waller, P., *Readers, Writers and Reputations: Literary Life in Britain, 1870–1918* (Oxford: Oxford University Press, 2006). See chap. 19 in 'In Cupid's Chains: Charles Garvice', 681–701; reference to Arnold Bennett, 681.

29. BBC Radio 4, Letter from America by Alistair Cooke, 'The Forgotten William le Queux', 13 May 1988, http://www.bbc.co.uk/programmes/articles/12VJn7Ghzkj3b8gC6CVHXpo/the-forgotten-william-le-queux-13-may-1988, accessed 2 August 2016.

30. Steve Holland's online biography is useful, http://bearalley.blogspot.co.uk/2010/02/charles-garvice.html, accessed 28 July 2015.

31. See Laura Sewell Matter's essay on Garvice, 'Pursuing the Great Bad Novelist', *Georgia Review* fall (2007): 445–59.

32. Sir Joseph, for example, in Garvice, C., *In Wolf's Clothing* (London: Hodder & Stoughton, 1908).

33. Garvice, *Her Heart's Desire* (London: Hodder & Stoughton 1908), 150.

34. Ibid, 469.

35. Ibid, 319.

36. Ibid, 446.

37. This is in essence the plot of Garvices's *In Wolf's Clothing*.

38. Waller, *op. cit.*, 685, 689.

39. See n. 24, *supra*.

40. Marie Corelli, 1855–1924 (born Mary Mackay) was hugely successful with her mystical and sentimental novels written in the closing decades of the nineteenth century. Her best known books were *A Romance of Two Worlds* (London: Richard Bentley and Son, 1886) and *The Sorrows of Satan* (London: Methuen, 1895). Her work was much derided by literary critics. 'Ouida', 1839–1908 (Maria Louise de la Ramée) was born in England but lived in Italy after 1974. Her *Under Two Flags* (1867) was a best-seller, considered racy at the time. She wrote some forty novels in a style which Helen Killoran, (who wrote her entry in the *Oxford Dictionary of National Biography*) memorably described as 'prurient romanticism'. Rhoda Broughton (1840–1920), another best-seller in her day, became famous for *Cometh Up as a Flower* (1843). Her novels featured independent-minded heroines who often had to choose between love and economic realities.

41. See for instance Stutfield, Hugh E. M., 'Tommyrotics', *Blackwoods Magazine* 157/June (1895): 833–45; also the same author's 'The Psychology of Feminism', *Blackwoods Magazine* 161/Jan. (1897): 104–17.

42. 'Victoria Cross' (Annie Sophie Cory), *Anna Lombard* (London: John Long, 1901).

43. See Brittain, Melisa, 'Dangerous Crossings: Victorian Feminism, Imperialist Discourse, and Victoria Cross's New Woman in Indigenous Space', MA thesis presented to Faculty of Graduate Studies, University of Guelph, ON, Canada, 1999, http://www.collectionscanada.gc.ca, accessed 2 August 2016.

44. Harraden, B., *Katharine Frensham* (London: Thomas Nelson and Sons, 1909). Thompson, *Dear Girl*, Eva's diary entry for 4 June 1913, 171.

45. See the entry on Beatrice Harraden in *Oxford Dictionary of National Biography*, written by Fred Hunter. Harraden (1864–1936) was a pupil at Cheltenham Ladies' College before studying at Queen's and Bedford Colleges, London. She had considerable public success with her first novel, *Ships that Pass in the Night* (1893). In the 1900s she became an energetic supporter of a number of suffrage organizations and a member of the Women's Social and Political Union.

46. See n. 10, *supra*.

47. Stead, W.T., 'Anna Lombard: A Novel of the Ethics of Sex', *Review of Reviews* 23 June (1901): 595–7.

48. Review of Katharine Frensham in *The Spectator*, 19 December 1903, 21, http://archive.spectator.co.uk/, accessed 28 July 2015.

49. Glyn, E., *Three Weeks* (New York: Duffield, 1907); Dell, Ethel M., *The Way of an Eagle* (London: Fisher Unwin, 1912).

50. Glyn, *Three Weeks*, 157.

51. Dell, P., *Nettie and Sissie: The Biography of Ethel M. Dell and her Sister Ella* (London: Hamish Hamilton, 1977), 33, 167. See also Hipsky, M., *Modernism and the Popular Romance in Britain, 1885–1925* (Athens, OH: Ohio University Press, 2011), 177.

52. Kent, Susan Kingsley, *Sex and Suffrage in Britain, 1860–1914* (London: Routledge, 1990), 57–8.

53. Stopes, Marie Carmichael, *Married Love: A New Contribution to the Solution of Sex Difficulties* (first published London: A. C. Fifield 1918; this edn London: G.P. Putnam's Sons, 1921).

54. Ibid., 24.

55. Ibid., 58.

56. Ibid., 57, 62.

57. Stopes, *Married Love*, Charts I and II, 68–9; 'woo before every separate act of coitus', 88.

58. Ibid., 92–3.

59. Stopes didn't use the term 'to come' as a synonym for climax: she spoke of 'the explosive completion of the act'; Stopes, *Married Love*, 55.

60. Ibid., also 95.
61. Delap, L., and Morgan, S. (eds), *Men, Masculinities and Religious Change in Twentieth Century Britain* (Basingstoke: Palgrave Macmillan, 2013), 184; Hall, Lesley A., *Hidden Anxieties: Male Sexuality 1900–1950* (Cambridge: Polity Press, 1991).
62. Quoted in Ross McKibbin's Introduction to Oxford World's Classics edition of Stopes's *Married Love* (Oxford: Oxford University Press 2004), xxxv.
63. Stopes, M., *Enduring Passion: Further New Contributions to the Solution of Sex Difficulties, being the Continuation of Married Love* (first published 1928; this edn London: Hogarth Press, 1953).
64. Ibid., 4.
65. Ibid.
66. Ibid., 5.
67. Hull, E.M., *The Sheik* (London: Eveleigh Nash & Grayson, 1919).
68. Leavis, *Fiction and the Reading Public*, 116.
69. Among a huge body of writing on *The Sheik*, an article by Sarah Wintle is particularly insightful in reassessing Q. D. Leavis's dismissal of the 'typist's daydream'. See Wintle, S., 'The Sheik: What can be made of a Daydream', *Women: A Cultural Review* 7/3 (1996): 291–302; see also Melman, B., *Women and the Popular Imagination in the Twenties, Flappers and Nymphs* (London: Macmillan, 1988). Connections between Marie Stopes and E. M. Hull are explored in Chow, K., 'Popular Sexual Knowledges and Women's Agency in 1920s England', *Feminist Review* 63/autumn (1999): 64–87.
70. King, Gilbert, 'The "Latin Lover" and His Enemies', *The Smithsonian*, 13 June 2012, http://www.smithsonianmag.com/history/the-latin-lover-and-his-enemies-119968944/, accessed 22 September 2014.
71. Lasky, Jesse L., *I Blow my Own Horn* (Garden City, NY, 1957), 148.

## Chapter 2

1. For ideas about women's sexuality and desire in the seventeenth century see Gowing, L., *Common Bodies: Women, Touch and Power in Seventeenth Century England* (New Haven, CT and London: Yale University Press, 2003), esp. 82 ff.
2. The Victorian physiologist Sir William Acton's observation that ('happily for society') the majority of women were 'not much troubled by sexual feelings of any kind' has been regularly cited as an illustration of contemporary belief in middle-class women as lacking in desire. This comes from Crozier, I., 'William Acton and the History of Sexuality: The Medical and Professional Context', *Journal of Victorian Culture* 5/1 (2000): 1–29.
3. Ibid.; see also Lecky, W.E.H. 'The Position of Women', in *History of European Morals*, vol. 2, *From Augustus to Charlemagne* (New York: D. Appleton & Co., 1895), 286–99.

4. Respectable Victorian women were supposed to behave with modesty. The degree of repression involved helps to explain the contemporary cultural fascination (among social critics and also feminists) with wild women, Bacchae, and maenads. On this theme see the particularly insightful essay by Yopie Prins, 'Greek Maenads, Victorian Spinsters', in Dellamora, R. (ed.), *Victorian Sexual Dissidence* (London: University of Chicago Press, 1999), 43–82.

5. Nancy F. Cott's article, 'Passionlessness: An Interpretation of Victorian Sexual Ideology, 1790-1850', originally *Signs* 4/2 (Winter 1978): 219–36, was one of the earliest attempts to explore the ways in which Victorian women might appropriate the idea of passionlessness in defence against gendered double standards of morality.

6. 'Currer Bell' (Charlotte Brontë), *Editor's Preface to the New Edition of Wuthering Heights and Agnes Grey by Ellis and Acton Bell* (London: Smith Elder & Co, 1850), xxvii–xxiii.

7. Charlotte's novels *The Professor* (1857) and *Villette* (1853) drew on her experiences in Brussels at the school run by Professor Constantin Héger and his wife in the early 1840s. Charlotte's passionate, tormented letters to Monsieur Héger, generally supposed to have been torn up by him and salvaged and pieced together by his wife, are now in the British Library (Add Ms 38732).

8. These ideas were first explored in an essay by Nancy F. Cott: Cott, 'Passionlessness', 219–36.

9. Stopes, Marie Carmichael, *Married Love: A New Contribution to the Solution of Sex Difficulties* (first published London: A.C. Fifield, 1918; this edn London: G.P. Putnam's Sons, 1921), 58.

10. Hull, E. M., *The Sheik* (first published London: Eveleigh Nash & Grayson, 1919; this edn London: Virago Press, 1996), 49.

11. Ibid., 140.

12. Mackrell, Judith, *Flappers: Six Women of a Dangerous Generation* (London: Macmillan, 2013).

13. See, *inter alia*, Wollen, P., 'Fashion/Orientalism/The Body', *New Formations* 1 (Spring 1987): 1–33.

14. On Josephine Baker see Mackrell, *Flappers*, 175–203.

15. Nava, M., 'The Cosmopolitanism of Commerce and the Allure of Difference: Selfridges, The Russian Ballet and the Tango, 1911-1914', *International Journal of Cultural Studies* 1/2 (1998): 163–96.

16. Davidson, James, '"Half Snake, Half Panther"', Review of Lucy Moore's *Nijinsky*', *London Review of Books* 35/18 (26 September 2013): 7–10.

17. Walkowitz, 'Vision of Salome'; see also Bland, Lucy, *Modern Women on Trial: Sexual Transgression in the Age of the Flapper* (Manchester: Manchester University Press, 2013).

18. Thompson, T. (ed.), *Dear Girl: The Diaries and Letters of Two Working Women, 1897–1917* (London: The Women's Press, 1987), extract from Ruth's diary for 11 July 1908, 120–1.

19. Ibid., 120.
20. Mackrell, J., 'When Flappers Ruled the Earth: How Dance helped Women's Liberation', *The Guardian*, 29 April 2013, http://www.theguardian.com/stage/2013/apr/29/dance-womens-liberation-flappers-1920s, accessed 2 August 2016.
21. Bland, *Modern Women on Trial*, see esp. chap. 1, 'The Case of the "Cult of the Clitoris": Treachery, Patriotism and English Womanhood'. See also Walkowitz, 'Vision of Salome'.
22. Dyhouse, C., *Girl Trouble: Panic and Progress in the History of Young Women* (London: Zed Books, 2013), see esp. chap. 2, 'Brazen Flappers, Bright Young Things and "Miss Modern"'.
23. Ibid., 71–2; Woollacott, A., '"Khaki Fever" and its Control: Gender, Class, Age and Sexual Morality on the British Home Front in the First World War', *Journal of Contemporary History* 29 (1994): 325–47.
24. Brader, C., '"A World on Wings": Young Female Workers and Cinema in World War I', *Women's History Review* 14/1 (2005): 99–117.
25. Dyhouse, *Girl Trouble*, 92; see also National Council of Public Morals, *The Cinema: Its Present Position and Future Possibilities; Being the Report of, and Chief Evidence Taken by the Cinema Commission of Inquiry instituted by the National Council of Public Morals* (London: Williams and Norgate, 1917).
26. Lawrence, D.H., 'Tickets, Please', in *The Complete Short Stories* (Phoenix Edn) (London: Heinemann, 1968), vol. 2, 334–46.
27. Loos, A., *Gentlemen Prefer Blondes: The Illuminating Diary of a Professional Lady* (New York: Boni & Liveright, 1925); Loos, *But Gentlemen Marry Brunettes* (New York: Boni & Liveright 1928). (This edn both texts published together by Penguin Books, 1998.)
28. Ibid., 93.
29. Ibid., 88–9.
30. Glyn, A., *Elinor Glyn: A Biography* (London: Hutchinson, 1955), 301–2; Glyn, E., *'It' and Other Stories* (London: Duckworth, 1927).
31. Kehr, D., 'A Wanton Woman's Ways Revealed, 71 Years Later', *New York Times*, 9 January 2005, http://www.nytimes.com/2005/01/09, accessed 3 August 2016.
32. Ibid. See also Doherty, T., *Hollywood's Censor: Joseph I. Breen and the Production Code Administration* (New York and Chichester, West Sussex: Columbia University Press, 2007), 46; Turan, K., *Never Coming to a Theatre Near You: A Celebration of a Certain Kind of Movie* (New York: Public Affairs, 2004), 370–3.
33. Basinger, J., *The Star Machine* (New York: Vintage, 2009); McDonald, P., *The Star System: Hollywood's Production of Popular Identities* (London and New York: Wallflower, 2000); DeCordova, R., *Picture Personalities: The Emergence of the Star System in America* (Champaign, IL: University of Illinois Press, 2001).
34. Carroll, D., *The Matinee Idols* (London: Peter Owen, 1972).
35. Walker, A., *Franz Liszt: The Virtuoso Years, 1811–1847* (Ithaca, NY: Cornell University Press, 1983), 289, 371–2, 380.

36. 'How Franz Liszt became the World's First Rock Star', NPR, 22 Oct 2011, http://www.npr.org/2011/10/22/141617637/how-franz-liszt-became-the-worlds-first-rock-star (accessed 6 August 2015).

37. Carroll, *Matinee Idols*, 15.

38. Ibid.

39. For the descriptions quoted see Botham, N. and Donnelly, P., *Valentino: The Love God* (New York: Ace Books, 1976); King, Gilbert, 'The "Latin Lover" and His Enemies', *The Smithsonian*, 13 June 2012, http://www.smithsonianmag.com/history/the-latin-lover-and-his-enemies-119968944/, accessed 22 September 2014; Leider, Emily W., *Dark Lover: The Life and Death of Rudolph Valentino* (London: Faber & Faber, 2003) is an excellent recent biography.

40. For contemporary comment on Valentino's funeral see (*inter alia*) http://www.britishpathe.com/video/rudolph-valentinos-funeral-aka-rudolphe-valentinos, accessed 2 August 2016.

41. See, for instance, the comments posted in response to the film clips and archival footage of Valentino on YouTube.

42. Hull, *The Sheik*, 2, 189.

43. Black, Gregory D., *Hollywood Censored: Morality Codes, Catholics and the Movies* (Cambridge: Cambridge University Press, 1994), 1, 226−8.

44. Ibid., 1.

45. Haskell, M., *From Reverence to Rape: The Treatment of Women in the Movies* (New York: Holt, Reinhart and Winston, 1974), 91.

46. Ibid. See also LaSalle, M., *Complicated Women: Sex and Power in Pre-Code Hollywood* (New York: St Martin's Press, 2000).

47. On Mitchell's novel, the film version of *Gone with the Wind* (1939) and its public reception both at the time of release and subsequently see Taylor, H., *Scarlett's Women: Gone with the Wind and its Female Fans* (London: Virago, 2014).

48. Mitchell, M., *Gone with the Wind* (London: Macmillan, 1936), 3.

49. Ibid., 564.

50. Ibid., 533.

51. 'Wilkes the Wimp', in Taylor, H. *Scarlett's Women*, 109−13.

52. Taylor, H. *Scarlett's Women*, 113 ff.

53. Mitchell, *Gone with the Wind*, 1016.

54. Ibid., 939.

55. Winsor, K., *Forever Amber* (first published 1944; this edn London: Penguin, 2002), film version by Twentieth Century Fox, 1947, starring Linda Darnell and Cornel Wilde.

56. Taylor, Charles, 'The bed-hopping novel that shocked America', *Salon*, 31 May 2003, http://www.salon.com/2003/05/31/winsor/, accessed 7 August 2015.

57. Guttridge, P., 'Obituary of Kathleen Winsor', *The Independent*, 29 May 2003, http://www.independent.co.uk/news/obituaries/kathleen-winsor-36575.html, accessed 7 August 2015.

58. Showalter, E., 'Emeralds on the Home Front', *The Guardian*, 10 August 2002, http://www.theguardian.com/books/2002/aug/10/featuresreviews. guardianreview19, accessed 2 August 2016.

59. See Attorney General vs The Book Named 'Forever Amber' and Others, 323 Mass. 302, 2 March–11 October 1948, http://masscases.com/cases/sjc/323/323mass302.html, accessed 7 August 2015.

60. Homberger, E., 'Forever Amber author who launched the bodice ripper boom' (obituary of Kathleen Winsor), *The Guardian*, 4 June 2003, http://www.theguardian.com/news/2003/jun/04/guardianobituaries.booksobituaries, accessed 2 August 2016.

61. Guttridge, *op.cit.*

62. Mitchell, *Gone with the Wind*, 103.

63. Mitchell became very frustrated by her publisher's concern to get the name of her heroine exactly right, snapping 'Personally, we could just call her Garbage O'Hara for all I care' at one point. See Brown, Ellen F., and Wiley, J. Jr, *Margaret Mitchell's Gone with the Wind: A Bestseller's Odyssey from Atlanta to Hollywood* (Lanham, MD: Taylor Trade Publishing), 33–4.

64. Taylor, H. *Scarlett's Women*, 5. Helen Taylor notes that Joan Collins's autobiography, *Past Imperfect* (London: Coronet, 1979) has seven references to *Gone with the Wind*, and that Collins's daughter Tara was named first after Scarlett's plantation home, and second, after the Ernest Dowson poem from which Mitchell's book takes its title: 'I have forgot much, Cynara! gone with the wind, Flung roses, roses riotously with the throng'.

65. Showalter, 'Emeralds on the Home Front', 2.

66. Dyhouse, *Glamour: Women, History, Feminism* (London: Zed Books, 2010), 81–90.

67. Steedman, C., *Landscape for a Good Woman: A Story of Two Lives* (London: Virago, 1986), 32.

68. Dyer, R., *Brief Encounter* (London: Palgrave Macmillan, BFI Film Classics, 1993) is a useful study of production history with an analysis of the film's widespread appeal.

69. Useful on *Dance Hall* is Christine Geraghty's *British Cinema in the Fifties: Gender, Genre and the 'New Look'* (London: Routledge, 2000), 16, 77–84; see also British Film Institute (BFI) *Screenonline* entry, http://www.screenonline.org.uk/film/id/587320/index.html, accessed 7 August 2015.

70. Jephcott, A.P., *Rising Twenty: Notes on some Ordinary Girls* (London: Faber & Faber, 1945), 68.

71. BFI Screenonline entry, *op. cit.*

72. Harper, S., 'Historical Pleasures: Gainsborough Costume Melodrama', in Landy, M. (ed.), *The Historical Film: History and Memory in Media* (London: Athlone Press, 2001), 98–125; see also Harper, *Picturing the Past: The Rise and Fall of the British Costume Film* (London: BFI, 1994).

73. BFI *Screenonline* entry for *The Seventh Veil*, http://www.screenonline.org.uk/film/id/441191/, accessed 7 August 2015.

74. http://www.imdb.com/title/tt0037035/taglines, accessed 7 August 2015.

75. Langhamer, C., *Women's Leisure in England, 1920–1960* (Manchester: Manchester University Press, 2000), 145.

76. Dyhouse, *Girl Trouble*, 124–6, 169–70.

77. See (inter alia) Whiteside, J., *Cry: The Johnnie Ray Story* (New York, NY: Barricade, 1994).

78. 'Frank Sinatra and the "bobby-soxers"', New York Correspondent to *The Guardian*, 10 January 1945, from 'Guardian Century', http://www.theguardian.com/century/1940-1949/Story/0,127764,00.html, accessed 2 August 2016.

79. Savage, J., 'The Columbus Day riot: Frank Sinatra is pop's first star', *The Guardian*, 11 June 2011, http://www.theguardian.com/music/2011/jun/11/frank-sinatra-pop-star, accessed 2 August 2016.

80. Ibid.

81. Lynskey, D., 'Beatlemania: "the screamers" and other tales of fandom', *The Observer*, 29 September 2013, http://www.theguardian.com/music/2013/sep/29/beatlemania-screamers-fandom-teenagers-hysteria, accessed 2 August 2016.

82. Johnson, P., 'The Menace of Beatlism', *New Statesman*, 28 February 1964, 326–7, quoted in Fowler, D., *Youth Culture in Modern Britain, c.1920–1970* (Basingstoke: Palgrave Macmillan, 2008), 171.

83. Faithfull, M., *Marianne Faithfull: An Autobiography* (New York: Cooper Square Press, 2000), 70.

84. Ibid.

85. MacCarthy, F., review by Philip Norman, *Mick Jagger* (London: Harper Collins, 2012), in *The Guardian*, 4 October 2012, http://www.theguardian.com/books/2012/oct/04/mick-jagger-philip-norman-review, accessed 2 August 2016.

86. Ehrenreich, B., Hess, E., and Jacobs, G., *Remaking Love; The Feminization of Sex* (New York: Anchor Press/Doubleday, 1986), 17–35.

87. Ibid., 6.

88. Kearney, Mary Celeste, *Girls Make Media* (New York and Abingdon: Routledge, 2006), 313–75.

## Chapter 3

1. Wootton, S., 'The Byronic in Janes Austen's *Persuasion* and *Pride and Prejudice*', *The Modern Language Review*, 102/1 (Jan 2007): 26–39; Brownstein, Rachel M., 'Romanticism, a Romance; Jane Austen and Lord Byron, 1813-1815', *Journal of the Jane Austen Society of North America, Persuasions* 16 (1994), http://www.jasna.org/persuasions/printed/number16/brownstein.pdf, accessed 14 August 2015.

2. Ibid.

3. Her first sight of Darcy's house leads Elizabeth to muse on the fact that 'to be mistress of Pemberley might be something', and again, that 'of this place ... I might have been mistress!' Austen, J., *Pride and Prejudice* (London: R.D. Bentley, 1853), 212–13.

4. Moskowitz, C., 'Urine Pheromone in Mice named after Jane Austen Character', *Livescience* 2 June 2010, http://www.livescience.com/10662-urine-pheromone-mice-named-jane-austen-character.html, accessed 14 August 2015.

5. Southam, B., 'Sir Charles Grandison and Jane Austen's Men', *Journal of the Jane Austen Society of North America, Persuasions* 18 (1996): 1–14, http://www.jasna.org/persuasions/printed/number18/southam.pdf, accessed 14 August 2015.

6. See for instance Dobson, A., *Samuel Richardson* (London: Macmillan, 1902), 90–2; Doody, M.A., *A Natural Passion: A Study of the Novels of Samuel Richardson* (Oxford: Clarendon Press, 1974).

7. Doody, *A Natural Passion*, 241.

8. Hilton, T., *John Ruskin* (New Haven, CT: Yale Nota Bene Press, 2002), 194–5; Flynn, Carol Houlihan, *Samuel Richardson: A Man of Letters* (Princeton, NJ: Princeton University Press, 2014), 324, n. 35.

9. Richetti, John J., *The Columbia History of the British Novel* (New York, NY and Chichester, West Sussex: Columbia University Press, 2013), 100.

10. Abbott, E. and Campbell, L. (eds), *The Life and Letters of Benjamin Jowett, M.A., Master of Balliol College, Oxford* (London: John Murray, 1897), 325, 335.

11. Southam, 'Sir Charles Grandison and Jane Austen's Men'.

12. Jane Austen letter to Fanny Knight, 23 March 1817 (Jane Austen Letters, Brabourne Edition, http://www.pemberley.com/janeinfo/brablt15.html#letter84, accessed 14 August 2015).

13. Southam, 'Sir Charles Grandison and Jane Austen's Men', 80–3.

14. There is a huge literature on Byron. See (*inter alia*), MacCarthy, F., *Byron: Life and Legend* (first published London: John Murray, 2002; this edn Faber & Faber, 2003); McDayter, G., *Byromania and the Birth of Celebrity Culture* (New York, NY: SUNY Press, 2009); Wilson, F. (ed.), *Byromania: Portraits of the Artist in Nineteenth- and Twentieth-century Culture* (London: Palgrave Macmillan, 1998).

15. 'Paston, G.' and Quennell, P., *'To Lord Byron' Feminine Profiles based upon unpublished letters, 1807–1824* (London: John Murray, 1939).

16. Ibid., Foreword, xi–xii.

17. Letters to Byron are now in the John Murray Collection at the National Library of Scotland. I understand from the curator David McClay that Byron's trophy hair collection remains at John Murray's premises, 50 Albemarle Street, London.

18. Soderholm, J., *Fantasy, Forgery and the Byron Legend* (Lexington, KY: University of Kentucky Press, 1996), 12–13, 31.

19. Lord Byron, *Don Juan in Sixteen Cantos with Notes* (Halifax, UK: Milner and Sowerby, 1837), http://www.gutenberg.org/files/21700/21700-h/21700-h.htm, accessed 14 August 2015.
20. I understand that this bust, like Byron's hair collection, remains at John Murray's offices at 50 Albemarle Street, London.
21. See, for instance, Quennell, *The Marble Foot: An Autobiography, 1905–1938* (London: Collins, 1976), 219.
22. Lamb, Lady Caroline, *Glenarvon* (first published 1816; this edn ed. Frances Wilson, London: Dent, Everyman, 1995). Frances Wilson's introduction to this text is illuminating; see also her essay '"An Exaggerated Woman": The Melodrama of Lady Caroline Lamb', in Wilson, *Byromania*; and Bordoni, S., 'Lord Byron and Lady Caroline Lamb', The Byron Study Centre, University of Nottingham, http://byron.nottingham.ac.uk/resources/digital/introductory/ByronandLamb.htm, accessed 16 August 2015.
23. Lamb, *Glenarvon*, 78.
24. Morrison, R. and Baldick, C. (eds), Introduction, in Polidori, J., *The Vampyre and Other Tales of the Macabre* (Oxford: Oxford University Press, 1997), 1–25.
25. The stories of 'George Egerton' (Mrs Mary Chavelita Dunne) are a good example. See for instance, her *Keynotes* (London: Elkin Mathews and John Lane, 1893). On 'New Woman' fiction generally see Richardson, A., *The New Woman in Fiction and in Fact: Fin de Siècle Feminisms* (London: Palgrave Macmillan, 2001), esp. Introduction. A recent attempt to disentangle fact from fiction in regard to the 'New Woman' can be found in Sutherland, G., *In Search of the New Woman: Middle-Class Women and Work in Britain, 1870–1914* (Cambridge: Cambridge University Press, 2015).
26. Brontë, E., *Wuthering Heights*, introduced by Whitley, J.S. (Hertfordshire: Wordsworth Editions, 1992), 109. Heathcliff insists that Isabella was deluded in abandoning the comforts of her home for him, 'picturing in me a hero of romance, and expecting unlimited indulgences from my chivalrous devotion. I can hardly regard her in the light of a rational creature', he continues, 'so obstinately has she persisted in forming a fabulous notion of my character, and acting on the false impressions she cherished.'
27. Morris, N., 'Pictures, Romance and Luxury: Women and British Cinema in the 1910s and 1920s', in Bell, M. and Williams, M. (eds), *British Women's Cinema* (Abingdon: Routledge, 2010), 19.
28. See Harris, E., *Britain's Forgotten Film Factory: The Story of Isleworth Studios* (Stroud: Amberley Publishing, 2012).
29. See Norma Talmadge Website, http://web.stanford.edu/~gdegroat/NT/oldreviews/sc.htm, accessed 16 August 2015.
30. Morris, 'Pictures, Romance and Luxury', 24.
31. Ibid.
32. Leider, E.W., *Dark Lover: The Life and Death of Rudolph Valentino* (London: Faber & Faber, 2003), 4, 112–13.

33. Ibid., 115. On June Mathis's role in shaping Valentino's performances of masculinity see Thomas J. Slater, 'June Mathis's Valentino Scripts: Images of Male "Becoming" after the Great War', *Cinema Journal* 50/1 (Fall 2010): 99–120.

34. Ibid., 205.

35. This anecdote has been endlessly recycled: for a recent version see Welsch, T., *Gloria Swanson: Ready for her Close-up* (Jackson, MS: University Press of Mississippi, 2013), 97.

36. Leider, *Dark Lover*, 134–5.

37. Ibid., 324.

38. Studlar, G., 'Valentino, 'Optic Intoxication,' and Dance Madness', in Cohan, S., and Hark, I. R., *Screening the Male: Exploring Masculinities in Hollywood Cinema* (London and New York, NY: Routledge, 1993), 27.

39. Pruette, L., 'Should Men be Protected?', *The Nation* 125: 200–1, cited in Studlar, *supra*.

40. Pruette, 'Should Men be Protected?', 201.

41. Studlar, 'Valentino, "Optic Intoxication"'; Hansen, M., 'Pleasure, Ambivalence, Identification: Valentino and Female Spectatorship', *Cinema Journal* 25/4 (summer 1986): 6–32; Anger, K., *Hollywood Babylon* (New York: Bell Publishing, 1981).

42. Leider, *Dark Lover*, 371–6.

43. On contradictions and Valentino's appeal see (*inter alia*) Leider, *Dark Lover*, 422.

44. Gordon, J. and Gordon, C., *Star-Dust in Hollywood* (London: G.G. Harrap and Co., 1930), 153.

45. Leider, *Dark Lover*, 118.

46. Garber, M., *Vested Interests: Cross Dressing and Cultural Anxiety* (New York, NY and London: Routledge, 1992), 309–10. Vintage 'Sheik' condom tins frequently come up for sale and images can be found on the web.

47. On attempts to clone successors to Valentino, see Basinger, J., *Silent Stars* (Hanover, NH: Wesleyan University Press, 2000), 303 ff.

48. On Novello, see Williams, *Ivor Novello, Screen Idol* (London: BFI Publishing, 2003), 11–19; Webb, Paul, *Ivor Novello: Portrait of a Star* (London: Haus Books, 2005).

49. Pitts, M. and Hoffman, F. (eds), *The Rise of the Crooners: Gene Austin, Russ Columbo, Bing Crosby, Nick Lucas, Johnny Marvin and Rudy Vallée* (Lanham, MD: Scarecrow Press, 2001). See esp. introduction by Ian Whitcomb, 'The Coming of the Crooners'.

50. Ibid.

51. Gellhorn, M., 'Rudy Vallée: God's Gift to Us Girls', *The New Republic*, 7 August 1929, 310–11.

52. Ibid., 311.

53. Ibid., 311: 'He is young, he is handsome, and tenderly, coaxingly he sings love-songs to every romance-silly female in these U.S.A.'
54. Lanza, J. and Penna, D., *Russ Columbo and the Crooner Mystique* (Los Angeles, CA: Feral House, 2002), 2, *passim*.
55. Simpson, P., *The Rough Guide to Cult Pop* (London: Haymarket/Penguin, 2003), 315.
56. Vinen, R., *National Service: A Generation in Uniform, 1945–1963* (London: Allen Lane, 2014).
57. Mankowitz, W., *Make me an Offer, Expresso Bongo and Other Stories* (London: Hutchinson Educational, 1961). The original story *Expresso Bongo* by Wolf Mankowitz and Julian More was published by Ace Books in 1960; first produced on stage 1958 and filmed in 1959.
58. Mankowitz, *Make Me an Offer*, 74.
59. Crowther, Bosley, New York Times, 13 April 1960, http://www.nytimes.com/movie/review, accessed 18 August 2015.
60. Mankowitz, *Make Me an Offer*, 87.
61. Rogan, J., *Starmakers and Svengalis* (London: Futura, 1988) has a useful chapter on Larry Parnes; see also 'Mr Parnes, Shillings and Pence', *Rock History*, October 2012, http://www.rockhistory.co.uk/cd-parnes-shillings-pence/, accessed 18 August 2015.
62. Rogan, *Starmakers and Svengalis*, 20.
63. Ibid. See also interview with Larry Parnes on Billy Fury website, http://www.billyfury.com/parnes/index.htm, accessed 18 August 2015.
64. National Film Board of Canada, https://www.nfb.ca/film/lonely_boy, accessed 18 August 2015.
65. See notes on *Privilege* on Peter Watkins's website, http://pwatkins.mnsi.net/privilege.htm; also notes on Watkins on BFI *Screenonline*, http://www.screenonline.org.uk/, both accessed 18 August 2015.
66. Whipple, A., 'Speaking for Whom? The 1971 Festival of Light and the Search for "the Silent Majority"', *Contemporary British History* 214/3 (2010): 319–39.
67. On Colonel Parker see (*inter alia*), Nash, Alanna, *The Colonel: The Extraordinary Story of Colonel Tom Parker and Elvis Presley* (London: Aurum, 2003).
68. Ibid., 125.
69. Ibid., 128, 149.
70. First issue of *Roxy*, 15 March 1958, in newspaper collection, British Library.
71. *Boyfriend*, October 1959, no. 2, British Library.
72. *Boyfriend*, May 1959, no 2.
73. *Boyfriend*, June 1959.
74. http://www.shopelvis.com/, accessed 2 August 2016.
75. http://jamesdean.com/store/, accessed 20 August 2015.
76. Card Corporation, US, https://www.card.com/james-dean, accessed 20 August 2015.

77. Sir Dirk Bogarde, obituary in *The Telegraph*, 10 May 1999, http://www.telegraph.co.uk/news/obituaries/7606375/Sir-Dirk-Bogarde.html, accessed 20 August 2015.

78. Vieira, M., *Hurrell's Hollywood Portraits: The Chapman Collection* (New York, NY: Harry N. Abrams, 1997), 175–6; Dyhouse, C., *Glamour: Women, History, Feminism* (London: Zed Books, 2010), 47.

79. Basinger, 'Disillusionment: Tyrone Power', in the same author's *Star Machine* (New York, NY: Vintage Books, 2009), 142–79.

80. 'Mr Frankie Vaughan in Startime', *The Times*, 31 March 1959, The Times Digital Archive, www.gale.cengage.co.uk, accessed 3 August 2016.

81. Ibid.

82. British Film Institute (BFI), Michael Brooke's *Screenonline* entry for *Stardust*, http://www.screenonline.org.uk/film/id/495155/, accessed 20 August 2015.

83. Hardy, Rebecca, 'Thrice-married David Essex on the emotional turmoil being a 70s pin-up caused – and why it still dogs him today', Mailonline, http://www.dailymail.co.uk/femail/article-2518842/David-Essex-emotional-turmoil-70s-pin-caused.html, 6 December 2013, accessed 20 August 2015.

84. Laurie, P., *The Teenage Revolution* (London: Anthony Blond, 1965), 54–5.

85. Ibid.

86. Ibid., 154.

87. Dyhouse, *Girl Trouble: Panic and Progress in the History of Young Women* (London: Zed Books, 2013), 78, 155–7; see also Jackson, C. and Tinkler, P., '"Ladettes" and "Modern Girls": "Troublesome" Young Femininities', *Sociological Review* 55/2 (2007): 251–72.

88. Laurie, *Teenage Revolution*, 154.

89. Goodman, M., 'Cosmo's Playboy', *Cosmopolitan*, April 1972.

90. Ibid.

91. http://www.fabioinc.com/; see also Rayner, J., 'Absolutely Fabio', *Observer*, 5 April 2009, http://www.theguardian.com/lifeandstyle/2009/apr/05/fabio-lanzoni, both accessed 20 August 2015.

92. Any image search will yield riches, but see esp. Davies, M., 'These Hilariously Outdated Fabio Bookcovers will Make your Day', *Jezebel*, 6 December 2013, http://jezebel.com/these-hilariously-outdated-fabio-book-covers-will-make-512731063, accessed 20 August 2015.

93. Lyall, S., 'Fabio; Please, Judge the Book by its Cover' *New York Times*, 23 September 1993, http://www.nytimes.com/1993/09/23/garden/on-location-with-fabio-please-judge-the-book-by-its-cover.html, accessed 20 August 2015.

94. Waller, D., *The Perfect Man: The Muscular Life and Times of Eugen Sandow, Victorian Strongman* (Brighton: Victorian Secrets, 2011).

95. Ibid., 9.

96. David Gandy's image advertised Dolce & Gabbana's perfume 'Light Blue' from 2007; David Beckham is associated with a range of perfumes, for men and also for women. The fragrances for men include 'Intimacy' and 'Instinct'.

## Chapter 4

1. See American Film Institute website, http://www.afi.com/100Years/songs. aspx, accessed 20 August 2015.
2. Oxford English Dictionary, digital version, http://oed.com,entry for Prince Charming, accessed 10 November 2013.
3. 'Phases of City Life', *New York Times*, 13 September 1891, http://nytimes.com, accessed 10 October 2013.
4. 'From Her Point of View', *New York Times*, 21 December 1890, http://nytimes. com, accessed 10 October 2013.
5. There are collections of Nelson memorabilia in the Royal Naval Museum, Portsmouth, in Norwich Castle Museum, and in the Norfolk Nelson Museum, Great Yarmouth. Collections of Wellington memorabilia are held in Apsley House and the Wellington Arch Museum, London. Many local museums hold memorabilia of these two Victorian figures, and items crop up regularly at auctions, fetching high prices today. In July 2015 a cloak allegedly worn by the Duke at Waterloo and given by him to Lady Caroline Lamb, following a brief affair, was sold by Sotheby's for some £38,000 (£47,500 including premium). It was purchased by the National Army Museum, http://www.nam.ac.uk/, accessed 3 August 2016. On Nelson's appeal to women and the ways in which he was marketed as a sex object see Williams, K., 'Nelson and Women: Marketing, Representation and the Female Consumer', in Cannadine, D., *Admiral Lord Nelson: Context and Legacy* (New York, NY and Basingstoke: Palgrave Macmillan, 2005), 67–89.
6. Carlyle, T., *On Heroes, Hero-Worship and the Heroic in History* (London: James Fraser, 1841).
7. Williams, 'Nelson and Women'.
8. See for instance Gaskell, E.C., *The Life of Charlotte Brontë* (London: Smith Elder and Co., 1957), 58, 94, 110; Alexander, C., 'Charlotte Brontë's "Anecdotes of the Duke of Wellington"', *Brontë Studies* 35/3 (November 2010): 208–14.
9. Gaskell, *Life of Charlotte Brontë*, 94.
10. Lemuel Francis Abbott (*c.*1760–1802) painted many portraits of Nelson. Two of the best known images are the National Portrait Gallery, NPG 394, http://www.npg.org.uk/collections, accessed 21 August 2015, painted around 1797, and the half-length portrait of around 1800 in the National Maritime Museum in Greenwich (BHC 2889), http://prints.rmg.co.uk/art/522225/Rear-Admiral-Horatio-Nelson-1st-Viscount-Nelson-1758-1805, accessed 3 August 2016; and the National Portrait Gallery's painting of Napoleon by Sir William Beechey, NPG 5798, from 1800.
11. The National Maritime Museum has a replica of Nelson's diamond chelengk (JEW0367), http://collections.rmg.co.uk/collections/objects/36519.html. The original was stolen from the Museum in 1950, http://hansard.millbanksystems.

com/lords/1951/jun/26/theft-of-nelson-relic, both accessed 2 August 2016. The chelengk as depicted by Lemuel Abbott is rather impressionistic.

12. Kauffmann, C.F. (rev. Susan Jenkins) *Catalogue of Paintings in the Wellington Museum, Apsley House* (London: English Heritage in association with Paul Holberton Publishing, 2009), 166–7. This catalogue has a reproduction of Lawrence's portrait (collection no. 85), https://www.english-heritage.org.uk/content/imported-docs/a-e/apsleyhouseartcatalogue.pdf, accessed 2 August 2016.

13. Conan Doyle, Sir Arthur, *The Complete Brigadier Gerard* (Edinburgh: Canongate, 1995), 113.

14. Adrian Adolph Greenberg ('Adrian') short biography, *New York Times*, http://www.nytimes.com/movies/person/79094/Adrian/biography, accessed 21 August 2015; see also Leese, E., *Costume Design in the Movies: An Illustrated Guide to the Work of 157 Great Designers* (Toronto, ON: Dover Publications, 1991), 19.

15. Psychologist J. C. Flügel famously referred to men turning their backs on bright, elaborate clothing at the end of the eighteenth century as 'the great masculine renunciation'. See Flügel, J.C., *The Psychology of Clothes* (London: Hogarth Press, 1930), 111.

16. On Brummel see Kelly, I., *Beau Brummel: The Ultimate Man of Style* (New York, NY: Free Press, 2006).

17. Sir Edwin Landseer, *Queen Victoria and Prince Albert at the Bal Costumé of 12 May 1942*, Royal Collection, Windsor, RCIN 404540.

18. Sir Edwin Landseer, *Windsor Castle in Modern Times; Queen Victoria, Prince Albert and Victoria, Princess Royal*, 1841–43, Royal Collection, Windsor, RCIN 406903.

19. Morris, M.T., *Madam Valentino: The Many Lives of Natacha Rambova* (New York, NY: Abbeville, 1991), 149, 152; Leese, *Costume Design in the Movies*, 47.

20. See OED online entry for 'gallant', www.oed.com, accessed 3 August 2016.

21. Egan, Pierce, *Life in London; or, the Day and Night Scenes of Jerry Hawthorne, Esq. and his elegant friend Corinthian Tom, accompanied by Bob Logic the Oxonian in their Rambles and Sprees through the Metropolis* (London: Sherwood Neely and Jones, Paternoster Row, 1821). There were many editions and imitators of this text.

22. Egan, *Life in London*, 41.

23. Ibid.

24. Egan, *Life in London*, 42.

25. Review in *Photoplay* October 1924, http://www.silentsaregolden.com/monsieurbeaucairereview.html, accessed 24 August 2015.

26. Ibid.

27. Leider, E., *Dark Lover: The Life and Death of Rudolph Valentino* (London: Faber & Faber, 2003), 286–9.

28. *Monsieur Don't Care*, 1924, see International Movie Database (IMDB) http://www.imdb.com/title/tt0015146/, accessed 2 August 2016; see also *Mud and*

*Sand*, 1922, (IMDB), http://www.imdb.com/title/tt0013416/, accessed 24 August 2015.

29. *Beau Brummel*, 1924, directed by Harry Beaumont, http://www.imdb.com/title/tt0014702/, accessed 2 August 2016.

30. Jordan, Stephen C., *Hollywood's Original Rat-Pack: The Bards of Bundy Drive* (Plymouth: Scarecrow Press, 2008), 131–2.

31. Morrison, Michael A., *John Barrymore; Shakespearian Actor* (Cambridge: Cambridge University Press, 1997), 131.

32. Heyer, G., *Powder and Patch* (London: Random House, 2011), 33.

33. Heyer, *Powder and Patch*, 35: 'Mastery thrilled her' although 'a mastery that offered to take all, giving nothing, annoyed her'.

34. Aiken Hodge, J., *The Private World of Georgette Heyer* (London: Arrow Books, 2006), 49 and *passim*.

35. Comment posted by Jodi Ralston, 14 November 2013, http://www.goodreads.com/book/show/311200.Powder_And_Patch (accessed 24 August 2015).

36. Aiken Hodge, *op. cit.* For a detailed exploration of Georgette Heyer's 'Mark I' and 'Mark II' heroes see also Warner, Celeste R., 'Heyer's Heroes: An Investigation into Georgette Heyer and her Literary "Mark" on the Regency Hero', MA thesis, University of Waikato, New Zealand, 2010.

37. Heyer, *These Old Shades* (London: Arrow Books, 2004), 1–2.

38. Heyer, *Regency Buck* (London: Arrow books, 2004), 12.

39. Egan, *Life in London*, chap. II.

40. Ibid.

41. The Four Horse Club was founded in 1808 and membership was highly select. See Kloester, J., *Georgette Heyer's Regency World* (London: Random House, 2011), 174. For more detail see Somerset, Henry Charles Fitzroy, 8th Duke of Beaufort, *Driving* (London: Longmans Green, 1889).

42. Heyer, *The Nonesuch* (London: Arrow Books, 2005), 45.

43. Heyer, *Regency Buck*, 232 ff.

44. Heyer, *The Nonesuch*, 99.

45. Cooper, Jilly, *Riders* (London: Arlington, 1985), *Rivals* (London: Bantam, 1988), and *Polo* (London: Bantam, 1991).

46. Brontë, C., *Jane Eyre* (London: Wordsworth Editions, 1992), 100.

47. Heyer, *The Nonesuch*, 175 ff.

48. 'Once Upon a Dream', a hit single from *Play It Cool* (1962), musical directed by Michael Winner.

49. *The Glass Slipper*, directed by Charles Walters, 1955, http://www.imdb.com/title/tt0048124/, accessed 2 August 2016.

50. *Cinderella Love*, published bi-monthly by Ziff Davis and later St John's Publishing Company, New York. See (*inter alia*) http://digitalcomicmuseum.com/index.php?cid=1156, accessed 24 August 2015; Grand Comics Database, http://www.comics.org/, accessed 17 November 2015.

51. Advertisement for Shell Petroleum from *Life Magazine*, 2 December 1946, reproduced by Sally Edelstein at http://envisioningtheamericandream.com/2012/06/01/queen-for-a-day/, accessed 24 August 2015. Thanks to Sally Edelstein for this information.

52. Revlon '"Cinderella's Pumpkin" Once Upon a Lifetime's Colour', reproduced at http://www.cosmeticsandskin.com/companies/revlon.php, accessed 24 August 2015.

53. Dyhouse, C., *Glamour: Women, History, Feminism* (London: Zed Books, 2010), 87.

54. Arch, N. and Marschner, J., *Royal Wedding Dresses* (London: Historic Royal Palaces, c.2011).

55. http://www.royal.gov.uk/HMTheQueen/TheQueenandspecialanniversaries/DiamondAnniversary/60facts.aspx, accessed 2 August 2016.

56. James, Robert Rhodes (ed.) *Chips: The Diaries of Sir Henry Channon* (London: Weidenfeld and Nicolson, 1967), 425, 438.

57. Ibid., 471.

58. Ibid., 475.

59. Ibid., 478.

60. Steedman, C., *Landscape for a Good Woman* (London: Virago, 1986), 11, 16.

61. Ibid., 9.

62. Woodhead, L., *War Paint: Elizabeth Arden and Helena Rubinstein, Their Lives, Their Times, Their Rivalry* (London: Virago, 2004), 280–2.

63. Ibid., 229–30, 272–3.

64. Heyman, C. David, *Poor Little Rich Girl: The Life and Legend of Barbara Hutton* (London: Hutchinson, 1985).

65. Ibid., 45, 304–5.

66. Ibid.

67. Eldridge, M., *In Search of a Prince: My Life with Barbara Hutton* (London: Sidgwick and Jackson, 1988).

68. *Woman's Own*, articles on Rita Hayworth, 11 and 18 September 1952.

69. See (*inter alia*) Haugland, H. Kristina, *Grace Kelly: Icon of Style to Royal Bride* (Philadelphia, PA and London: Philadelphia Museum of Art and Yale University Press, 2006).

70. Garber, M., *Vested Interests; Cross Dressing and Cultural Anxiety* (New York, NY and London: Routledge, 1992), 357, 359.

71. 'Mr Liberace's First London Concert: Fancy Dress at the Festival Hall', *The Times* (London, England) 2 October 1956, 3, The Times Digital Archive, Web 15 February 1915, www.gale.cengage.co.uk, accessed 3 August 2016.

72. Ibid.

73. Ibid. The comment is worth quoting in full, it is so ambivalent. 'With all his finery and his almost natural strawberries and cream complexion, he is a quiet, shy little man, ready to dwell at length on his early life and his indebtedness to God and the Public. He has a quiet sense of humour and

is ready to laugh at himself. He did not swank or slobber, or flash diamond rings shaped like grand pianos at his admirers.'

74. The two pieces by 'Cassandra' (William Connor) were published in the *Daily Mirror* on 26 September and 18 October 1956.

75. Ibid.; on the affair generally see Pyron, Darden Asbury, *Liberace, An American Boy* (Chicago, IL: University of Chicago Press, 2000), extracts from Connor's articles reproduced, 225, 226. See also Barker, Revel, with a Foreword by Baird, Vera, *Crying All the Way to the Bank: Liberace versus Cassandra and Daily Mirror* (Brighton: Revel Barker, 2009).

76. *The Times* followed the case in detail. See (*inter alia*), 'High Court of Justice', *The Times* (London, England) 9 June, 14. See also 11 June and 16 June 1959, The Times Digital Archive, Web 15 February 2015, www.gale.cengage.co.uk, accessed 3 August 2016.

77. Quoted in *The Times*, 9 June, *loc. cit.*

78. Pyron, *Liberace*, 226 ff, 229–30 and *passim*.

79. 'Mr Liberace Finds the Right Note' *The Times* (London, England) 26 September 1956. The Times Digital Archive, Web 15 February 2015, www. gale.cengage.co.uk, accessed 3 August 2016.

80. 'High Court of Justice', *The Times* (London, England) 9 June: 14 The Times Digital Archive, Web 15 February 2015, www.gale.cengage.co.uk, accessed 3 August 2016.

81. Garber, *Vested Interests*, 363.

82. Pyron, *Liberace*, 156, 170, 193.

83. There are useful obituaries in the *New York Times* (by Richard Severo), 22 May 2000, http://www.nytimes.com/2000/05/22/books/barbara-cartland-98-best-selling-author-who-prized-old-fashioned-romance-dies.html, and in *The Telegraph*, 22 May 2000, http://www.telegraph.co.uk/news/obituaries/culture-obituaries/books-obituaries/1366803/Dame-Barbara-Cartland.html, both accessed 25 August 2015. See also Cloud, H., *Barbara Cartland: Crusader in Pink* (Long Preston, Yorkshire: Magna Print Books, 1979). For a more academic approach see Sales, R., 'The Loathsome Lord and the Disdainful Dame: Byron, Cartland and the Regency Romance', in Wilson, F. (ed.), *Byromania: Portraits of the Artist in Nineteenth- and Twentieth-Century Culture* (London: Palgrave Macmillan, 1998), 166–83.

84. I haven't been able to trace the origin of this quote but it is widely reproduced, see for instance, 'Clive James: 30 Classic Quotes' in *The Telegraph*, 11 May 2015, http://www.telegraph.co.uk/culture/tvandradio/9347061/Clive-James-30-classic-quotes.html, accessed 25 August 2015.

85. Cloud, *Barbara Cartland*, 21–2.

86. Ibid., 53, 57.

87. Ibid., 56.

88. Ibid., 80.

89. Ibid., 50–1.

90. Ibid., 54; Sales, 'The Loathsome Lord'.
91. Cartland, B., *I Search for Rainbows* (London: Hutchinson and Co., 1967), 94–5.
92. Ibid.
93. Cartland, *The Passion and the Flower* (London: Pan Books, 1978), 28–30.
94. Cloud, *Barbara Cartland*, 23.
95. See, for instance, https://www.pinterest.com/mirandaeast37/barbara-cartlands-covers/, accessed 2 August 2016.
96. For an early discussion of women's competing roles in work and family in the 1950s see Myrdal, A. and Klein, V., *Women's Two Roles: Home and Work* (London: Routledge and Kegan Paul, 1956); a more recent study is Spencer, S., *Gender, Work and Education in Britain in the 1950s* (Basingstoke: Palgrave Macmillan, 2005).
97. Novels by Penelope Mortimer focusing on domestic entrapment include *The Bright Prison* (London: Michael Joseph, 1956), *Daddy's Gone A-Hunting* (London: Michael Joseph, 1965), and *The Pumpkin Eater* (London: Hutchinson, 1962) which was made into a successful film in 1964.
98. Haase, D. (ed.), *Fairy Tales and Feminism: New Approaches* (Detroit, MI: Wayne State University Press, 2004).
99. For instance, Rosemary Stones' compilation, *More to Life than Mr Right: Stories for Young Feminists* (London: Piccadilly Press, 1985).
100. 'Cinders Jilts Prince Charming', *Daily Mirror*, 30 October 1987, digital archive, www.ukpressonline.co.uk, accessed 23 February 2015.
101. Ibid.
102. Canby, V., 'Screen: Glass Slipper into Sow's Ear', *New York Times*, 5 November 1976, http://www.nytimes.com/movie/review, accessed 25 August 2015.
103. Ibid.
104. Chamberlain, R., *Shattered Love: A Memoir* (New York: Harper Collins, 2003), 55; see also photographs and comments on http://www.richardchamberlain.net, accessed 25 August 2015.
105. Perrick, P., 'A-Level or Glass Slipper?', *The Times* (London, England), 13 June 1983, www.gale.cengage.co.uk, accessed 3 August 2016.
106. See for instance Bastin, Giselle, 'There were Three of us in this Biography so it was a Bit Crowded: The Biography of a Suitor and the Rhetoric of Romance in Diana: Her Story', *Journal of Popular Romance Studies* 1/1 (2010), http://jprstudies.org/tag/princess-diana/, accessed 25 August 2015.
107. 'Adam Ant', born Stuart Leslie Goddard, see Ant, A., *Stand and Deliver: The Autobiography* (London: Pan, 2007).
108. Lodge, G., 'Cinderella Review—Kenneth Branagh's perky, pretty cupcake of a fairytale', *The Guardian*, 13 February 2015.
109. Cook, H., *The Long Sexual Revolution: English Women, Sex and Contraception 1800–1975* (Oxford: Oxford University Press, 2004).
110. *The Princess Bride*, 1987, directed by Rob Reiner, based on book by William Goldman.

111. *Into the Woods* (2014), Disney film version of musical based on Broadway production of the same name by Stephen Sondheim and James Lapine, directed by Rob Marshall.

## Chapter 5

1. du Maurier, D., 'The Menace', in *The Breaking Point*, short stories with an introduction by Sally Beauman (London: Virago, 2009), 202.
2. Ibid., 203.
3. George du Maurier (1834–96) was a cartoonist for *Punch* magazine and a writer best known for *Trilby* (1894), the story of which centred on the relationship between a young girl and a Jewish rogue, Svengali, who hypnotizes and seduces her. Under his control she becomes a famous singer. The novel was adapted for the stage and there have been many film versions. G. du Maurier's earlier novel, *Peter Ibbetson* (1891) was also a modest success and adapted for stage and screen.
4. Forster, M., *Daphne du Maurier* (London: Arrow Books, 2007), see esp. Part One, 'The Golden Girl, 1907-1932', and 4–7. D. du Maurier's short story, 'The Matinée Idol' portrays Gerald as an affectionate, demanding man for whom life was always a matter of 'pretending to be someone else'. D. du Maurier, *The Rebecca Notebook and Other Memories* (London: Gollancz, 1981), 72 ff.
5. Forster, *Daphne du Maurier*, 8.
6. Douglass, P., *Lady Caroline Lamb: A Biography* (New York, NY and Basingstoke: Palgrave Macmillan, 2004), 104.
7. Cartland, B., *We Danced All Night* (London: Hutchinson, 1970), 16.
8. Cloud, H., *Barbara Cartland: Crusader in Pink* (Long Preston, Yorkshire: Magna Print Books, 1979), 21.
9. Heyer, G., *Devil's Cub* (first published London: Heinemann 1932; this edn London: Arrow Books, 2004).
10. Heyer, *Devil's Cub*, 198.
11. See, for instance, Georgette Heyer Fans' Discussion, 'Who is Your favourite Hero in a Heyer Novel and Why?' Goodreads.com, http://www.goodreads.com/topic/show/903940-who-is-your-favorite-hero-in-a-heyer-novel-why, accessed 26 August 2015.
12. Ness, Mari 'Refining the Rake as Hero: Georgette Heyer's *Devil's Cub*', posted 16 October 2012, http://www.tor.com/2012/10/16/refining-the-rake-as-hero-devils-cub-by-georgette-heyer/, accessed 3 August 2016.
13. Heyer, G., *Venetia* (first published London: Heinemann, 1958; this edn London: Arrow Books, 2004), 22.
14. Dyhouse, C., *Girl Trouble; Panic and Progress in the History of Young Women* (London: Zed Books, 2013), 124–5.
15. Heyer, *Venetia*, 32–3.
16. Ibid., 29.

17. Ibid., 30.

18. Ibid., 108.

19. Ibid.

20. Ibid., 64.

21. Ibid., 94.

22. British Government Art Collection, George Gordon Byron by Thomas Phillips, 1814. See http://artuk.org/discover/artworks/george-gordon-byron-6th-baron-byron-157543, accessed 3 August 2016; see also Nation.al Portrait gallery, http://www.npg.org.uk/collections/search/portrait/mw00991/George-Gordon-Byron-6th-Baron-Byron, accessed 3 August 2016. The Albanian costume is now in Bowood House, Wiltshire. Art historian Sir David Piper quipped that the Phillips portrait looked like Lord Byron as played by Errol Flynn; MacCarthy, F., *Byron: Life and Legend* (London: Faber & Faber, 2003), 216.

23. For Byron's letter to his mother (from Prevesa, 12 November 1809) describing the clothes, see Elsie, R., *Texts and Documents of Albanian History*, http://www.albanianhistory.net/1809_Byron/index.html, accessed 3 August 2016.

24. Aronson, T., *Victoria and Disraeli; The Making of a Romantic Partnership* (London: Thistle Publishing, 2014); See also Crewe, T., 'Disraeli's Flowery History', https://history.blog.gov.uk/2013/04/29/disraelis-flowery-history/, accessed 28 August 2015.

25. Aronson, *Victoria and Disraeli*, 116, 162 186, 248, and *passim*.

26. Ibid., 301–5.

27. Ibid., 303.

28. James, H., *Daniel Deronda: A Conversation*, reprinted in Leavis, F.R., *The Great Tradition* (New York: Doubleday, 1954).

29. Basu, Shrabani, *Victoria and Abdul: The True Story of the Queen's Closest Confidant* (Stroud: The History Press, 2011).

30. Laurits Regner Tuxen (1853–1927), oil portrait of The Munshi Abdul Karim, signed and dated 1887, in Royal Collection, Osborne House (RCIN 403836), https://www.royalcollection.org.uk/collection/403836/the-munshi-abdul-karim-1863-1909; Rudolf Swoboda (1859–1914) oil portrait of Abdul Karim, signed and dated 1888, Osborne House (RCIN 403831), https://www.royalcollection.org.uk/collection/403831/the-munshi-abdul-karim-1863-1909; Baron Heinrich von Angeli (1840–1925) signed portrait of Munshi dated 1890, also in Durbar Corridor, Osborne House (RCIN 406915), https://www.royalcollection.org.uk/collection/406915/the-munshi-abdul-karim-1863-1909, all accessed 28 August 2015.

31. Basu, *Victoria and Abdul*, 2, 19.

32. *Peg's Paper*, 15 April 1939.

33. *Peg's Paper*, 1 April 1939.

34. Said, Edward W., *Orientalism* (New York: Vintage, 1979). Feminist scholars have queried and amplified Said's interpretations as they relate to women. See (for example), Melman, B., *Women's Orients: English Women and the Middle*

East 1718–1918: Sexuality, Religion and Work (Ann Arbor, MI: University of Michigan Press, 1992); Lewis, R., Gendering Orientalism: Race, Femininity and Representation (London: Routledge, 2013).

35. Teo, Hsu-Ming, Desert Passions: Orientalism and Romance Novels (Austin, TX: University of Texas Press, 2012).

36. Ibid., 3.

37. Harum Scarum, 1965, directed by Gene Nelson, http://www.imdb.com/title/tt0059255/, accessed 3 August 2016.

38. Winspear, V., Palace of the Peacocks (London: Mills and Boon, 1969).

39. There is a huge amount of material relating to Violet Winspear in the Mills and Boon Archive at the University of Reading.

40. Teo, Desert Passions, 203 ff., 214–16.

41. Ibid., 10, chap. 9.

42. Jordan, P., Falcon's Prey (London: Mills and Boon, 1981).

43. Conran, S., Lace (London: Sidgwick and Jackson, 1982). The book was notorious for a scene involving goldfish abuse.

44. Hughes, Sarah, 'Shirley Conran's Lace is a Feminist Bonkbuster', The Guardian, 11 June 2012, http://www.theguardian.com/books/the-womens-blog-with-jane-martinson/2012/jun/11/shirley-conran-lace-feminist-bonkbuster, accessed 3 August 2016.

45. See Harlequin Kimani website: http://www.harlequin.com/, accessed 3 August 2016.

46. Miyao, Daisuke, Sessue Hayakawa: Silent Cinema and Transnational Stardom (Durham, NC: Duke University Press, 2007).

47. Hull, E.M., The Sheik (London: Virago, 2002), 204.

48. Blanch, L., The Wilder Shores of Love (first published 1954; this edn New York: Carroll & Graf, 2002).

49. See Blanch, The Wilder Shores, chap. 2; also Lovell, Mary S., A Scandalous Life: The Biography of Jane Digby (London: Fourth Estate, 1998).

50. Burroughs, Edgar Rice, Tarzan of the Apes (first appeared in magazine form, then as a book published by A. C. McClurg in 1914. For more detailed publishing history see http://www.erbzine.com/mag4/0483.html, accessed 1 September 2015). The first screen version was a silent film directed by Scott Sidney and starring Elmo Lincoln in 1918.

51. Copy of Louise Gerard, Jungle Love: A Tropical Tangle, with original dustjacket (n. d., c.1924) in Mills and Boon collection at University of Reading.

52. King Kong, original film 1933, starring Fay Wray, directed by Merian C. Cooper and Ernest B. Schoedsack, with screenplay/story idea and input by Edgar Wallace.

53. A good example would be the film version (1959) of Tennessee Williams's play, Suddenly, Last Summer, starring Elizabeth Taylor and Montgomery Clift. Sebastian's garden speaks volumes about his sexuality.

54. See (*inter alia*) Boyle, Sheila Tully and Bunie, Andrew, *Paul Robeson: The Years of Promise and Achievement* (Boston, MA: University of Massachusetts Press, 2005), 254–60.

55. Ibid., 254. See also Gordon, L., *Nancy Cunard, Heiress, Muse, Political Idealist* (New York, NY: Columbia University Press, 2007), 149 ff; Moynagh, M. (ed.) *Nancy Cunard: Essays on Race and Empire* (New York, NY: Broadview Press, 2002).

56. Breese, C., *Hutch* (London: Bloomsbury, 1999), 45–6, 105, 111–13.

57. See, for instance, Breese, *Hutch*, 199–200.

58. Williams, S., *Colour Bar: The Triumph of Seretse Khama and his Nation* (London: Penguin, 2007).

59. In Britain, *Sapphire* (1959, directed by Basil Dearden) and *Flame in the Streets* (1961, directed by Roy Ward Baker), explored the impact of the 'colour bar' on personal relationships.

60. Lord Byron, *The Corsair: A Tale* (London: John Murray, 1814), l, ix, l. 225. On pirate history and representation of pirates see (*inter alia*) Cordingley, D., *Under the Black Flag: The Romance and Reality of Life among the Pirates* (London: Random House, 2006); Rennie, N., *Treasure Neverland: Real and Imaginary Pirates* (Oxford: Oxford University Press, 2013).

61. *Captain Blood*, 1935, Warner Brothers production directed by Michael Curtiz and starring Errol Flynn and Olivia de Havilland.

62. du Maurier, D. *Frenchman's Creek* (London: Gollancz, 1941). The name Jean-Benoit Aubery is borrowed from George du Maurier's *Peter Ibbetson*.

63. Meikle, D., *Johnny Depp: A Kind of Illusion* (London: Reynolds and Hearn, 2004), 324, 346.

64. For representations, and interesting stories about Blackbeard (Edward Teach) see http://www.golden-age-of-piracy.com/infamous-pirates/edward-teach.php, accessed 3 August 2016.

65. British Library website information about the history of the Newgate Calendar, http://www.bl.uk/learning/histcitizen/21cc/crime/media1/calendar1/facts1/facts.html, accessed 2 September 2015.

66. White, Barbara, 'Duval, Claude, d.1670', *Oxford Dictionary of National Biography* (Oxford: Oxford University Press, 2004), online edition, January 2008, http://www.oxforddnb.com/view/article/8333, accessed 2 September 2015. Less reliably, see http://www.stand-and-deliver.org.uk/highwaymen/new gate_duval.htm, accessed 2 September 2015.

67. Heyer, G., *Black Moth* (first published 1921; this edn London: Arrow Books, 2004).

68. Winsor, K., *Forever Amber* (first published 1944; this edn London: Penguin, 2002), 151, 168.

69. King-Hall, M., *Life and Death of The Wicked Lady Skelton* (first published London: Peter Davies, 1944; this edn *The Wicked Lady*, London: May Fair Books, 1961). Screen version of *The Wicked Lady*, Gainsborough Studios, 1945,

directed by Leslie Arliss and starring Margaret Lockwood, James Mason, and Patricia Roc. The film was hugely successful, attracting an audience of some 18.4 million.

70. *Forever Amber* (film) 1947, directed by Otto Preminger and starring Linda Darnell and Cornel Wilde.

71. Cartland, B., *Cupid Rides Pillion* (London: Arrow Books, 1969), film *The Lady and the Highwayman* (made for television) directed by John Hough, 1989, starring Hugh Grant and Lysette Anthony.

72. Famous women pirates included Anne Bonney and Mary Read. See Cordingley, D., *Seafaring Women: Adventures of Pirate Queens, Female Stowaways and Sailors' Wives* (London: Random House, 2007).

73. Ibid., see also film, *The Spanish Main* (1945), directed by Frank Borzage and starring Paul Henreid and Maureen O'Hara.

74. Frayling, C., *Vampyres: Lord Byron to Count Dracula* (London: Faber & Faber, 1992); McConnell-Scott, A., *The Vampyre Family: Passion, Envy and the Curse of Byron* (London: Canongate, 2013).

75. Ibid., see also Frayling, 'Dracula: The Man Behind the Cape', *The Guardian*, 4 May 2012, http://www.theguardian.com/books/2012/may/04/dracula-man-behind-cape-christopher-frayling, accessed 3 August 2016.

76. Dyer, L., 'P is for Paranormal, Still', *Publishers' Weekly*, 24 May 2010, http://www.publishersweekly.com/pw/by-topic/new-titles/adult-announcements/article/43272-p-is-for-paranormal-still.html, accessed 2 September 2015.

77. Rice, Anne, *Interview with the Vampire* (New York, NY: Alfred A. Knopf, 1976) was first in the series of the Vampire Chronicles, adapted for film in 1994.

78. Film version of *Dark Shadows*, directed by Tim Burton and starring Johnny Depp as Barnabas Collins, 2012; *People* magazine 'Sexiest Man Alive' votes 2003, 2009, http://www.people.com/people/package/article/0,,20315920_20320494,00.html, accessed 3 August 2016.

79. See, for instance, Gold, Tanya, 'Why have teenage girls been bitten by the Edward Cullen bug to devour the Twilight novels?' *The Guardian*, 13 November 2009, http://www.theguardian.com/books/2009/nov/13/twilight-vampires-teenage-girls, accessed 3 August 2016.

80. 'Twilight, Take Me Away; Teenage Vampires and the Mothers who Love Them' *New York* Magazine, 15 November 2009, http://nymag.com/movies/features/62027/; see also Twilight Moms Facebook and Twitter pages, accessed 7 September 2015.

81. Gold, 'Teenage girls', 2.

82. Stephen King, interview with Emma Brockes published in *The Guardian*, 21 September 2013, http://www.theguardian.com/books/2013/sep/21/stephen-king-shining-sequel-interview, accessed 3 August 2016.

## Chapter 6

1. Langhamer, C., *The English in Love: The Intimate Story of an Emotional Revolution* (Oxford: Oxford University Press, 2013).

2. Ibid, 37–8, and *passim*; see also Claire Langhamer's 'Afterword' in Harris, A. and Willem Jones, T. (eds), *Love and Romance in Britain, 1918–1970* (Basingstoke: Palgrave Macmillan, 2015), 245–52.

3. Oxford English Dictionary, digital version, http://www.oed.com/view/Entry/292748?redirectedFrom=soul-mate#eid, accessed 8 September 2015.

4. On classical ideas about soulmates in Aristophanes and Plato see, for instance, Dover, K.J., 'Aristophanes' Speech in Plato's *Symposium*', *Journal of Hellenic Studies* 86 (1966): 41–50.

5. Eliot, G., *Adam Bede* (New York, NY: Harper and Brothers, 1860), 447.

6. Federico, A., *Idol of Suburbia: Marie Corelli and Late Victorian Literary Culture* (Charlottesville, VA: University of Virginia Press, 2000); Ransom, T., *The Mysterious Miss Corelli: Queen of Victorian Bestsellers* (Stroud: Sutton Publishing, 1999).

7. See material on Corelli by Whalen, K., at Bryn Mawr, 'A Novel Life: The Marie Corelli Collection', which includes an evocative postcard image of Marie in her gondola on the River Avon at Stratford, http://www.brynmawr.edu/library/mirabile/mirabile2/corelli.html, accessed 8 September 2015; Corelli now has a dedicated website, http://mariecorelli.org.uk/, accessed 8 September 2015.

8. Corelli, M. *The Sorrows of Satan, or The Strange Experiences of One Geoffrey Tempest, Millionaire*, is said to have broken all previous sales records when first published by Methuen in 1895: it had gone through sixty-eight editions by 1936.

9. Federico, *Idol of Suburbia*, 139.

10. du Maurier, G., *Peter Ibbetson* (New York: Harper, 1891), available at Internet Archive https://archive.org/details/peteribbetsonwi00maurgoog, 249, accessed 8 September 2015.

11. Ibid., 415.

12. Kennedy, M., *The Constant Nymph* (London: Heinemann, 1924).

13. Jordan, Stephen C., *Hollywood's Original Rat-Pack: The Bards of Bundy Drive* (Plymouth: Scarecrow Press, 2008), 131–2.

14. *Forever*, film version of *Peter Ibbetson* (1921), directed by George Fitzmaurice, starring Wallace Reid and Elsie Ferguson, based on G. du Maurier's novel and stage adaptation by John Nathaniel Raphael; 1935 film version of *Peter Ibbetson* directed by Henry Hathaway starring Gary Cooper and Ann Harding.

15. Film versions of *The Constant Nymph*; 1928 version directed by Adrian Brunel and starring Ivor Novello and Mabel Poulton, http://www.screenonline.org.uk/film/id/506343/index.html, accessed 8 September 2015; 1933 version directed by Basil Dean and starring Brian Ahern and Victoria Hopper, http://

www.imdb.com/title/tt0024998/; and 1943 version directed by Edmund Golding and starring Charles Boyer and Joan Fontaine, http://www.imdb.com/title/tt0035751/, both accessed 8 September 2015.

16. On Novello generally see Williams, M., *Ivor Novello: Screen Idol* (London: BFI Publishing, 2003); see also Macnab, G., *Searching for Stars: Stardom and Screen Acting in British Cinema* (London and New York, NY: Cassell, 2000), 34–59.

17. *The Man Without Desire*, directed by Adrian Brunel, 1923, see http://www.screenonline.org.uk/film/id/506532/, accessed 8 September 2015.

18. *The Lodger*, 1926, and *Downhill*, 1927, both directed by Alfred Hitchcock, http://www.screenonline.org.uk/film/id/438120/, accessed 3 August 2016, and http://www.screenonline.org.uk/film/id/437747/, accessed 8 September 2015.

19. Macnab, *Searching for Stars*, 48, 51; see also the same author's 'Homme Fatal' in *The Guardian*, 10 January 2004, http://www.theguardian.com/film/2004/jan/10/1, accessed 3 August 2016.

20. *The Rat* (1925), directed by Graham Cutts and based on a play by Ivor Novello and Constance Collier (under shared pen-name of David L'Estrange), http://www.screenonline.org.uk/film/id/493450/index.html, accessed 8 September 2015; Eileen Ascroft, 'I Deliver a Fan-Letter . . . To the Man who has Won a Million Hearts!' *The Daily Mirror*, 3 November 1937, 14. See also Williams, M., 'War-Torn Dionysus: The Silent Passion of Ivor Novello', in Higson, A. (ed.), *Young and Innocent? The Cinema in Britain 1896–1930* (Exeter: University of Exeter Press, 2002), 256 ff.

21. *The Daily Mirror*, Advert for New Weekly Paper, *Joy*, 10 February 1925, 6.

22. Ibid.

23. Meyers, J., *Gary Cooper: American Hero* (New York, NY: Cooper Square Press, 2001), 131.

24. See, for instance, *New York Times* review by Andre Sennwald, 8 November 1935, http://www.nytimes.com/, accessed 9 September 2015; user reviews on International Movie Database, http://www.imdb.com/title/tt0026866/, accessed 3 August 2016.

25. McCullough, C., *The Thorn Birds* (New York: Harper and Row, 1977).

26. McCullough, *Thorn Birds* (this edn London: Futura, 1980), 71.

27. Ibid, 150.

28. Ibid., 252.

29. Ibid., 354.

30. Chamberlain, R., *Shattered Love: A Memoir* (New York, NY: HarperCollins, 2004).

31. *Suddenly, Last Summer* (1958) directed by Joseph Mankiewicz and starring Montgomery Clift, Elizabeth Taylor and Katharine Hepburn.

32. *Freud: A Secret Passion* (1962). The screenplay was originally by Jean-Paul Sartre but Sartre quarrelled with director John Huston and his name was withdrawn from the credits. There is interesting material in the Huston

family archives, in the James Hardiman Library, NUI Galway, see http://nuiarchives.blogspot.ie/2012/09/huston-sartre-and-freud-scenario. html, accessed 11 September 2015.

33. *Captain Blood* (1935) directed by Michael Curtiz and starring Errol Flynn and Olivia de Havilland.

34. *The Rains Came* (1939) directed by Clarence Brown, starring Tyrone Power and Myrna Loy.

35. Digby, Anne, *The Evolution of British General Practice, 1850–1948* (New York, NY: Oxford University Press, 1999).

36. *Doctor in the House* (1954) see BFI website, Screenonline, http://www. screenonline.org.uk/film/id/457556/, accessed September 11 2015.

37. Harmetz, A., 'Dirk Bogarde, 78, Matinee Idol Turned Serious Actor, Dies', *New York Times*, 9 May 1999, http://www.nytimes.com/1999/05/09/nyregion/dirk-bogarde-78-matinee-idol-turned-serious-actor-dies.html, See also 'Idol of the Odeons', http://dirkbogarde.co.uk/, accessed 11 September 2015.

38. London Weekend Television ran a comedy series, *Doctor in the House*, 1969–70.

39. Faust, Frederick Schiller (Max Brand), first introduced the character Doctor Kildare in a magazine story published in *Cosmopolitan* in 1936. The story, 'Internes Can't Take Money' was the basis of a film of the same name, starring Joel McCrea as *Dr Kildare* and Barbara Stanwyck as Janet Haley, in 1937. See Easton, R. and J. (eds), *The Collected Stories of Max Brand* (Lincoln, NE and London: University of Nebraska Press, 1994).

40. The NBC TV series, *Dr Kildare*, ran from 1961–66 and was produced by MGM Television. The series was highly successful and established Richard Chamberlain as a star.

41. *Emergency Ward Ten* hospital drama series, 1957–65, full cast and details on IMDB, http://www.imdb.com/title/tt0159870/fullcredits/, accessed 11 September 2015.

42. *Casualty*, long-running British medical drama series running on BBC since 1986; *Holby City*, a spin-off from the main series, began in 1999.

43. Douglas, Lloyd C., *Magnificent Obsession* (New York, NY: Houghton Mifflin, 1929); 1935 film of same name, Universal Studios, starring Irene Dunne and Robert Taylor, 1954 version with Jane Wyman and Rock Hudson.

44. *Change of Habit*, 1969 American musical drama directed by William A. Graham and starring Elvis Presley and Mary Tyler Moore.

45. See, for instance, 'Interacting with Autism, *Change of Habit*' http://www. interactingwithautism.com/section/understanding/media/representations/ details/31, accessed 14 September 2015; Mercer, J., 'Coercive Restraint Theories: A Dangerous Alternative Mental Health Intervention', *MedGenMed* 7/3 (2005): 6. Published online, http://www.ncbi.nlm.nih.gov/pmc/articles/ PMC1681667/, accessed 14 September 2015.

46. 'Nurse Janet and the Forty Bachelors', *Romeo*, 21 December 1957.

47. Dixon, Jay, *The Romance Fiction of Mills and Boon, 1909-1990s* (London: UCL Press, 1999), 16.

48. McAleer, J., *Passion's Fortune: The Story of Mills and Boon* (Oxford: Oxford University Press, 1999), 120, 189, 216, and *passim*.

49. Betty Neels biography at Harlequin.com, http://www.harlequin.com/author.html?authorid=160, accessed 14 September 2015.

50. Neels, B., *Sister Peters in Amsterdam* (Richmond: Mills and Boon, 1969). See list of publications at http://www.fictiondb.com/author/betty-neels~5527.htm, accessed 3 August 2016.

51. See, for instance, *The Uncrushable Jersey Dress: Conquering the World, One Betty Neels at a Time*, http://everyneelsthing.blogspot.co.uk/, accessed 14 September 2015.

52. Neels, B., *Amazon in an Apron* (Richmond, Mills and Boon, 1969); subsequently reissued twice as *Nurse in Holland* (1970) and *A Match for Sister Maggy* (1999).

53. See http://everyneelsthing.blogspot.co.uk/, accessed 14 September 2015.

54. This line is from Neels, B., *Britannia All at Sea* (Richmond: Mills and Boon, 1979).

55. Heyer, G., *Venetia* (London: Heinemann, 1958).

56. Heyer, G., *Cotillion* (London: Heinemann, 1953).

57. Heyer, G., *A Civil Contract* (London: Heinemann, 1961).

58. See (*inter alia*) Giles, J., *Women, Identity and Private Life in Britain, 1900–1950* (Basingstoke: Macmillan, 1995); and the same author's *The Parlour and the Suburb: Domestic Identities, Class, Femininity and Modernity* (Oxford: Berg, 2004).

59. Ryan, D., *The Ideal Home Through the Twentieth Century: 'Daily Mail' Ideal Home Exhibition* (London: Hazar Publishing, 1997).

60. *The Man in The Grey Flannel Suit*, 1956 (American spelling 'Gray'), directed by Nunnally Johnson and based on a best-selling novel by Sloan Wilson.

61. Mortimer, P., *Daddy's Gone A-Hunting* (London: Michael Joseph, 1958); *The Pumpkin Eater* (London: Hutchinson, 1962).

62. Friedan, B., *The Feminine Mystique* (London: Victor Gollancz, 1963).

63. Greer, G., *The Female Eunuch* (London: Paladin, 1971), 224.

64. Bessel, R. and Schumann, D. (eds), *Life After Death: Approaches to a Cultural and Social History of Europe during the 1940s and 1950s* (Cambridge: Cambridge University Press, 2003); Langhamer, C., Spencer, S., and Tinkler, P. 'Revisioning the History of Girls and Women in Britain in the long 1950s', *Women's History Review* Special Issue (2016): Advance Online.

65. Dyhouse, C., *Girl Trouble: Panic and Progress in the History of Young Women* (London: Zed, 2013), esp. chaps 4 and 5.

66. Gott, R., 'Poster Boy' in *The Guardian*, 3 June 2006, http://www.theguardian.com/artanddesign/2006/jun/03/art.art, accessed 3 August 2016; also 'Alberto Korda: The Photographer behind the Face of Ernesto Che Guevara', Art History Archive, http://www.arthistoryarchive.com/arthistory/photography/Alberto-Korda.html, accessed 14 September 2015.

67. http://www.jamesdean.com/, accessed 14 September 2015.

68. Hedges, C., 'Tariq Ali: The Time is Right for a Palace Revolution', http://www.informationclearinghouse.info/article41146.htm, accessed 14 September 2015; see also Richards, K., *Life* (New York, NY and London: Little, Brown and Co., 2010), 235, 249.

69. Baxter, B., 'Paul Newman Obituary' in *The Guardian*, 27 September 2008, points out that Newman's philanthropy was on the grand scale. See also Levy, S., *Paul Newman: A Life* (New York, NY: Three Rivers Press, 2005).

70. Lifton, D., '46 Years Ago: John Lennon and Yoko Ono Begin "Bed-In for Peace"' ultimateclassicrock.com, 25 March 2015, http://ultimateclassicrock.com/john-lennon-yoko-ono-bed-in/; Archer, M. 'What Has John Lennon and Yoko Ono's Bed-In Taught Us?', The Guardian, 25 March 2009, http://www.theguardian.com/artanddesign/2009/mar/24/lennon-ono-bed-in-40-years, both accessed 3 August 2016.

71. 'Teen-Age Girls Choose Como as "Crooner of the Year"' *The Pittsburgh Press*, 19 September 1943, https://news.google.com/newspapers, accessed 14 September 2015.

72. '20 Year Olds' Ideal: Perry Como, Their Choice, Enacts Perfect Spouse' *Life Magazine*, 41/26 (24 December 1956): 143–5.

73. *Boyfriend*, 13 June 1959, 10–11. Como is described as 'the 47 year old dream-boat' whose fans' ages ranged 'between 9 and 90'.

74. One of the best examples is Stronach, A., *A Newnham Friendship* (London: Blackie and Son, 1901).

75. Reed, J., *Ten Days That Shook the World* (New York, NY: Boni and Liveright, 1919); *Reds* 1981, directed by and starring Warren Beatty with Diane Keaton as Louise Bryant.

76. *Wagon Train*, American TV Western series running 1957–65 and originally starring Ward Bond as Major Seth Adams and Robert Horton as scout Flint McCullough. There were 284 episodes in eight seasons and the series was hugely popular on both sides of the Atlantic. *Rawhide*, American TV Western series running 1959–65 starring Eric Fleming as trail leader Gil Favor and Clint Eastwood as Rowdy Yates.

77. Kanfer, S., *Somebody: The Reckless Life and Remarkable Career of Marlon Brando* (New York, NY: Alfred Knopf, 2008) 190–3, 200 ff., and *passim*; see also filmed version of 1963 Civil Rights Roundtable discussion (28 August 1963) between Brando, Sidney Poitier, James Baldwin, Harry Belafonte and others, available on youtube, https://www.youtube.com, accessed 3 August 2016; Schickel, R., *Clint Eastwood: A Biography* (New York, NY: Vintage, 1996).

78. See for instance 'George Clooney and a History of Humanitarianism' in Borgen Magazine, 25 November 2013, http://www.borgenmagazine.com, accessed 15 September 2015.

79. Miller, J., *Women Writing About Men* (London: Virago, 1986).

80. Ibid., 144.

81. Ibid.
82. Neels, B., *The End of the Rainbow* (Richmond: Mills and Boon, 1974), 74.
83. See comments on http://www.goodreads.com/, citation here from posting by 'Leona', 12 May 2013, accessed 15 September 2015.

## Chapter 7

1. Geddes, P. and Thomson, J.A., *The Evolution of Sex* (London: Walter Scott, 1889).
2. Ibid., 267.
3. Spencer, H., *Principles of Sociology* (London: Williams and Norgate, 1876), vol. 1, see esp. part III, 'Domestic Relations'.
4. Ibid., 792.
5. See for instance Dyhouse, C., *Girl Trouble: Panic and Progress in the History of Young Women* (London: Zed Books, 2013), 54–8.
6. Wells, H.G., *Ann Veronica: A Modern Love Story* (London: Fisher Unwin, 1909); Lewis, J., 'Intimate Relations between Men and Women: The Case of H. G. Wells and Amber Pember Reeves,' *History Workshop Journal* 37/1 (1994): 76–98.
7. Wells, *Ann Veronica*, 254.
8. London, J., *The Call of the Wild* (first published 1903; this edn London: Heinemann, 1912); Burroughs, Edgar Rice, *Tarzan of the Apes* (first published in *All-Story Magazine*, October 1912; this edn New York: Grosset and Dunlap, 1914, available Internet Archive), first film version of Tarzan of the Apes, directed by Scott Sidney with Elmo Lincoln as Tarzan, 1918; 1933 film *King Kong* directed by Merian C. Cooper and Ernest B. Shoedsack.
9. Google Ngrams graph of the use of phrases in a corpus of books through time, see https://books.google.com/ngrams/info, accessed 4 August 2016.
10. Huxley, A., *Point Counter Point* (first published 1928; this edn London: Vintage 2004), 405, 430.
11. Sark, Sylvia, *Take Me! Break Me!* (London: Mills and Boon, 1938) copy with original dustjacket in Reading University Archives. See also the papers of Edith Maud Hull in the Women's Library, London University, London School of Economics (Ref. EMH), which include early editions of her books in original florid dustjackets.
12. On Oliver Reed see Sellers, R., *What Fresh Lunacy is This?: The Authorized Biography of Oliver Reed* (London: Constable, 2014) which offers to provide new insights into 'a man seen by many as merely a brawling, boozing hellraiser' (http://www.amazon.co.uk/, accessed 16 September 2015); on Harris see Callan, Michael Feeney, *Richard Harris: Sex, Death and the Movies: An Intimate History* (London: Robson Books, 2003). Callan describes his subject as a man 'who just bawled. He bawled and bawled and went on doing so until his fading days' (ibid., 2). Russell Crowe's bad behaviour

constantly made headlines in the popular press in the early 2000s and he allegedly penned an 800-word apology for it to Sydney's *Daily Telegraph* in 2009, see *Daily Mail* Reporter, "'I'm embarrassed, and accept responsibility for my bad behaviour" says an apologetic Russell Crowe in 800-word letter to fans', 16 September 2009, http://www.dailymail.co.uk, accessed 16 September 2015. Jeremy Clarkson was reported as having been sacked from the popular television show, *Top Gear*, by the BBC in March 2015, following 'an unprovoked physical attack on a producer', http://www.bbc.co.uk/news, 25 March 2015, accessed 16 September 2015.

13. See, for instance, http://www.alpha-dream.com/AlfaMaschio_F.php. This allegedly best-selling product has been advertised as 'the Bad Boy' formula for men, which blends eight different pheromones to give off a message of 'sexual superiority' to women, http://www.pheromoneessentials.com, accessed 16 September 2015. See also https://www.pheromones.co.uk/, accessed 4 August 2016.

14. *Love Story* (1944) directed by Leslie Arliss, starring Stewart Granger, Margaret Lockwood, and Patricia Roc. Stewart Granger was one of the most popular male leads in British cinema in the 1940s. On the glamour of airmen generally see Francis, M., *The Flyer: British Culture and the Royal Airforce, 1939–45* (Oxford: Oxford University Press, 2008).

15. Heyer, G., *These Old Shades* (London: Arrow Books, 2004).

16. Coward, R., *Female Desire: Women's Sexuality Today* (London: Paladin, 1984).

17. Ibid., 194.

18. *The Unabridged Journals of Sylvia Plath, 1960–1962*, edited by Karen V. Kukil (New York: Anchor Books, 2000).

19. Ibid., 20.

20. Ibid., 174.

21. Ibid., 182.

22. Sark, *Take Me! Break Me!* 35, 41, 62, and *passim*.

23. Russell, A., 'Island of Desire', *Glamour* issue 1, 12 March 1938.

24. Ibid.

25. See for instance Dixon, J., *The Romance Fiction of Mills and Boon, 1909-1990s*, (London: UCL Press, 1999), 143 ff. There are interesting discussions in Thurston, C., *The Romance Revolution, Erotic Novels for Women and the Quest for a New Sexual Identity* (Urbana and Chicago, IL: University of Illinois Press, 1987); and Krentz, J. A., *Dangerous Men and Adventurous Women: Romance Writers on the Appeal of the Romance* (Philadelphia, PA: University of Pennsylvania Press, 1992).

26. Ginty, M.M., 'Our Bodies, Ourselves Turns 35 Today', Women's ENews, 4 May 2004, http://womensenews.org/story/health/040504/our-bodies-ourselves-turns-35-today. The book has since generated its own website, see http://www.ourbodiesourselves.org/, which has a useful section on history; 16 September 2015.

27. Comfort, A., *The Joy of Sex: A Gourmet Guide to Lovemaking* (London: Quartet, 1972).

28. Levy, A., 'Doing It: A New Edition of *The Joy of Sex*', *New Yorker*, 5 January 2009, http://www.newyorker.com/magazine/2009/01/05/doing-it, accessed 16 September 2015.

29. Ibid.

30. Jong, E., *Fear of Flying* (New York, NY: Holt, Rinehart and Winston, 1973); Friday, N., *My Secret Garden: Women's Sexual Fantasies* (London: Quartet, 1975), and *Forbidden Flowers: More Women's Sexual Fantasies* (London: Arrow, 1994).

31. Hite, S., *The Hite Report: A Nationwide Study of Female Sexuality* (New York, NY and London: Macmillan, 1977); Kinsey, A. (et al.), *Sexual Behaviour in the Human Male* (Philadelphia, PA and London: W.B. Saunders, 1948), and *Sexual Behaviour in the Human Female* (Philadelphia, PA: Saunders, 1953).

32. Friday, N., *Women on Top: How Real Life has Changed Women's Sexual Fantasies* (first published London: Hutchinson, 1991; this edn London: Arrow Books, 2012), 8.

33. Cloud, H., *Barbara Cartland: Crusader in Pink* (Long Preston: Magna Print Books, 1979), 54.

34. Woodiwiss, K., *The Flame and the Flower* (New York, NY: Avon Books, 1972); see also Thurston, *The Romance Revolution*, 18 ff; Radway, J., *Reading the Romance: Women, Patriarchy and Popular Literature* (Chapel Hill, NC: University of North Carolina Press, 1984).

35. Violet Winspear, 1928–89, wrote some seventy romance novels published by Mills and Boon 1961–87. She developed a close relationship with Alan Boon, and much of her correspondence with Boon has been preserved in the Mills and Boon archive now housed at the University of Reading.

36. Violet Winspear, undated letter to Alan Boon (*c.*April 1971), Mills and Boon Archive, University of Reading.

37. Don Raul Cesar de Romanos appears in Winspear's *Tawny Sands* (Richmond: Mills and Boon, 1970).

38. Tellex [sic] Report, transcript of broadcast *Why is the Romantic Novel so popular?* for programme 'Happily Ever After', Radio 4, 5 September 1971, presented by Benedict Nightingale, in Mills and Boon Archive, University of Reading.

39. *Radio Times*, 30 July 1970, 10–11.

40. Winspear was desperately upset by the *Radio Times* feature. She thought that the photo made her look like 'an ugly old dyed up bat . . . with man mania, who can't get what the Rolling Stones are always singing about'. (Winspear to Alan Boon, 1 August 1970). A year later she told Alan that 'Parkin has the bitterest face I've ever seen . . . she started gunning for me the moment I told her how much I could make writing "sloppy love stories" Her Words!' (Letter to Alan Boon, 15 March 1971), Mills and Boon Archive.

41. Quoted in *Radio Times*, 30 July 1970.

42. Undated, typescript *News Letter* (7 pages) from Violet Winspear, Mills and Boon Archive.

43. Ibid., 4.
44. Ibid.
45. Ibid., 5.
46. Winspear, *News Letter*, 4.
47. Violet wasn't too keen on Katherine Whitehorn, either, whom she saw as another middle-class feminist prone to criticizing working-class women for finding pleasure in romance fiction (undated correspondence (*c.*1970–71) with Alan Boon, Mills and Boon Archive.
48. Winspear, letter to Alan Boon dated 5 December 1971, Mills and Boon Archive.
49. Winspear, letter to Alan Boon, undated, *c.*1972, Mills and Boon Archive.
50. Winspear, undated postcard to Alan Boon, undated letter from *c.*1970, Mills and Boon Archive.
51. Winspear's correspondence with Alan Boon continually reverts to this kind of explanation and reasoning.
52. Cuttings files, 1972, Mills and Boon Archive.
53. Haskell, M., 'Rape: The 2,000-Year-Old Misunderstanding', originally published in *Ms.*, November 1976, reprinted in the same author's *Holding My Own in No-Man's Land: Women and Men, Film and Feminists* (Oxford: Oxford University Press, 1997), 127–37, 127.
54. Ibid., 128.
55. Modleski, T., *Loving with a Vengeance: Mass Produced Fantasies for Women* (Hamden, CT: Archon Books, 1982), 48, 50.
56. Heyer, G., *The Transformation of Philip Jettan* (London: Mills and Boon, 1923); subsequently republished (minus the final chapter) as *Powder and Patch* (London: Random House, 2011).
57. Dell, Ethel M., *The Way of an Eagle* (London: Fisher Unwin, 1912).
58. Barclay, F., *The Rosary* (New York, NY and London: G. P. Putnam's Sons, 1909).
59. James, E.L., *Fifty Shades of Grey* (London: Arrow Books, 2011).
60. Winsor, K., *Star Money* (New York: Appleton-Century Crofts, 1950; this edn London: Macdonald, 1950).
61. Ibid., 420.
62. Dyhouse, *Girl Trouble*, esp. chaps 4–6, 197–210, 246–50.
63. For the dramatic changes in age of marriage in relation to access to birth control see Dyhouse, C., *Students: A Gendered History* (London and New York, NY: Routledge, 2006), 92–4, 103–7.
64. 'Petticoat Guide: What Every Girl Should Know', *Petticoat*, March 1966.
65. Cilla Black, quoted in *Honey*, April 1970.
66. *Buffy the Vampire Slayer*, American TV series which aired 1997–2003. Writer–director Joss Whedon famously set out to create a girl character who would resist victimhood, and the series quickly achieved cult status, particularly among young women.

67. *Labyrinth* (1986), a musical adventure fantasy film directed by Jim Henson. It met with a mixed critical reception when first screened but has since acquired something of a cult following.

68. For an insightful essay on the appeal of *Labyrinth* see Hubbard, A., 'Labyrinth and David Bowie', Bill Douglas Cinema Museum (University of Exeter) website, posted 24 October 2013, http://www.bdcmuseum.org.uk/news/labyrinth-and-david-bowie-by-amy-hubbard/. See also discussion on Girls Underground blog, http://girls-underground.com/tag/labyrinth/, both accessed 18 September 2015.

69. A feature 'Modern Families' in *The New York Times*, 2 December 2014, looks at changes in divorce rates through time, showing how rates peaked in the 1970s and 1980s, but have declined significantly over the last twenty years, http://www.nytimes.com/2014/12/02/upshot/the-divorce-surge-is-over-but-the-myth-lives-on.html. For the UK see Wilson, B. and Smallwood, S., *The Proportion of Marriages Ending in Divorce*, Office for National Statistics, 2008; Sedghi, A. and Rogers, S., 'Divorce Rate Data, 1858 to Now: How has it Changed?' *The Guardian*, 6 February 2014, http://www.theguardian.com/news/datablog/2010/jan/28/divorce-rates-marriage-ons, both accessed 18 September 2015. In Britain, key legislative changes were the Divorce Reform Act of 1969 and the Matrimonial Causes Act of 1973, which made the process of getting a divorce easier. In the 1970s and 1980s petitions for divorce were more likely to be filed by women. See also Lewis, J., 'Marriage', chap. 5 in Zweiniger-Bargielowska, I., (ed.) *Women in Twentieth Century Britain: Social, Cultural and Political Change* (Harlow: Longman, 2001).

70. Mortimer, P., *Daddy's Gone A-Hunting* (London: Michael Joseph, 1958); *The Pumpkin Eater* (London: Hutchinson, 1962).

71. Collins, J., *The World is Full of Married Men* (London: W.H. Allen, 1968).

72. Ward, C., 'Jackie . . . Looking a Little *Younger* Each Day', *Daily Mirror*, 24 May 1974, 7.

73. Fallows, G., 'And Now . . . It's the Five Year Itch', *Daily Mirror*, 16 November 1977, 7.

74. For 'Queen of Sleaze' designation see (*inter alia*) *Daily Mirror*, 7 March 1988, 13. The *Mirror* wasn't kind to Collins. Paul Callan described her as sliding across the *Daily Mirror* foyer like 'some sensual serpent'. Callan, P., 'The Vamp: Real-Life Confessions of Jackie Collins', *Daily Mirror*, 22 June 1979, 17.

75. Bradford, Barbara Taylor, *A Woman of Substance* (Bath: Chivers, 1979; this edn London: HarperCollins, 1993).

76. Ibid., 766.

77. Conran, S., *Lace* (London: Sidgwick and Jackson, 1982; this edn Edinburgh: Canongate, 2012), 548.

78. Ibid., 548.

79. Krantz, J., *I'll Take Manhattan* (London: Bantam Press, 1986).

80. Ibid., 186.

81. Ibid., 244.
82. Jaffe, R., *The Best of Everything* (New York, NY: Simon and Schuster, 1958); *Mr Right is Dead* (New York, NY: Simon and Schuster 1965).
83. McCarthy, M., *The Group* (London: Weidenfeld and Nicolson, 1963); Mailer, N., 'The Mary McCarthy Case', *The New York Review of Books*, 17 October 1963, http://www.nybooks.com/, accessed 21 September 2015.
84. Candace Bushnell's column for the *New York Observer*, 1994–96, gave rise to the HBO television series, *Sex and the City* (1998–2004).
85. See, for instance, Gold, T., 'Sorry Sisters, But I Hate Sex and the City', *The Telegraph*, 21 May 2010, http://www.telegraph.co.uk/, accessed 21 September 2015; Felski, R., (ed.), *Doing Time: Feminist Theory and Postmodern Culture* (New York, NY and London: New York University Press, 2000), see esp. chap. entitled 'Judith Krantz, Author of the Cultural Logics of Late Capitalism'.
86. Philips, D., *Women's Fiction 1945–2005, Writing Romance* (London: Continuum, 2007), see chap. 6, 'Shopping for Men: The Single Woman Novel'.

## Chapter 8

1. See the very detailed entry for 'Romance' and the word's history and various forms in the Oxford English Dictionary, http://www.oed.com/, accessed 6 August 2016.
2. Bentley, P., *'O Dreams, O Destinations': An Autobiography* (London: Victor Gollancz, 1962).
3. Ibid., 35.
4. Ibid., 36.
5. Ibid., 36–7.
6. Ibid., 42–3.
7. Ibid., 47.
8. Ibid., 111.
9. Didion, J., 'John Wayne, a Love Song', in the same author's *Slouching towards Bethlehem* (Harmondsworth: Penguin, 1974).
10. Pratt, Jean Lucey, ed. Simon Garfield, *A Notable Woman: The Romantic Journals of Jean Lucey Pratt* (Edinburgh: Canongate, 2015), 481, 404, 412.
11. Ferguson, R., *The Brontës went to Woolworths* (London: Benn, 1931; this edn London: Bloomsbury, 2009).
12. Ibid., 4.
13. Kearney, Mary Celeste, *Girls Make Media* (New York: Routledge, 2013), 36–7; Duffet, M., *Understanding Fandom: An Introduction to the Study of Media Fan Culture* (New York, NY and London: Bloomsbury Academic, 2013).
14. Mark Abrams, *The Teenage Consumer* (London: Press Exchange, 1959); Laurie, P., *The Teenage Revolution* (London: Anthony Blond, 1965).
15. Ehrenreich, B., Hess, E., and Jacobs, G., *Remaking Love; The Feminization of Sex* (New York, NY: Anchor Press/Doubleday, 1986), 17–35.

16. See McRobbie, A. and Garber, J. 'Girls and Subcultures', in Hall, S. and Jefferson, T. (eds), *Resistance Through Rituals: Youth Subcultures in Postwar Britain* (London: Harper Collins, 1976). For a more recent discussion see Kearney, Mary Celeste, 'Productive Spaces: Girls' Bedrooms as Sites of Cultural Production', *Journal of Children and Media* 1/2 (2007): 126–41.

17. Pearson, A., *I Think I Love You* (London: Chatto and Windus, 2010).

18. The fourteen-year-old girl who tragically lost her life was Bernadette Whelan. The concert at the White City Stadium was on 26 May 1974. The crowd surged forward towards the stage and fans were trampled underfoot: some 750 girls were treated for injuries or hysteria on the night.

19. Jones, L., 'David Cassidy Ruined my Life', *Daily Mail*, 16 December 2006, accessed online, http://www.dailymail.co.uk/, 21 September 2015.

20. Freud, Emma, 'David Cassidy, my No.1 Dreamboat Santa', *The Guardian*, 22 December 2012, http://www.theguardian.com/, accessed 5 August 2016.

21. 'I was a Teenage Heartthrob', episode 1, David Cassidy, presented by Nina Myskow, BBC Radio 2, 30 December 2012.

22. Rolling Stone and Bailey, A., *The Big Four: David Cassidy, David Bowie, Marc Bolan and Michael Jackson* (London and New York, NY: Wise Publications, 1973). There's a description of Bolan on p. 23, 'down on his knees in the last ecstatic throes of sheer carnal crotch rock, like a sinister little angel out of the densest and most exotic prison visions of Jean Genet, with glitter round his eyes and stars in his hair and dressed in satin and sequins and girls' shoes from Anello and Davide's'.

23. Albertine, V., *Clothes, Music, Boys: A Memoir* (London: Faber & Faber, 2014), 44.

24. Ibid.

25. Ibid., 49, 69.

26. Jones, L., 'David Cassidy Ruined my Life', *Daily Mail*, 16 December 2006, *supra*.

27. Who Was Your First Heartthrob?' Gransnet Forums, http://www.gransnet.com, accessed 4 November 2013.

28. Ibid., posted by 'glammanana', 6 October 2012.

29. Ibid., posted by 'LullyDully', 30 January 2013.

30. Ibid., posted by 'gillybob', 31 January 2013.

31. Ibid., posted by 'Goose', 30 January 2013.

32. Ibid., posts dated 30 January 2013, 5 October 2012 and *passim*.

33. Hale, B., 'Cliff Richard and his £1m Shadows', MailOnline, http://dailymail.co.uk, 3 June 2010, accessed 28 June 2012.

34. Weaver, M., 'Problems with young ones? Get wired for sound', *The Guardian*, 7 June 2007, http://www.guardian.co.uk, accessed 5 August 2016.

35. Sieczkowski, C., 'Lauren Adkins, Las Vegas Student, to Marry Robert Pattinson Cardboard Cut-out for Thesis Project', *Huffington Post*, www.huffingtonpost.

com, 12 April 2012, accessed 23 September 2015. Adkin's draft MA thesis 'Love is Overtaking Me', at http://vamped.org/wp-content/uploads/2014/10/thesis-draft_-41513.pdf, accessed 23 September 2015.

36. Hogg, A., Interview with Lauren Adkins, 2 October 2014, http://vamped.org/2014/10/02/interview-with-lauren-adkins/, accessed 23 September 2015.

37. Pearson, A., 'The Immovable Mr Darcy', *Intelligent Life*, Jan/Feb 2013, http://moreintelligentlife.com, accessed 25 June 2014.

38. Ibid.

39. Carey, J., 'The Damning First Proposal', *Intelligent Life*, Jan/Feb 2013, http://moreintelligentlife.com, accessed 25 June 2014.

40. Foulds, A., 'Jane Austen's Alpha Male', *Intelligent Life*, Jan/Feb 2013, http://moreintelligentlife.com, accessed 25 June 2014.

41. McAleer, J., *Passion's Fortune: The Story of Mills and Boon* (Oxford: Oxford University Press, 1999), 2.

42. 'The Power of Love: 100 Years of Romantic Fiction' *The Independent*, 2 February 2008, http://www.independent.co.uk, accessed 23 September 2015.

43. Modleski, T., *Loving with a Vengeance: Mass Produced Fantasies for Women* (Hamden, CT: Archon Books, 1982); Radway, J., *Reading the Romance: Women, Patriarchy and Popular Literature* (Chapel Hill, NC: University of North Carolina Press, 1984); transcript of broadcast *Why is the romantic novel so popular?* for BBC Radio 4 programme 'Happily Ever After', 5 September 1971, presented by Benedict Nightingale, in Mills and Boon Archive, University of Reading.

44. Sheridan, Richard Brinsley, *Letters*, ed. Price, C. (Oxford: Clarendon Press, 1966), vol. 1, 61), cited in Oxford English Dictionary online, http://www.oed.com/, accessed 23 September 2015.

45. Radway, *Reading the Romance, passim*.

46. Modleski, T., *Loving with a Vengeance*; for a useful discussion of feminist thinking about romance see Gill, R., *Gender and the Media* (Cambridge: Polity, 2007), esp. chap. 7, 'Postfeminist Romance'.

47. *Where the Heart Roams*, produced and directed by Csicsery, G., 1987. Released on DVD 2006, see http://www.zalafilms.com, accessed 5 August 2016.

48. Csicsery, G., interviewed July 2012, POV website 'Documentaries with a point of view', http://www.pbs.org/pov/wheretheheartroams/, accessed 24 September 2015.

49. 'Wayback Whensday: The RT Convention Train', *Romantic Times* book reviews, 9 November 2013, http://www.rtbookreviews.com, accessed 24 September 2015.

50. See 'The Inside Scoop on *Romantic Times Magazine*', 14 October 2013, 'Writers in The Storm' blog, https://writersinthestorm.wordpress.com/2013, accessed 21 September 2015.

51. Ibid.

52. http://jprstudies.org/.

53. 'Leona', review of Violet Winspear's *The Honey is Bitter*, posted 27 July 2012 on https://www.Goodreads.com., accessed 25 September 2015.

54. Ibid., posted 6 April 2010 by 'Dina' on https://www.Goodreads.com, accessed 25 September 2015.

55. 'Beth F.', review of Woodiwiss, K., *The Flame and the Flower*, posted 18 March 2011 on https://www.Goodreads.com, accessed 5 August 2016.

56. Giles, J., '"You Meet 'Em and That's It"; Working Class Women's Refusal of Romance between the Wars in Britain', in Pearce, L. and Stacey, J. (eds), *Romance Revisited* (London: Lawrence and Wishart, 1995).

57. Szreter, S., and Fisher, K., *Sex before the Sexual Revolution: Intimate Life in England 1918–1963* (Cambridge: Cambridge University Press, 2010).

58. Ibid., 45, 167, 179, and *passim*.

59. Giles, '"You Meet 'Em"', 288.

60. Szreter and Fisher, *Sex before the Sexual Revolution*, 178–9.

61. On this theme see Cook, H., *The Long Sexual Revolution: English Women, Sex and Contraception 1800–1975* (Oxford: Oxford University Press, 2004).

62. For general discussion of these issues see Dyhouse, C., *Girl Trouble: Panic and Progress in the History of Young Women* (London: Zed Books, 2013).

63. Graphs showing age at marriage in England and Wales, 1941–1997 can be found in Dyhouse, *Students: A Gendered History* (London and New York, NY: Routledge, 2006), 93.

64. Angel, K., *Unmastered: A Book on Desire, Most Difficult to Tell* (London: Allen Lane, 2012).

65. Laing, O., review of K. Angel's *Unmastered*, *The Guardian*, 2 September 2012, http://www.theguardian.com, accessed 24 September 2015.

66. Giddens, A., *The Transformation of Intimacy: Sexuality, Love and Eroticism in Modern Societies* (Cambridge: Polity, 1992).

67. Smith, A. and Duggan, M., 'Online Dating and Relationships', Pew Research Center, 21 October 2013, http://www.pewinternet.org, accessed 24 September 2015.

68. See, for instance, Arvidsson, A., '"Quality Singles": Internet Dating and the Work of Fantasy', *New Media and Society* 8/4 (August 2006): 671–90.

69. Pearce and Stacey, *Romance Revisited*, 15–16.

70. Ibid., 11.

71. Brooke, S., '"A Certain Amount of Mush": Love, Romance, Celluloid and Wax in the Mid-Twentieth Century', in Harris, A. and Willem Jones, T. (eds.), *Love and Romance in Britain, 1918–1970* (Basingstoke: Palgrave Macmillan, 2015), 81–99, 94.

72. An internet search shows the song to be a lasting favourite on karaoke nights.

73. Williams, K., 'Nelson and Women: Marketing, Representation and the Female Consumer', in Cannadine, D., *Admiral Lord Nelson: Context and Legacy* (New York, NY and Basingstoke: Palgrave Macmillan, 2005).

74. Cadogan, M., *And Then Their Hearts Stood Still: An Exuberant Look at Romantic Fiction Past and Present* (London: Macmillan, 1994).

75. Ibid., 227.

76. Ibid.

77. This is particularly the case in *Grey*, the fourth volume in the series. James, E.L., *Grey* (London: Arrow Books, 2015).

78. Gordon, B., 'Mr Darcy with nipple-clamps', *The Telegraph*, 18 June 2015, http://www.telegraph.co.uk/, accessed 28 September 2015.

79. Colgan, J., 'Christian Grey Indulges his Inner Psychopath', *The Guardian*, 18 June 2015, http://www.theguardian.com/, accessed 28 September 2015.

80. McMahon, B., 'E.L. James on Fifty Shades: Christian Grey is Fantasy—We Really Want Men Doing Washing-Up', *Daily Mirror*, 19 June 2015, http://www.mirror.co.uk/, accessed 28 September 2015.

81. Colgan, *op.cit.*

82. Syrian writer Samar Yazbek was quoted in *The Guardian* as having observed that some young Muslim girls, who were 'also creatures of the West', 'love the fantasy of the virile Arab warrior on the horse with a gun'. 'This is a cliché and a fantasy and they come because it is erotic and exotic', she continued, 'they are bored in the West and they need to rebel. But they do not understand Islam or Syria and they are making things worse for the women who live here.' Hussey, A., 'Samar Yazbek: "Syria has been Hung, Drawn and Quartered"', *The Guardian*, 28 June 2015, http://www.theguardian.com, accessed 28 September 2015. British comedian and columnist Shazia Mirza has been widely reported for expressing similar ideas; see, for instance, '"ISIS fighters are the One Direction of Islam": Jihadi brides are suckers for terrorists' bad boy sex appeal, says British Muslim Comic', *Daily Mail*, 22 February 2016, http://www.dailymail.co.uk/, accessed 3 March 2016. For a contrasting view see Khan, D., 'For Isis women it's not about "jihadi brides": it's about escape', *The Guardian*, 21 June 2015, http://www.theguardian.com/, accessed 22 February 2016.

83. *Harum Scarum*, 1965, discussed in Chapter 5 (this volume).

84. Beck, Melinda, 'Inside the Brains of Bieber Fans' *The Wall Street Journal*, 26 June 2012, http://www.wsj.com/, accessed 16 October 2015.

85. This is a problem discussed recently in Ansari, A., *Modern Romance* (New York, NY: Penguin Random House, 2015).

# SELECT BIBLIOGRAPHY AND SOURCES

## Archives and Collections

Bill Douglas Collection, Cinema Museum, University of Exeter.
Digital Comics Museum (http://digitalcomicmuseum.com/).
Grand Comics Database (http://www.comics.org/).
Internet Movie Database [IMDb] (http://www.imdb.com/).
Mills and Boon Archive, University of Reading.
Special Collections, University of Sussex, including Mass Observation Archive, The Keep, East Sussex.
Women's Library, London School of Economics.

## Magazines and Periodicals

*Boyfriend*
*Cinderella Love* (published in USA, Ziff Davis, later St John Publishing Company, 1950–1955)
*Cosmopolitan*
*Date*
*Girls' Cinema*
*Glamour* (published by C. Arthur Pearson, later Glamour and Peg's Paper)
*Glamour* (published by Condé Nast)
*Heart Throbs* (published in USA: Quality Comics, 1949–57; DC Comics, 1957–72)
*Honey*
*Jackie*
*Marilyn*
*Mirabelle*
*My Guy*
*Oh Boy and Fab*
*Oracle*
*Peg's Paper*
*Petticoat*
*Photoplay*

*Picture Post*
*Picturegoer*
*Red Star*
*Romeo*
*Roxy*
*Valentine*

## Films

*The Adventures of Robin Hood* (Michael Curtiz, William Keighley, 1938)
*As Long as They're Happy* (J. Lee Thompson, 1955)
*Baby Face* (Alfred E. Green, 1933)
*Beau Brummel* (Harry Beaumont, 1924)
*The Black Pirate* (Albert Parker, 1926)
*Blood and Sand* (Fred Niblo, 1922)
*The Blueback Hussar* (Jack Bond, 2013)
*Brief Encounter* (David Lean, 1945)
*Bye Bye Birdie* (George Sidney, 1963)
*Camille* (Ray C. Smallwood, 1921)
*Camille* (George Cukor, 1936)
*Captain Blood* (Michael Curtiz, 1935)
*Caravan* (Arthur Crabtree, 1946)
*Change of Habit* (William A. Graham, 1969)
*Cinderella* (Clyde Geronimi, Hamilton Luske, and Wilfred Jackson, 1950)
*Cinderella* (Kenneth Branagh, 2015)
*The Constant Nymph* (Adrian Brunel, 1928)
*The Constant Nymph* (Edmund Goulding, 1943)
*Crazy About One Direction* (Daisy Asquith for Channel 4, 2013)
*Dance Hall* (Charles Crichton, 1950)
*Dark Shadows* (Tim Burton, 2012)
*Doctor in the House* (Ralph Thomas, 1954)
*Downhill* (Alfred Hitchcock, 1927)
*The Eagle* (Clarence Brown, 1925)
*Expresso Bongo* (Val Guest, 1959)
*Flame in the Streets* (Roy Ward Baker, 1961)
*Forever* (George Fitzmaurice, 1921)
*Forever Amber* (Otto Preminger, 1947)
*The Four Horsemen of the Apocalypse* (Rex Ingram, 1921)
*Freud: A Secret Passion* (John Huston, 1962)
*Gentlemen Prefer Blondes* (Howard Hawks, 1953)
*The Glass Slipper* (Charles Walters, 1955)
*Gone with the Wind* (David O. Selznick, 1939)
*Harum Scarum* (Gene Nelson, 1965)

*Interview with the Vampire* (Neil Jordan, 1994)
*Into the Woods* (Rob Marshall, 2014)
*It* (Clarence G. Badger, 1927)
*King Kong* (Merian C. Cooper, Ernest B. Schoedsack, 1933)
*Labyrinth* (Jim Henson, 1986)
*The Lady and the Highwayman* (John Hough, 1989)
*Lady Caroline Lamb* (Robert Bolt, 1972)
*The Lodger* (Alfred Hitchcock, 1927)
*Lonely Boy* (Wolf Koenig and Roman Kroitor, 1962)
*Love Story* (Leslie Arliss, 1944)
*Madonna of the Seven Moons* (Arthur Crabtree, 1945)
*Magnificent Obsession* (John M. Stahl, 1935)
*Magnificent Obsession* (Douglas Sirk, 1954)
*The Man in Grey* (Leslie Arliss, 1943)
*The Man in the Grey Flannel Suit* (Nunnally Johnson, 1956)
*The Man without Desire* (Adrian Brunel, 1923)
*The Merry Widow* (Erich von Stroheim, 1925)
*Monsieur Beaucaire* (Sidney Olcott, 1924)
*Monsieur Don't Care* (Scott Pembroke, 1924)
*Now, Voyager* (Irving Rapper, 1942)
*Peter Ibbetson* (Henry Hathaway, 1935)
*Pirates of the Caribbean: The Curse of the Black Pearl* (Gore Verbinski, 2003)
*Play It Cool* (Michael Winner, 1962)
*The Princess Bride* (Rob Reiner, 1987)
*Privilege* (Peter Watkins, 1967)
*The Pumpkin Eater* (Jack Clayton,1964)
*The Rains Came* (Clarence Brown, 1939)
*The Rat* (Graham Cutts, 1925)
*Rebel without a Cause* (Nicholas Ray, 1955)
*Red Headed Woman* (Jack Conway, 1932)
*Reds* (Warren Beatty, 1981)
*Robin Hood* (Allan Dwan, 1922)
*Sapphire* (Basil Deardon, 1959)
*The Seventh Veil* (Compton Bennett, 1945)
*The Sheik* (George Melford, 1921)
*The Slipper and the Rose* (Bryan Forbes, 1976)
*The Spanish Main* (Frank Borzage, 1945)
*Stardust* (Michael Apted, 1974)
*A Streetcar Named Desire* (Elia Kazan, 1951)
*Suddenly, Last Summer* (Joseph B. Mankiewicz, 1959)
*Svengali* (Archie Mayo, 1931)
*That'll Be the Day* (Claude Watham, 1973)
*Viva Zapata!* (Elia Kazan, 1952)

*Where the Heart Roams* (George Csicsery, 1982)
*The Wicked Lady* (Lesley Arliss, 1945)
*The Wild One* (László Benedek, 1953)
*Wuthering Heights* (William Wyler, 1939)

## Books and Articles

Abbott, E. and Campbell, L. (eds), *The Life and Letters of Benjamin Jowett, M.A., Master of Balliol College, Oxford* (London: John Murray, 1897).

Abrams, M., *The Teenage Consumer* (London: Press Exchange, 1959).

Albertine, V., *Clothes, Music, Boys: A Memoir* (London: Faber & Faber, 2014).

Alexander, C., 'Charlotte Brontë's "Anecdotes of the Duke of Wellington"', *Brontë Studies* 35:3, November 2010, 208–14.

Anderson, G., *The White Blouse Revolution: Female Office Workers Since 1870* (Manchester: Manchester University Press, 1988).

Anderson, R., *The Purple Heart Throbs; The Sub-Literature of Love* (London: Hodder and Stoughton, 1974).

Angel, K., *Unmastered: A Book on Desire, Most Difficult to Tell* (London: Allen Lane, 2012).

Anger, K., *Hollywood Babylon* (New York, NY: Bell Publishing, 1981).

Ansari, A., *Modern Romance* (New York, NY: Penguin Random House, 2015).

Arch, N., and Marschner, J., *Royal Wedding Dresses* (London: Historic Royal Palaces, *c.* 2011).

Aronson, T., *Victoria and Disraeli; The Making of a Romantic Partnership* (London: Thistle Publishing, 2014).

Arvidsson, A., '"Quality Singles": Internet Dating and the Work of Fantasy', *New Media and Society* 8:4, August 2006, 671–90.

Auerbach, N., *Our Vampires, Ourselves* (London: University of Chicago Press, 1995).

Barclay, F., *The Rosary* (New York, NY and London: G. P. Putnam's Sons, 1909).

Barker, Revel, with a foreword by Baird, Vera, *Crying All the Way to the Bank: Liberace versus Cassandra and Daily Mirror* (Brighton: Revel Barker, 2009).

Basinger, J., *A Woman's View: How Hollywood spoke to Women 1930–1960* (London: Chatto, 1994).

Basinger, J., *Silent Stars* (Hanover, NE: Wesleyan University Press, 2000).

Basinger, J., *The Star Machine* (New York, NY: Vintage, 2009).

Bastin, Giselle, 'There were Three of Us in this Biography so it was a Bit Crowded: The Biography of a Suitor and the Rhetoric of Romance in Diana: Her Story,' *Journal of Popular Romance Studies* 1:1, 2010.

Basu, Shrabani, *Victoria and Abdul: The True Story of the Queen's Closest Confidant* (Stroud: The History Press, 2011).

Bederman, G., *Manliness and Civilisation: A Cultural History of Gender and Race in the United States, 1880–1917* (Chicago, IL and London: University of Chicago Press, 1995).

Bell, M. and Williams, M. (eds), *British Women's Cinema* (Abingdon: Routledge, 2010).

Belsey, C., *Desire: Love Stories in Western Culture* (Oxford: Blackwell, 1994).

Bentley, P., 'O *Dreams, O Destinations': An Autobiography* (London: Victor Gollancz, 1962).

Berger, John, *Ways of Seeing* (London: Penguin, 1972).

Bessel, R., and Schumann, D. (eds), *Life After Death: Approaches to a Cultural and Social History of Europe during the 1940s and 1950s* (Cambridge: Cambridge University Press, 2003).

Black, Gregory D., *Hollywood Censored: Morality Codes, Catholics and the Movies* (Cambridge: Cambridge University Press, 1994).

Blanch, L., *The Wilder Shores of Love* (New York, NY: Carroll & Graf, 2002).

Bland, Lucy, *Modern Women on Trial: Sexual Transgression in the Age of the Flapper* (Manchester: Manchester University Press, 2013).

Botham, N. and Donnelly, P., *Valentino: The Love God* (New York, NY: Ace Books, 1976).

Bowring, J. and O'Brien, M., *The Art of Romance; Mills and Boon and Harlequin Cover Designs* (Munich, Berlin, London, and New York, NY: Prestel, 2008).

Boyle, Sheila Tully and Bunie, Andrew, *Paul Robeson: The Years of Promise and Achievement* (Boston, MA: University of Massachusetts Press, 2005).

Brader, C., '"A World on Wings": Young Female Workers and Cinema in World War I', *Women's History Review* 14:1, 2005, 99–117.

Bradford, Barbara Taylor, *A Woman of Substance* (Bath: Chivers, 1979).

Breese, C., *Hutch* (London: Bloomsbury, 1999).

Brittain, Melisa, 'Dangerous Crossings: Victorian Feminism, Imperialist Discourse and Victoria Cross's New Woman in Indigenous Space', MA thesis, Faculty of Graduate Studies, University of Guelph, Canada, 1999.

Brontë, C., *Jane Eyre* (London: Wordsworth Editions, 1992).

Brown, Ellen F. and Wiley J. Jr, *Margaret Mitchell's Gone with the Wind: A Bestseller's Odyssey from Atlanta to Hollywood* (Lanham, MD: Taylor Trade Publishing, 2011).

Burchell, M., *Wife to Christopher* (London: Mills and Boon, 1936).

[Lord] Byron, *The Corsair: A Tale* (London: John Murray, 1814).

Cadogan, M., *And Then Their Hearts Stood Still: An Exuberant Look at Romantic Fiction Past and Present* (London: Macmillan, 1994).

Callan, Michael Feeney, *Richard Harris: Sex Death and the Movies: An Intimate History* (London: Robson Books, 2003).

Cannadine, D., *Admiral Lord Nelson: Context and Legacy* (New York, NY and Basingstoke: Palgrave Macmillan, 2005).

Carlyle, T., *On Heroes, Hero-Worship and the Heroic in History* (London: James Fraser, 1841).

Carpenter, E., *Love's Coming of Age: A Series of Papers on the Relations of the Sexes* (Manchester: Labour Press, 1896).

Carroll, D., *The Matinee Idols* (London: Peter Owen, 1972).

Cartland, B., *I Search for Rainbows* (London: Hutchinson, 1967).

Cartland, B., *Cupid Rides Pillion* (London: Arrow Books, 1969).

Cartland, B., *We Danced All Night* (London: Hutchinson, 1970).

Cartland, B., *The Passion and the Flower* (London: Pan Books, 1978).

Chamberlain, R., *Shattered Love: A Memoir* (New York, NY: Harper Collins, 2003).

Chow, K., 'Popular Sexual Knowledges and Women's Agency in 1920s England' in *Feminist Review* 63, Autumn 1999, 64–87.

Christiansen, R., *Romantic Affinities: Portraits from an Age 1780–1930* (London: Bodley Head, 1988).

Cloud, H., *Barbara Cartland: Crusader in Pink* (Long Preston, Yorkshire: Magna Print Books, 1979).

Cocks, H., 'The Cost of Marriage and the Matrimonial Agency in late Victorian Britain', *Social History* (38:1, 2013, 66–88).

Cohan, S. and Hark, I.R., *Screening the Male: Exploring Masculinities in Hollywood Cinema* (London and New York, NY: Routledge, 1993).

Collins, J., *The World is Full of Married Men* (London: W.H. Allen, 1968).

Collins, M., *Modern Love; An Intimate History of Men and Women in Twentieth Century Britain* (London: Atlantic, 2001).

Comfort, A., *The Joy of Sex: A Gourmet Guide to Lovemaking* (London: Quartet, 1972).

Conan Doyle, Arthur, *The Complete Brigadier Gerard* (Edinburgh: Canongate, 1995).

Conran, S., *Lace* (London: Sidgwick and Jackson, 1982).

Cook, H., *The Long Sexual Revolution: English Women, Sex and Contraception 1800–1975* (Oxford: Oxford University Press, 2004).

Cooper, J., *Riders* (London: Arlington, 1985).

Cooper, J., *Rivals* (London: Bantam, 1988).

Cooper, J., *Polo* (London: Bantam, 1991).

Cordingley, D., *Under the Black Flag: the Romance and Reality of Life among the Pirates* (London: Random House, 2006).

Cordingley, D., *Seafaring Women: Adventures of Pirate Queens, Female Stowaways and Sailors' Wives* (London: Random House, 2007).

Corelli, M., *A Romance of Two Worlds* (London: Richard Bentley and Son, 1886).

Corelli, M., *The Sorrows of Satan* (London: Methuen, 1895).

Cory, Annie Sophie ('Victoria Cross'), *Anna Lombard* (London: John Long, 1901).

Cott, N.F., 'Passionlessness: An Interpretation of Victorian Sexual Ideology, 1790–1850', originally published in *Signs* 4:2, winter 1978, 219–36.

Coward, R., *Female Desire: Women's Sexuality Today* (London: Paladin, 1984).

Crozier, I., 'William Acton and the History of Sexuality: The Medical and Professional Context', *Journal of Victorian Culture* 5:1, 2000, 1–29.

Dawson, G., *Soldier Heroes: British Adventure, Empire and the Imagining of Masculinities* (London: Routledge, 1994).

DeCordova, R., *Picture Personalities: The Emergence of the Star System in America* (Champaign, IL: University of Illinois Press, 2001).

Delap, L. and Morgan, S. (eds), *Men, Masculinities and Religious Change in Twentieth Century Britain* (Basingstoke: Palgrave Macmillan, 2013).

Dell, Ethel M., *The Way of an Eagle* (London: Fisher Unwin, 1912).

Dell, P., *Nettie and Sissie: The Biography of Ethel M. Dell and her sister Ella* (London: Hamish Hamilton, 1977).

Dellamora, R. (ed.), *Victorian Sexual Dissidence* (London: University of Chicago Press, 1999).

Digby, Anne, *The Evolution of British General Practice, 1850–1948* (New York, NY: Oxford University Press, 1999).

Dixon, Jay, *The Romance Fiction of Mills and Boon, 1909–1990s* (London: UCL Press, 1999).

Dobson, A., *Samuel Richardson* (London: Macmillan, 1902).

Doherty, T., *Hollywood's Censor: Joseph I. Breen and the Production Code Administration* (New York, NY and Chichester: Columbia University Press, 2007).

Doody, M.A., *A Natural Passion: A Study of the Novels of Samuel Richardson* (Oxford: Clarendon Press, 1974).

Douglass, P., *Lady Caroline Lamb: A Biography* (New York, NY and Basingstoke: Palgrave Macmillan, 2004).

du Maurier, Daphne, *Frenchman's Creek* (London: Gollancz, 1941).

du Maurier, Daphne, *The Rebecca Notebook and Other Memories* (London: Gollancz, 1981).

du Maurier, Daphne, *The Breaking Point*, short stories with an introduction by Sally Beauman (London: Virago, 2009).

Duffet, M., *Understanding Fandom: An Introduction to the Study of Media Fan Culture* (New York, NY and London: Bloomsbury Academic, 2013).

Dyhouse, C., *Girls Growing Up in Late Victorian and Edwardian England* (London: Routledge & Kegan Paul, 1981).

Dyhouse, C., *Feminism and the Family in England, 1880–1939* (Oxford: Basil Blackwell, 1989).

Dyhouse, C., *Students: A Gendered History* (London and New York, NY: Routledge, 2006).

Dyhouse, C., *Glamour: Women, History, Feminism* (London: Zed Books, 2010).

Dyhouse, C., *Girl Trouble, Panic and Progress in the History of Young Women* (London: Zed Books, 2013).

Egan, Pierce, *Life in London; or, the Day and Night Scenes of Jerry Hawthorne, Esq. and his elegant friend Corinthian Tom, accompanied by Bob Logic the Oxonian in their Rambles and Sprees through the Metropolis* (London: Sherwood Neely and Jones, Paternoster Row, 1821).

Ehrenreich, B., Hess, E., and Jacobs, G., *Remaking Love; The Feminization of Sex* (New York, NY: Anchor Press/Doubleday, 1986).

Eldridge, M., *In Search of a Prince: My Life with Barbara Hutton* (London: Sidgwick and Jackson, 1988).

Eliot, G., *Adam Bede* (New York, NY: Harper and Brothers, 1860).

England, K. and Boyer, K., 'Women's Work: The Feminisation and Shifting Meanings of Clerical Work', *Journal of Social History* 43:2, Winter 2009, 307–40.

Faithfull, M., *Marianne Faithfull: An Autobiography* (New York, NY: Cooper Square Press, 2000).

Federico, A., *Idol of Suburbia: Marie Corelli and Late Victorian Literary Culture* (Charlottesville, VA: University of Virginia Press, 2000).

Felski, R. (ed.,) *Doing Time: Feminist Theory and Postmodern Culture* (New York, NY and London: New York University Press, 2000).

Ferguson, R., *The Brontës Went to Woolworths* (London: Benn, 1931).

Flint, K., *The Woman Reader, 1837–1914* (Oxford: Clarendon Press, 1995).

Flügel, J.C., *The Psychology of Clothes* (London: Hogarth Press, 1930).

Flynn, Carol Houlihan, *Samuel Richardson: A Man of Letters* (Princeton, NJ: Princeton University Press, 2014).

Forster, M., *Daphne du Maurier* (London: Arrow Books, 2007).

Fowler, D., *Youth Culture in Modern Britain, c.1920–1970* (Basingstoke: Palgrave Macmillan, 2008).

Francis, M., 'The Domestication of the Male? Recent Research on Nineteenth and Twentieth Century British Masculinity', *Historical Journal* 45:3, September 2002, 637–52.

Francis, M., *The Flyer: British Culture and the Royal Airforce, 1939–45* (Oxford: Oxford University Press, 2008).

Frantz, S.G. and Rennhak, K. (eds), *Women Constructing Men: Female Novelists and Their Male Characters 1750–2000* (Lanham, MD: Lexington Books, 2009).

Frayling, C., *Vampyres: Lord Byron to Count Dracula* (London: Faber & Faber, 1992).

Frenier, Marian Darce, *Good-bye Heathcliff: Changing Heroes, Heroines, Roles and Values in Women's Category Romances* (New York, NY: Greenwood Press, 1988).

Friday, N., *My Secret Garden: Women's Sexual Fantasies* (London: Quartet, 1975).

Friday, N., *Forbidden Flowers: More Women's Sexual Fantasies* (London: Arrow, 1994).

Friday, N., *Women on Top: How Real Life has Changed Women's Sexual Fantasies* (London: Arrow Books, 2012).

Friedan, B., *The Feminine Mystique* (London: Gollancz, 1963).

Garber, M., *Vested Interests: Cross Dressing and Cultural Anxiety* (New York, NY and London: Routledge, 1992).

Garvice, C., *Her Heart's Desire* (London: Hodder & Stoughton, 1908).

Garvice, C., *In Wolf's Clothing* (London: Hodder & Stoughton, 1908).

Gaskell, E.C., *The Life of Charlotte Brontë* (London: Smith Elder and Co., 1957).

Geddes, P. and Thomson, J.A., *The Evolution of Sex* (London: Walter Scott, 1889).

Geraghty, C., *British Cinema in the Fifties: Gender, Genre and the 'New Look'* (London: Routledge, 2000).

Gerard, L., *Jungle Love: A Tropical Tangle* (London: Mills and Boon, n.d., c.1924).

Giddens, A., *The Transformation of Intimacy: Sexuality, Love and Eroticism in Modern Societies* (Cambridge: Polity, 1992).

Giles, J., *Women, Identity and Private Life in Britain, 1900–1950* (Basingstoke: Macmillan, 1995).

Giles, J., *The Parlour and the Suburb: Domestic Identities, Class, Femininity and Modernity* (Oxford: Berg, 2004).

Gill, R., *Gender and the Media* (Cambridge: Polity, 2007).

Gledhill, C. (ed.), *Stardom; Industry of Desire* (London: Routledge, 1991).

Glyn, A., *Elinor Glyn: A Biography* (London: Hutchinson, 1955).

Glyn, E., *Three Weeks* (New York, NY: Duffield, 1907).

Glyn, E., *'It' and Other Stories* (London: Duckworth, 1927).

Gordon, J. and C., *Star-Dust in Hollywood* (London: G.G. Harrap, 1930).

Gordon, L., *Nancy Cunard, Heiress, Muse, Political Idealist* (New York, NY: Columbia University Press, 2007).

Gowing, L., *Common Bodies: Women, Touch and Power in Seventeenth Century England* (New Haven, CT and London: Yale University Press, 2003).

Greer, G., *The Female Eunuch* (London: Paladin, 1971).

Gullace, Nicoletta F., 'White Feathers and Wounded Men: Female Patriotism and the Memory of the Great War', *Journal of British Studies* 36, April 1997.

Haase, D. (ed.), *Fairy Tales and Feminism: New Approaches* (Detroit, MI: Wayne State University Press, 2004).

Hall, Lesley A., *Hidden Anxieties: Male Sexuality 1900–1950* (Cambridge: Polity Press, 1991).

Hansen, M., 'Pleasure, Ambivalence, Identification: Valentino and Female Spectatorship', *Cinema Journal* 25:4, Summer 1986, 6–32.

Hapgood, L., *Margins of Desire: The Suburbs in Fiction and Culture, 1880–1925* (Manchester: Manchester University Press, 2005).

Harper, S., *Picturing the Past: The Rise and Fall of the British Costume Film* (London: BFI, 1994).

Harraden, B., *Katharine Frensham* (London: Thomas Nelson and Sons, 1909).

Harris, A. and Willem Jones, T. (eds), *Love and Romance in Britain, 1918–1970* (Basingstoke: Palgrave Macmillan, 2015).

Harris, E., *Britain's Forgotten Film Factory: The Story of Isleworth Studios* (Stroud: Amberley Publishing, 2012).

Haskell, M., *From Reverence to Rape: The Treatment of Women in the Movies* (New York, NY: Holt, Reinhart and Winston, 1974).

Haskell, M., *Holding My Own in No-Man's Land: Women and Men, Film and Feminists* (Oxford: Oxford University Press, 1997).

Haugland, H. Kristina, *Grace Kelly: Icon of Style to Royal Bride* (Philadelphia, PA and London: Philadelphia Museum of Art and Yale University Press, 2006).

Heyer, G., *The Transformation of Philip Jettan* (London: Mills and Boon, 1923).

Heyer, G., *Cotillion* (London: Heinemann, 1953).

Heyer, G., *A Civil Contract* (London: Heinemann, 1961).

Heyer, G., *Black Moth* (London: Arrow Books, 2004).

Heyer, G., *Devil's Cub* (London: Arrow Books, 2004).

Heyer, G., *Regency Buck* (London: Arrow Books, 2004).

Heyer, G., *These Old Shades* (London: Arrow Books, 2004).

Heyer, G., *Venetia* (London: Arrow Books, 2004).

Heyer, G., *The Nonesuch* (London: Arrow Books, 2005).

Heyer, G., *Powder and Patch* (London: Random House, 2011).

Heyman, C. David, *Poor Little Rich Girl: The Life and Legend of Barbara Hutton* (London: Hutchinson, 1985).

Higson, A. (ed.), *Young and Innocent? The Cinema in Britain 1896–1930* (Exeter: University of Exeter Press, 2002).

Hilton, T., *John Ruskin* (New Haven, CT: Yale Nota Bene Press, 2002).

Hipsky, M., *Modernism and the Popular Romance in Britain, 1885–1925* (Athens, OH: Ohio University Press, 2011).

Hite, S., *The Hite Report: A Nationwide Study of Female Sexuality* (New York and London: Macmillan, 1977).

Hodge, J. Aiken, *The Private World of Georgette Heyer* (London: Arrow Books, 2006).

Holden, K., *The Shadow of Marriage: Singleness in England 1914–1960* (Manchester: Manchester University Press, 2007).

Hull, E.M., *The Sheik* (London: Eveleigh Nash & Grayson, 1919).

Huxley, A., *Point Counter Point* (London: Vintage, 2004).

Jackson, C. and Tinkler, P., '"Ladettes" and "Modern Girls": "Troublesome" Young Femininities', *Sociological Review* 55:2, 2007, 251–72.

Jaffe, R., *The Best of Everything* (New York, NY: Simon and Schuster, 1958).

Jaffe, R., *Mr Right is Dead* (New York, NY: Simon and Schuster 1965).

James, E.L. (Erika Leonard/Mitchell), *Fifty Shades of Grey* (2011), *Fifty Shades Darker* (2012), *Fifty Shades Freed* (2012) and *Grey* (2015). All now published London: Arrow Books.

James, Robert Rhodes (ed.), *Chips: The Diaries of Sir Henry Channon* (London: Weidenfeld and Nicolson, 1967).

Jephcott, A.P., *Rising Twenty: Notes on Some Ordinary Girls* (London: Faber & Faber, 1948).

Jones, Ernest, *Sigmund Freud, Life and Work: Vol. 2, Years of Maturity, 1901–1919* (London: Hogarth Press, 1955).

Jong, E., *Fear of Flying* (New York, NY: Holt, Rinehart and Winston, 1973).

Jordan, P., *Falcon's Prey* (London: Mills and Boon, 1981).

Jordan, Stephen C., *Hollywood's Original Rat-Pack: The Bards of Bundy Drive* (Plymouth: Scarecrow Press, 2008).

Kanfer, S., *Somebody: The Reckless Life and Remarkable Career of Marlon Brando* (New York, NY: Alfred Knopf, 2008).

Kastan, Davis Scott (ed.), *The Oxford Encyclopedia of British Literature* (Oxford: Oxford University Press, 2006).

Kauffmann, C.F. (revised by Susan Jenkins), *Catalogue of Paintings in the Wellington Museum, Apsley House* (London: English Heritage in association with Paul Holberton Publishing, 2009).

Kearney, Mary Celeste, 'Productive Spaces: Girls' Bedrooms as Sites of Cultural Production', *Journal of Children and Media* 1:2, 2007, 126–41.

Kearney, Mary Celeste, *Girls Make Media* (New York, NY: Routledge, 2013).

Keeble, N.H., *The Cultural Identity of Seventeenth Century Woman: A Reader* (London and New York, NY: Routledge, 2002).

Kelly, I., *Beau Brummel: The Ultimate Man of Style* (New York, NY: Free Press, 2006).

Kennedy, M., *The Constant Nymph* (London: Heinemann, 1924).

Kent, Susan Kingsley, *Sex and Suffrage in Britain, 1860–1914* (London: Routledge, 1990).

King-Hall, M., *Life and Death of The Wicked Lady Skelton* (London: Peter Davies, 1944).

Kinsey, A. (et al.), *Sexual Behaviour in the Human Male* (Philadelphia, PA and London: W.B. Saunders, 1948).

Kinsey, A. (et al.), *Sexual Behaviour in the Human Female* (Philadelphia, PA: W.B. Saunders, 1953).

Kline, Wendy, *Bodies of Knowledge: Sexuality, Reproduction and Women's Health in the Second Wave* (Chicago, IL: University of Chicago Press, 2010).

Kloester, J., *Georgette Heyer's Regency World* (London: Random House, 2011).

Krantz, J., *I'll Take Manhattan* (London: Bantam Press, 1986).

Krentz, J.A., *Dangerous Men and Adventurous Women: Romance Writers on the Appeal of the Romance* (Philadelphia, PA: University of Pennsylvania Press, 1992).

Lamb, [Lady] Caroline, *Glenarvon* (London: Dent, Everyman, 1995).

Landy, M. (ed.), *The Historical Film: History and Memory in Media* (London: Athlone Press, 2001).

Langford, W., *Revolutions of the Heart: Gender, Power and the Delusions of Love* (New York, NY and London: Routledge, 1999).

Langhamer, C., *Women's Leisure in England, 1920–1960* (Manchester: Manchester University Press, 2000).

Langhamer, C., *The English in Love: The Intimate Story of an Emotional Revolution* (Oxford: Oxford University Press, 2013).

Langhamer, C., Spencer, S., and Tinkler, P., 'Revisioning the History of Girls and Women in Britain in the long 1950s', Women's History Review Special Issue, 2016, Advance Online DOI: 10.1080/09612025.2015.1123025.

Lanza, J. and Penna, D., *Russ Columbo and the Crooner Mystique* (Los Angeles, CA: Feral House, 2002).

LaSalle, M., *Complicated Women: Sex and Power in Pre-Code Hollywood* (New York, NY: St Martin's Press, 2000).

LaSalle, M., *Dangerous Men: Pre-code Hollywood and the Birth of the Modern Man* (New York, NY: Thomas Dunne Books, 2002).

Lasky, Jesse L., *I Blow my Own Horn* (Los Angeles, CA: Doubleday, 1957).

Laurie, P., *The Teenage Revolution* (London: Anthony Blond, 1965).

Lawrence, D.H., *The Complete Short Stories* (Phoenix Ed.) (London: Heinemann, 1968).

Leavis, F.R., *The Great Tradition* (New York, NY: Doubleday, 1954).

Leavis, Q.D., *Fiction and the Reading Public* (London: Penguin, 1979).

Leese, E., *Costume Design in the Movies: An Illustrated Guide to the Work of 157 Great Designers* (Toronto, ON: Dover Publications, 1991).

Leider, Emily W., *Dark Lover: The Life and Death of Rudolph Valentino* (London: Faber & Faber, 2003).

Lewis, J. (ed.), *Labour and Love: Women's Experience of Home and Family 1850–1914* (Oxford: Blackwell, 1986).

Lewis, Jane, 'Intimate Relations between Men and Women: The Case of H.G. Wells and Amber Pember Reeves', *History Workshop Journal* 37: 1, 1994, 76–98.

Lewis, Jon, *The Road to Romance and Ruin: Teen Films and Youth Culture* (New York, NY: Routledge, 1992).

Lewis, R., *Gendering Orientalism: Race, Femininity and Representation* (London: Routledge, 2013).

Levy, S., *Paul Newman: A Life* (New York, NY: Three Rivers Press, 2005).

Loos, A., *Gentlemen Prefer Blondes: The Illuminating Diary of a Professional Lady* (New York, NY: Boni & Liveright, 1925).

Loos, A., *But Gentlemen Marry Brunettes* (New York, NY: Boni & Liveright, 1928).

Lovell, Mary S., *A Scandalous Life: The Biography of Jane Digby* (London: Fourth Estate, 1998).

Lutz, D., *The Dangerous Lover: Gothic Villains, Byronism and the Nineteenth Century Seduction Narrative* (Columbus, OH: Ohio State University Press, 2006).

McAleer, J., 'Scenes from Love and Marriage: Mills and Boon and the Popular Reading Industry in Britain, 1908-1950', *Twentieth Century British History* 1:3, 1990, 264–88.

McAleer, J., *Passion's Fortune: The Story of Mills and Boon* (Oxford: Oxford University Press, 1999).

McAleer, J., 'Love, Romance and the NHS', in Griffiths, C., Nott, J., and Whyte, W. (eds), *Classes, Cultures and Politics: Essays in British History for Ross McKibbin* (Oxford: Oxford University Press, 2011).

MacCarthy, F., *Byron: Life and Legend* (London: John Murray, 2002).

McCarthy, M., *The Group* (London: Weidenfeld and Nicolson, 1963).

McConnell-Scott, A., *The Vampyre Family: Passion, Envy and the Curse of Byron* (London: Canongate, 2013).

McCracken, Scott, *Pulp: Reading Popular Fiction* (Manchester: Manchester University Press, 1998).

McCullough, C., *The Thorn Birds* (New York, NY: Harper and Row, 1977).

McDayter, G., *Byromania and the Birth of Celebrity Culture* (New York, NY: Suny Press, 2009).

McDonald, P., *The Star System: Hollywood's Production of Popular Identities* (London and New York, NY: Wallflower, 2000).

Mackrell, Judith, *Flappers: Six Women of a Dangerous Generation* (London: Macmillan, 1913).

Macnab, G., *Searching for Stars: Stardom and Screen Acting in British Cinema* (London and New York, NY: Cassell, 2000).

McRobbie, A., *'Jackie': An Ideology of Adolescent Femininity* (Birmingham: Centre for Contemporary Cultural Studies, 1977).

McRobbie, A., *Feminism and Youth Culture: From Jackie to Just Seventeen* (Basingstoke: Macmillan Education, 1991).

McRobbie, A. and Garber, J., 'Girls and Subcultures' in Hall, S. and Jefferson, T. (eds), *Resistance Through Rituals: Youth Subcultures in Postwar Britain* (London: Harper Collins, 1976).

McRobbie, A. and Nava, M. (eds), *Gender and Generation* (Basingstoke: Macmillan, 1982).

Mankowitz, W., *Make Me an Offer, Expresso Bongo and Other Stories* (London: Hutchinson Educational, 1961).

Mansfield, K., *Collected Stories of Katherine Mansfield* (London: Penguin, 2007).

Matter, Laura Sewell, 'Pursuing the Great Bad Novelist', *Georgia Review* LXI: 3, fall 2007, 445–59.

Meikle, D., *Johnny Depp: A Kind of Illusion* (London: Reynolds and Hearn, 2004).

Melman, B., *Women and the Popular Imagination in the Twenties, Flappers and Nymphs* (London: Macmillan, 1988).

Melman, B., *Women's Orients: English Women and the Middle East 1718–1918: Sexuality, Religion and Work* (Ann Arbor, MI: University of Michigan Press, 1992).

Metzl, Johnathan, '"Mother's Little Helper": The Crisis of Psychoanalysis and the Miltown Resolution', *Gender and History* 15:2, August 2003, 240–67.

Meyers, J., *Gary Cooper: American Hero* (New York, NY: Cooper Square Press, 2001).

Miller, J., *Women Writing about Men* (London: Virago, 1986).

Mitchell, M., *Gone with the Wind* (London: Macmillan, 1936).

Miyao, Daisuke, *Sessue Hayakawa: Silent Cinema and Transnational Stardom* (Durham, NC: Duke University Press, 2007).

Modleski, T., *Loving with a Vengeance: Mass Produced Fantasies for Women* (Hamden, CT: Archon Books, 1982).

Morris, M.T., *Madam Valentino: The Many Lives of Natacha Rambova* (New York, NY: Abbeville, 1991).

Morrison, Michael A., *John Barrymore; Shakespearian Actor* (Cambridge: Cambridge University Press, 1997).

Mortimer, P., *Daddy's Gone A-Hunting* (London: Michael Joseph, 1958).

Mortimer, P., *The Pumpkin Eater* (London: Hutchinson, 1962).

Moynagh, M. (ed.) *Nancy Cunard: Essays on Race and Empire* (New York, NY: Broadview Press, 2002).

Myrdal, A. and Klein, V., *Women's Two Roles: Home and Work* (London: Routledge and Kegan Paul, 1956).

Nash, Alanna, *The Colonel: The Extraordinary Story of Colonel Tom Parker and Elvis Presley* (London: Aurum, 2003).

National Council of Public Morals, *The Cinema: Its Present Position and Future Possibilities; Being the Report of, and Chief Evidence Taken by the Cinema Commission of Inquiry instituted by the National Council of Public Morals* (London: Williams and Norgate, 1917).

Nava, M., 'The Cosmopolitanism of Commerce and the Allure of Difference: Selfridges, The Russian Ballet and the Tango, 1911-1914', *International Journal of Cultural Studies* 1:2, 1998, 163–96.

Neels, B., *Amazon in an Apron* (Richmond: Mills and Boon, 1969).

Neels, B., *Sister Peters in Amsterdam* (Richmond: Mills and Boon, 1969).

Neels, B., *The End of the Rainbow* (Richmond: Mills and Boon, 1974).

Neels, B., *Britannia All At Sea* (Richmond: Mills and Boon, 1979).

Nelson, Jennifer, *More than Medicine: A History of the Feminist Women's Health Movement* (New York, NY and London: New York University Press, 2015).

Nicholson, V., *Singled Out: How Two Million Women Survived Without Men after the First World War* (London: Viking, 2007).

Norman, P., *Mick Jagger* (London: Harper Collins, 2012).

'Paston, G.' and Quennell, P., *'To Lord Byron': Feminine Profiles based upon unpublished letters, 1807–1824* (London: John Murray, 1939).

Pearce, L. and Stacey, J. (eds), *Romance Revisited* (London: Lawrence and Wishart, 1995).

Pearson, A., *I Think I Love You* (London: Chatto and Windus, 2010).

Penley, C., 'Feminism, Psychoanalysis and the Study of Popular Culture', in Grossberg, L., Nelson, C., and Treichler, P. (eds), *Cultural Studies* (New York, NY and London: Routledge, 1992).

Phegley, J., *Courtship and Marriage in Victorian England* (Santa Barbara, CA and London: Praeger [an imprint of ABC- CLIO], 2012).

Philips, D., *Women's Fiction 1945–2005, Writing Romance* (London: Continuum, 2007).

Pitts, M. and Hoffman, F. (eds), *The Rise of the Crooners: Gene Austin, Russ Columbo, Bing Crosby, Nick Lucas, Johnny Marvin and Rudy Vallée* (Lanham, MD: Scarecrow Press, 2001).

Plath, S. (edited by Karen V. Kukil), *The Unabridged Journals of Sylvia Plath, 1960–1962* (New York, NY: Anchor Books, 2000).

Polidori, J., *The Vampyre and Other Tales of the Macabre* (Oxford: Oxford University Press, 1997).

Pratt, Jean Lucey (ed. Simon Garfield), *A Notable Woman: The Romantic Journals of Jean Lucey Pratt* (Edinburgh: Canongate, 2015).

Prioleau, B., *Swoon: Great Seducers and Why Women Love Them* (New York, NY: W. W. Norton and Company, 2013).

Prouty, O. Higgins, *Now, Voyager* (Bath: Chivers, 1975).

Pyron, Darden Asbury, *Liberace: An American Boy* (Chicago, IL: University of Chicago Press, 2000).

Quennell, P., *The Marble Foot: An Autobiography, 1905–1938* (London: Collins, 1976).

Radway, J., *Reading the Romance: Women, Patriarchy and Popular Literature* (Chapel Hill, NC: University of North Carolina Press, 1984).

Ransom, T., *The Mysterious Miss Corelli: Queen of Victorian Bestsellers* (Stroud: Sutton Publishing, 1999).

Reed, J., *Ten Days That Shook the World* (New York, NY: Boni and Liveright, 1919).

Regis, P., *A Natural History of the Romance Novel* (Philadelphia, PA: University Of Pennsylvania Press, 2003).

Rennie, N., *Treasure Neverland: Real and Imaginary Pirates* (Oxford: Oxford University Press, 2013).

Rice, Anne, *Interview with the Vampire* (New York, NY: Alfred A. Knopf, 1976).

Richards, K., *Life* (New York, NY and London: Little, Brown, 2010).

Richardson, A., *The New Woman in Fiction and in Fact: Fin de Siècle Feminisms* (London: Palgrave Macmillan, 2001).

Richetti, John J., *The Columbia History of the British Novel* (New York, NY and Chichester, West Sussex: Columbia University Press, 2013).

Robins, D., *Women Who Seek* (London: Mills and Boon, 1928).

Rogan, J., *Starmakers and Svengalis* (London: Futura, 1988).

Rotundo, E. Anthony, *American Manhood: Transformations in Masculinity from the Revolution to the Modern Era* (New York, NY: Basic Books, 1993).

Rowbotham, S., *Edward Carpenter: A Life of Liberty and Love* (London: Verso, 2008).

Ryan, D., *The Ideal Home Through the Twentieth Century: 'Daily Mail' Ideal Home Exhibition* (London: Hazar Publishing, 1997).

Said, Edward W., *Orientalism* (New York, NY: Vintage, 1979).

Sanders, Lise Shapiro, *Consuming Fantasies: Labor, Leisure and the London Shopgirl, 1880–1920* (Columbus, OH: Ohio State University Press, 2006).

Sark, Sylvia, *Take Me! Break Me!* (London: Mills and Boon, 1938).

Schickel, R., *Clint Eastwood: A Biography* (New York, NY: Vintage, 1996).

Schreiner, O., *The Story of an African Farm: A Novel* (London: Hutchinson, 1883).

Segal, L., *Is the Future Female? Troubled Thoughts on Contemporary Feminism* (London: Virago, 1987).

Sellers, R., *What Fresh Lunacy is This? The Authorized Biography of Oliver Reed* (London: Constable, 2014).

Simpson, P., *The Rough Guide to Cult Pop* (London: Haymarket/Penguin, 2003).

Slater, Thomas J., 'June Mathis's Valentino Scripts: Images of Male "Becoming" after the Great War', *Cinema Journal* 50:1, Fall 2010, 99–120.

Soderholm, J., *Fantasy, Forgery and the Byron Legend* (Lexington, KY: University of Kentucky Press, 1996).

Somerset, Henry Charles Fitzroy, 8th Duke of Beaufort, *Driving* (London: Longmans Green, 1889).

Spencer, H., *Principles of Sociology* (London: Williams and Norgate, 1876).

Spencer, S., *Gender, Work and Education in Britain in the 1950s* (Basingstoke: Palgrave-Macmillan, 2005).

Spicer, A., *Typical Men: The Representation of Masculinity in British Popular Culture* (London: I.B. Tauris, 2001).

Stead, W.T., 'Anna Lombard: A Novel of the Ethics of Sex', *Review of Reviews* 23, June 1901, 595–7.

Steedman, C., *Landscape for a Good Woman: A Story of Two Lives* (London: Virago, 1986).

Stones, R., *More to Life than Mr Right: Stories for Young Feminists* (London: Piccadilly Press, 1985).

Stopes, Marie Carmichael, *Married Love: A New Contribution to the Solution of Sex Difficulties* (London: A. C. Fifield, 1918).

Stopes, Marie Carmichael, *Enduring Passion: Further New Contributions to the Solution of Sex Difficulties, being the Continuation of Married Love* (London: G. Putnam's Sons, 1928).

Stott, A. McConnell, *The Vampyre Family: Passion, Envy and the Curse of Byron* (Edinburgh: Canongate, 2013).

Stronach, A., *A Newnham Friendship* (London: Blackie and Son, 1901).

Studlar, G., *This Mad Masquerade: Stardom and Masculinity in the Jazz Age* (New York, NY: Columbia University Press, 1996).

Stutfield, Hugh E.M., 'Tommyrotics', *Blackwoods Magazine* 157, June, 1895, 833–45.

Stutfield, Hugh E.M., 'The Psychology of Feminism', *Blackwoods Magazine* 161, January 1897, 104–17.

Sutherland, G., *In Search of the New Woman: Middle-Class Women and Work in Britain, 1870–1914* (Cambridge: Cambridge University Press, 2015).

Szreter, S. and Fisher, K., *Sex before the Sexual Revolution: Intimate Life in England 1918–1963* (Cambridge: Cambridge University Press, 2010).

Taylor, H., *Scarlett's Women: Gone with the Wind and its Female Fans* (London: Virago, 2014).

Teo, Hsu-Ming, *Desert Passions: Orientalism and Romance Novels* (Austin, TX: University of Texas Press, 2012).

Thompson, T. (ed.), *Dear Girl: The Diaries and Letters of Two Working Women, 1897–1917* (London: The Women's Press, 1987).

Thurston, C., *The Romance Revolution, Erotic Novels for Women and the Quest for a New Sexual Identity* (Urbana and Chicago, IL: University of Illinois Press, 1987).

Todd, S., *Young Women, Work and Family in England 1918–1950* (Oxford: Oxford University Press, 2005).

Turan, K., *Never Coming to a Theatre near You: A Celebration of a Certain Kind of Movie* (New York, NY: Public Affairs, 2004).

Tweedie, Mrs A., *Women and Soldiers* (London: John Lane Bodley Head, 1918).

Vieira, M., *Hurrell's Hollywood Portraits: The Chapman Collection* (New York, NY: Harry N. Abrams, 1997).

Vinen, R., *National Service: A Generation in Uniform, 1945–1963* (London: Allen Lane, 2014).

Vivanco, L., 'Feminism and Early Twenty-First Century Harlequin Mills and Boon Romances', *Journal of Popular Culture* 45:5, 2012, 1060–89.

Walker, A., *Franz Liszt: The Virtuoso Years, 1811–1847* (Ithaca, NY: Cornell University Press, 1983).

Walkowitz, Judith R., 'The "Vision of Salome": Cosmopolitanism and Erotic Dancing in Central London, 1908–1918', *The American Historical Review* 108:2, April 2003, 337–76.

Wallace, D., *The Woman's Historical Novel: British Women Writers 1900–2000* (Houndmills: Palgrave Macmillan, 2005).

Waller, D., *The Perfect Man: The Muscular Life and Times of Eugen Sandow, Victorian Strongman* (Brighton: Victorian Secrets, 2011).

Waller, P., *Readers, Writers and Reputations: Literary Life in Britain, 1870–1918* (Oxford: Oxford University Press, 2006).

Webb, Paul, *Ivor Novello: Portrait of a Star* (London: Haus Books, 2005).

Wells, H.G., *Ann Veronica: A Modern Love Story* (London: Fisher & Unwin, 1909).

Welsch, T., *Gloria Swanson: Ready for her Close-up* (Jackson, MS: University Press of Mississippi, 2013).

Whipple, A., 'Speaking for Whom? The 1971 Festival of Light and the Search for "the Silent Majority"', *Contemporary British History* 214:3, 2010, 319–39.

Whiteside, J., *Cry: The Johnnie Ray Story* (New York, NY: Barricade, 1994).

Williams, M., *Ivor Novello, Screen Idol* (London: BFI Publishing, 2003).

Williams, S., *Colour Bar: The Triumph of Seretse Khama and his Nation* (London: Penguin, 2007).

Wilson, F. (ed.), *Byromania: Portraits of the Artist in Nineteenth- and Twentieth-Century Culture* (London: Palgrave Macmillan, 1998).

Winsor, K., *Star Money* (New York, NY: Appleton-Century Crofts, 1950).

Winsor, K., *Forever Amber* (London: Penguin, 2002).

Winspear, V., *Blue Jasmine* (London: Mills and Boon, 1969).

Winspear, V., *Palace of the Peacocks* (London: Mills and Boon, 1969).

Wintle, S., 'The Sheik: What Can be Made of a Daydream', *Women: A Cultural Review* 7: 3, 1996, 291–302.

Wollen, P., 'Fashion/ Orientalism/The Body', *New Formations* 1, spring 1987, 1–33.

Woodhead, L., *War Paint: Elizabeth Arden and Helena Rubinstein, Their Lives, Their Times, Their Rivalry* (London: Virago, 2004).

Woodiwiss, K., *The Flame and the Flower* (New York, NY: Avon Books, 1972).

Woollacott, A., '"Khaki Fever" and its Control: Gender, Class, Age and Sexual Morality on the British Home Front in the First World War', *Journal of Contemporary History* 29, 1994, 325–47.

Wootton, S., 'The Byronic in Janes Austen's *Persuasion* and *Pride and Prejudice*', *The Modern Language Review* 102:1, Jan 2007, 26–39.

Zimmeck, M., 'Jobs for the Girls: The Experience of Clerical Work for Women, 1850-1914', in John, Angela V. (ed.), *Unequal Opportunities: Women's Employment in England 1800–1918* (Oxford: Blackwell, 1986).

Zweiniger-Bargielowska, I. (ed.) *Women in Twentieth Century Britain: Social, Cultural and Political Change* (Harlow: Longman, 2001).

# PICTURE ACKNOWLEDGEMENTS

19th era/Alamy Stock Photo: **5**; AF Archive/Alamy Stock Photo: **6**, **17**; Keystone Pictures USA/Alamy Stock Photo: **4**, **24**; Photos 12/Alamy Stock Photo: **18**; Pictorial Press Ltd/Alamy Stock Photo: **3**, **11**; ZUMA Press, Inc./Alamy Stock Photo: **22**; author's photograph, image by kind permission of Bill Douglas Cinema Museum, University of Exeter: **2**; Manchester Art Gallery/Bridgeman Images: **19**; The British Library Board (General Reference Collection P.P.6004.sal.): **1**, **16**; Martin O'Neill/Mary Evans Picture Library: **7**; Heritage Images/Glowimages.com: **10**; Grand Comics Database (CC BY 3.0): **12**; iStock.com/TonyBaggett: **9**; courtesy of Pan Macmillan: **14**; ITV/REX Shutterstock: **8**; Allan Ballard/Scopefeatures.com: **20**; courtesy of Earl Spencer and Michael O'Mara Books Ltd: **15**; Jane Bown/Observer/TopFoto: **25**; courtesy of University of Reading, Special Collections: **23**; Allan Warren (CC BY-SA 3.0): **13**

# INDEX